AF444610

EXPLORING MICHIGAN'S SUNSET COASTS

CROSS VILLAGE

TO

NEW BUFFALO

LENKK PRESS
Copyright © 2022 by Julie Albrecht Royce
Cover Design: Bob Royce
Holland Lighthouse Cover Photo: Gary Martin, www.coastalbeacons.com
Editor: Violet Moore
ISBN 979-8-9855037-2-2

To my grandchildren—
Lauren, Ezra, Noah, Kaelin, and Kohler.

Thank you for the laughter and hugs and kisses. Thank you for the memories I tuck away and pull out when I need a smile. I cherish the adventures we've shared.

FOLLOWING LAKE MICHIGAN'S MILLION DOLLAR SUNSETS

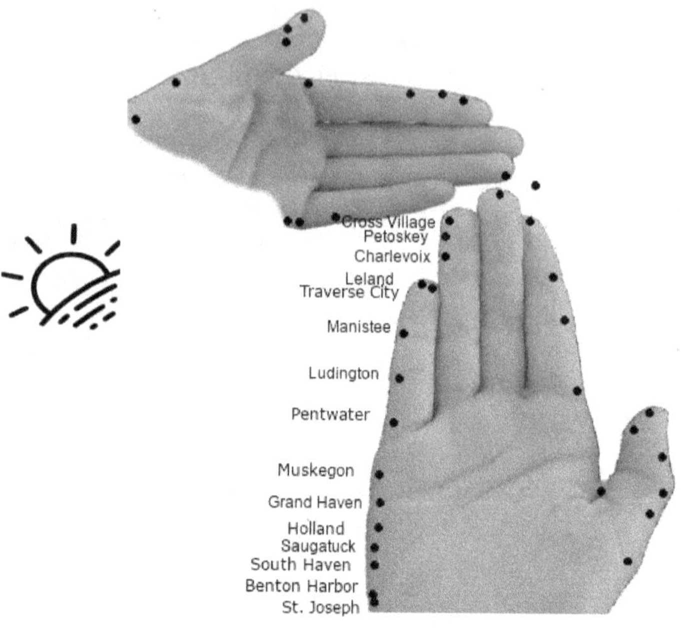

THE FIVE LARGEST CITIES OF THE SUNSET COASTS

MUSKEGON 36,565

HOLLAND 33,137

TRAVERSE CITY 15.902

GRAND HAVEN 11,383

MUSKEGON HEIGHTS 10,730

CONTENTS

Book Three
Exploring Michigan's Sunset Coasts

(Mackinac Island and Mackinaw City are included in Book One (*Exploring Michigan's Sunrise Coasts*) of this series.

INTRODUCTION AND OVERVIEW

Julie Royce wrote and compiled two travel books in the early 2000s. The first was devoted to Michigan's Thumb where she was born and raised. The second covered Lake Michigan's Sunset Coast. She intended to make the Upper Peninsula the subject of a book, but her plans were delayed.

After several years, she returned her attention to her home state, but by then travelers obtained information about lodging, restaurants, and shopping using phone apps and online searches.

The upside of the internet is immediacy. By the time the earlier travel books were published, several places had closed or been replaced by new businesses. Only the background and local stories remained interesting.

Thus was born the idea of a traveler's companion to Michigan's Great Lakes waterways. It would encompass a journey starting on I-75 in Michigan's southeast corner, traveling along Lake Erie, the Detroit River, Lake St. Clair, the St. Clair River, Lake Huron, the St. Marys River, the southern coast of Lake Superior, and Lake Michigan to Michigan's most southwestern point.

It would not include hotels, motels, restaurants, or other places that go out of business often. The few art galleries mentioned have been screened to include those with a long history and operating as these travel books were researched. With COVID-19 and the business climate, it is wise to call if a specific gallery is your reason for a trip. Otherwise, walk the small town and you'll likely find that if one gallery has closed, another has sprung up to replace it.

Royce started the project with the intention of one comprehensive volume, but as the information grew to 900 pages, she divided it into three books: *Exploring Michigan's Sunrise Coasts, Exploring Michigan's Upper*

Peninsula Coasts, and *Exploring Michigan's Sunset Coasts.*

Exploring Michigan's Sunset Coasts includes city histories, museums, parks, beaches, lighthouses, ghost stories, shipwrecks, tales about the famous or infamous with ties to the lakeshores, disasters that shaped the state, and movies and books set along the Lake Michigan coastline. (For example, Petoskey and the surrounding cities are the settings for several of the Nick Adams stories by Ernest Hemingway.)

The author hopes that this volume sprinkles flavor on the places you visit, and that your adventures along Michigan's waterways add many unique experiences to your travel repertoire.

Royce did not add a bibliography. Much of what is included in this guide is stories—no way to prove or disprove the truth. While she tried to research carefully, this is not meant to be a reference book.

Legends. The following categories have been included, as applicable, for each city or stop:

- MUSEUMS
- BEACHES, PARKS, AND TRAILS
- OTHER STOPS TO CONSIDER
- LIGHTHOUSES
- SHIPWRECKS
- THE FAMOUS OR INFAMOUS FROM EACH CITY
- BOOKS AND MOVIES WITH TIES TO CITIES
- GHOST STORIES

LAKE MICHIGAN
"The delightfullest lake in the world."

Lake Michigan's eastern shore is the western border of Michigan's lower peninsula.

In the mid-1600s, French adventurer and fur trader Pierre Esprit Radisson gazed at the vast sapphire waters of Lake Michigan and proclaimed it "the delightfullest lake in the world."

Sitting on a sugar-sand beach in Grand Haven or Pentwater, mesmerized by the gentle waves, it is easy to watch the sun slip beyond the horizon and lose yourself in the splendor of Lake Michigan. Statistics seem too cold, too trivial, and too impersonal to describe the grandeur of the great lake. Its statistics are impressive. By volume, Lake Michigan is the second-largest Great Lake, next to Superior. It is approximately 118 miles wide and 307 miles long with more than 1,600 miles of shoreline, or about the same distance as from Traverse City to Albuquerque, New Mexico. The lake reaches 925 feet at its deepest point and averages a depth of 297 feet. It has 22,300 square miles of surface water. Its drainage basin covers portions of Illinois, Indiana, Michigan, and Wisconsin and is twice as large as the area of its surface water. Lake Michigan is the only Great Lake that lies completely enveloped by the United States.

There is no separation of the waters between Lake Michigan and Lake Huron. The latter provides Lake Michigan's only natural outlet and connects it to the Atlantic Ocean and international trade by way of the St. Lawrence Seaway. The Illinois Waterway links Lake Michigan to the Mississippi River and the Gulf of Mexico.

Lake Michigan is the receptacle for the Muskegon, Grand, Kalamazoo, Fox, and Menominee Rivers. The Chicago River at one time flowed into Lake Michigan, but its course was reversed in 1900 using a series of canal locks, increasing the river's flow from Lake Michigan and causing it to empty into the newly completed Chicago Sanitary and Ship Canal.

Together, the Great Lakes contain about 84% of North America's surface freshwater supply and 21% of the world's fresh water supply. The lakes contain 5,500 cubic miles or six quadrillion gallons of water. Lake Michigan holds 1,180 cubic miles and 1,287,272,400,000,000 gallons of water—give or take a few hundred thousand gallons. If the water from the Great Lakes could be spread evenly across the continental United States the depth would reach 9½ feet. No matter how you look at it, that is a lot of water.

The history of Lake Michigan is also the history of the people and land at its shore. Pastoral scenes painted by streams, barns, silos, dairy cattle, orchards, vineyards, wheat fields, small vegetable gardens, harbors, ships, and quaint towns roll up to the water's shore. They are all props in the drama of the great lake, Michigan.

Explorer Rene-Robert Cavelier Sieur de La Salle struggled with French bureaucrats and politicians to gain permission for his bold plan to expand the French Empire and increase trade in the New World. Finally, on August 7, 1679, La Salle after obtaining the necessary rights and financial backing to build his ship, the green timbered, 50-ton *Le Griffon*, set sail for the Great Lakes in search of the shortcut to China.

La Salle was the first explorer to sail all of the Great Lakes. His destiny was to captain and sail *Le Griffon* from Buffalo at the head of the Niagara River on Lake Erie westward, past Cleveland to Detroit, through the Detroit River and Lake St. Clair, up Huron to the Straits of Mackinac to Green Bay. There, on the shores of Lake Michigan, he left *Le Griffon* in the charge of his pilot who would take her, loaded with furs, on the return trip that would earn La Salle enough money to clear his debts and finance future endeavors. He expected his ambitious plan would secure him a place in history.

La Salle continued exploring the east coast of Lake Michigan to Chicago and across the southern end of the lake by the dune country to what is now St. Joseph. Given the scarcity of food, inclement weather, uncharted course, and other hardships he endured, it is a miracle he lived to report the magnificent lake system he had navigated. His journey was assisted by Native Americans who provided him with food and guidance.

In 1679 months after the *Le Griffon's* voyage began, La Salle learned she had disappeared. It is generally believed the ship went down in a violent Lake Huron storm, but no sign of her crew or cargo was ever discovered. In spite of this tragic loss, La Salle's ventures were not wasted effort. They revealed a path for trading—although not to China—and made the Great Lakes accessible.

Today, Lake Michigan is a resort paradise and a tourist destination featuring small, quaint shops, gourmet restaurants, swimming, sailing, dunes, wineries, and orchards. But for the first 200 years after Europeans arrived, Lake Michigan's shoreline was prized by the French for its importance in the fur trade. Mink, muskrat, martin, and otter were trapped, but beaver pelts were the coveted commodity of the era.

The wealth that accompanied the fur trade caused men to organize companies, recruit explorers, outfit ships, and set sail for a land where they knew hardships awaited. Winters of ice and snow and freezing gales whipping with a ferocity unlike anything they experienced in France or England awaited them. The land was primitive. Food would elude them. Some Native American tribes, like the Iroquois, might fiercely try to thwart their efforts. Despite the dangers, early fur traders, believing there were fortunes to be made, were not dissuaded by the risks.

By the mid-1700s, a trade route ran along the western coast of Lake Michigan between the forts at St. Joseph and Michilimackinac. The French caught the fur trade fever early and seemed less intent on colonizing and moving families into their new trade areas than their British counterparts who brought settlements to the new land. French, English, and Native Americans spread traps and trading posts over a huge area of the Great Lakes. In the 1780s, it is estimated that pelts valued at a million dollars in that days' currency were sold at fur markets in New York City, London, and Paris each year. By 1800 six million pelts sold for a few cents to $500 for especially beautiful specimens.

The Hudson Bay Company, the Northwest Company, and the Canadian Mackinaw Company were all formed to exploit the fur industry of the Great Lakes and Canada. The most prominent fur trader was John Jacob Astor. A butcher's son born in 1763 in Germany, he left at sixteen to seek a fortune and made his way to America via London. For four months, he was trapped in the Chesapeake Bay aboard a ship solidly frozen in the January ice of 1784.

During his months aboard, Astor spent time listening to his fellow passengers and crew and learning the art of the fur trade. He discovered how furs could be picked up in odd lots at the wharves of New York. He stored the knowledge of bartering with Native Americans for a few knives and beads and blankets to obtain the valuable pelts. He learned how to judge the value of the pelts, how to sort and pack them, and how to sell them. Astor was a astute student, keen on learning the tools of what would become his trade. Through his shrewd, if not always scrupulous, business practices, he created a fur monopoly and rode its economic wave until it broke beneath the crush of the lumbering tide. Astor bought the Mackinaw Company and absorbed it into his new American Fur Company. By the late 1700s, Astor's new company operated 20 trading posts in Western Michigan, including his principal post, Gabagouache, current day Grand Haven.

Initially, many Native Americans believed the fur trade was a way to obtain goods never before available to them. In time, however, the fur trade proved disastrous to the survival of the indigenous people. It depleted the local wildlife and caused violent conflict between tribes that battled to curry favor with European fur traders. Perhaps the worst of the evils to befall the Anishinaabe because of their contact with European fur traders was illness. Having no immunity to many of the diseases the Europeans carried, the Native Americans fell victim to scourges including scarlet fever, diphtheria, typhoid fever, whooping cough, measles, and influenza. About half the Huron population was wiped out by 1638 when disease accompanied the French into Native American villages. In 1639 the Odawa were caught in the grip of the most pernicious of the diseases, a massive smallpox epidemic.

Native Americans became pawns in the fierce battle between the French and the British to control the lucrative fur trade. Then the 1776 War of Independence caught them between two English-speaking groups, the British and those former British subjects who now identified themselves as Americans.

In the years following the war, Americans used questionable land deals and military force to claim much Native American land. Alarmed by the advance of the *Chemokmon*, or Big Knives as some Native Americans called the American militiamen, the tribes around the lakes looked to the British for support. The British, who still held forts in the region, supplied the Native Americans with arms.

When the British and Americans found themselves again at war in 1812, most Native Americans sided with the British. They battled Americans before the United States declared war on Great Britain. Chief Tecumseh, who had lost most of his ancestral Shawnee territory in Ohio to the Americans, convinced the tribes to the north and west that they would soon suffer the same fate if they did not band with him against the Big Knives. Tecumseh was joined in his fight by the Ojibwe, Odawa, Pottawatomie, Winnebago, Menominee, Sauk, and Fox.

The early battles favored the Native Americans, and they overwhelmed the soldiers at the forts of Detroit, Mackinac (formerly Michilimackinac), and Chicago where approximately 600 Pottawatomie killed scores of American soldiers and a few civilians. These assaults provoked the Americans who launched devastating attacks against tribal villages in Michigan. By 1814 when the British were pushed back into Canada and defeated, the embattled tribes found themselves without allies. Life for the Great Lakes tribes had always been a struggle, but now their very existence was endangered.

After the War of 1812, the American hostility toward the Native Americans ensured that federal authorities would pressure them relentlessly to yield territory. The end of the war brought settlers across the Ohio border, many of them were farmers attracted by the rich soil at the southern end of the Great Lakes. By 1830 the settlers outnumbered the native people by about twenty-five to one. Many tribes had already surrendered most of their land.

In 1819 Lewis Cass, Michigan's territorial governor, traveled to Saginaw to convince Ojibwe leaders to relinquish their remaining Michigan land. He brought along a company of U.S. Army troops and a shipment of gifts that included nearly 200 gallons of liquor. When the meeting was over the Ojibwe had signed away about six million acres of land in Michigan in exchange for tribal reserves of about 100,000 acres plus a small sum as an annual annuity.

In the 1822 Treaty of Chicago, Native Americans were divested of their remaining rights to the land in the area of Southwestern Michigan. In exchange, they received $5,000 per year for 20 years. With that deal in place, the majority of Native Americans began their trek west of the Mississippi. Some who had adapted to European ways stayed behind and formed small communities of their own along the eastern shore of Lake Michigan where they had lived and hunted for centuries.

In the 1800s, when fur-bearing animals became scarce and the fur trade was in its death throes, the entrepreneurial spirit was stirred by another natural resource. (See Lake Michigan in *Exploring Michigan's Upper Peninsula Coasts* for additional discussion of the lumber era.) Farmers, eager to provide a space for crops, played a minor role in the massive devastation of Michigan's forests when compared to that of the great lumber barons who invaded port towns like Grand Haven and Muskegon. After the lumber barons cut the forests, the cities they created looked for a new way to survive. Manistee, for example, turned the cleared land into farms for fruit orchards, Traverse City turned to cherry canning, and Muskegon turned to foundries.

Lumbering brought a cast of rough and tumble men to the western Michigan lakeshore region. Silver Jack, as John Driscoll was known, was a huge man who traveled to the Saginaw mills when he was eighteen years old. He lumbered in Muskegon, and his reputation grew as he went from one lumber camp to the next. He was said to be an expert in the Hell's Half Mile school of fighting: gouging out eyes, head butting, kicking, fist-punching, wrestling, and "putting the boots to a man," which meant driving the sharp calks or spikes into his opponent's face and giving him scars for life, or in some cases, killing him.

Still, most legends, including those that swirled around Silver Jack, insisted that lumbermen, even those of fabled violence, had a good streak buried just beneath the surface. Jack's friends described him as lovable, generous, and kindly and claimed he stood up against bullies on behalf of the weak. Someone with Jack's boot planted in his face might have disagreed.

Jack was also said to be a staunch defender of his watered-down Catholic faith. An old lumberjack ballad tells the story of a fight provoked by fellow lumberman, Bobby Waite's assertion that the Bible was fiction and hell nothing more than a lot of humbug. The slur on the religion of Jack's mother earned Bobby Waite a forty-minute fight with the not-so-gentle giant who pummeled him with iron fists, chewed off his ear, and otherwise defended his religion as he believed any good Christian should.

While everyday lumbermen were described as a bellicose, but benevolent bunch, those who became lumber barons were almost revered. They evolved into prestigious citizens of coastal communities, wearing a cloak of 1800s genteel glamour. Charles H. Hackley was one such lumber baron, and his benefactions continue to brighten the modern complexion of Muskegon today. Hackley arrived in the spring of 1856 ready to seek his timber fortune. He was nineteen years old when his steamship pulled alongside the sawdust heaps of Muskegon harbor. He had seven dollars in his pocket. He began working in the mills the day he arrived. Three years later, he and his father bought a share of a sawmill. Like other lucky lumber barons, Hackley found his fortune. Homes of wealthy lumber barons still overlook Muskegon

Lake and the dunes along Lake Michigan. Hackley's is one of the more elegant and is now a museum.

The fishing industry ran parallel with both fur trade and lumbering and survived when both faltered. However, lake pollution and invasive species including the sea lamprey and zebra mussel took their toll on commercial fishing in the Great Lakes. The lamprey, first introduced to the lakes in 1936, attaches its sucking mouth with razor-sharp teeth to a host and then feeds on its blood. Lake trout, once one of the most sought-after species caught in the lakes, had no natural defense against the lamprey. By the mid-1950s, lamprey had nearly eliminated the native population of trout in Lake Michigan and significantly reduced other species. Even when the lamprey did not succeed in killing trout, the predator still wreaked havoc. Often sport anglers reeled in a beautiful trout with lamprey hanging from its sides. Such a damaged trout wasn't likely to become an evening meal.

The zebra mussel was first discovered in Lake St. Clair in 1988. It was believed introduced to the lakes in the ballast water of ocean-going ships traveling the St. Lawrence Seaway, although it could have entered attached to chains and anchors of ocean vessels. The zebra mussel adversely affected the lakes' ecosystem causing widespread economic loss running in the billions of dollars each year from damaged harbors, boats, and power plants where the microscopic larvae made it directly into the facilities. The ruffe and spiny waterflea may have also hopped a ride in the ballast of ocean vessels.

Each played a role in upsetting the delicate balance of the water's natural system. More than 140 non-indigenous species of plants and animals have been established in the Great Lakes since the 1800s. Even those that were intentionally introduced often came at the expense of something that was already there.

Native species have been replaced with introduced fish such as smelt, alewife, and Pacific salmon. The alewife entered the upper Great Lakes through the Welland Canal that connects Lakes Erie and Ontario and was first found in Lake Michigan in 1949. When the trout population in Lake Michigan was nearly destroyed by the lamprey, the alewife no longer had a natural predator and eventually became an estimated 85 percent of the fish population. Herring, yellow perch, and emerald shiner populations were decimated. Predators to the alewife were desperately needed and resulted in stocking Lake Michigan with Coho salmon in 1966 and Chinook salmon in 1967. Sportfishing regained popularity as local anglers began catching salmon.

Recent reports from Lake Michigan suggest that commercial fisheries and sport anglers are again finding abundant populations of whitefish and trout. The status of the yellow perch is less certain. Hopefully, the past has yielded valuable lessons about how to manage the fish population so that Michigan can again boast successful commercial fisheries and world-class sportfishing that is one important draw for the tourist industry.

Tourism is an important cog in the gear of Lake Michigan's economy. After the lumber industry was extinguished like the fur industry before it, the Lake Michigan shoreline developed a more stable and less environmentally destructive means of supporting itself. Today, vineyards and orchards dot the countryside and resorts and tourism thrive.

The immigrants who sought their fortunes in fur or lumber brought with them customs and traditions, and along with the original people, they wove a colorful cultural tapestry. Today's visitors enjoy the fruits of these earlier inhabitants' labors from the orchards to the wines to the grains. Visitors also appreciate enduring celebrations from the Tulip Festival in Holland to the Greek and Irish Festivals in Muskegon to the Pow Wows in Grand Haven and along the Leelanau Peninsula.

Lake Michigan is called the Gold Coast because of the expensive homes, cottages, upscale shops, gourmet restaurants, and yachts that grace its shores. Every shore town caters to the whims and needs of visitors, no matter how extravagant their taste. But the million-dollar sunsets cost nothing and are there for everyone to enjoy.

<<>>

(Mackinac Island and Mackinaw City are included in Book One of this travel series, *Exploring Michigan's Sunrise Coasts.*)

1. CROSS VILLAGE

Cross Village is a census-designated place with a 2020 population of 95.

In 1675 Father Jacques Marquette, who figured prominently in the history of Cross Village, Mackinaw City, and St. Ignace, raised a large white cross on a cliff overlooking Lake Michigan at the site of what would become Cross Village. He wanted the symbol visible from the shore far into Lake Michigan. Today, a replica of Father Marquette's cross stands at the edge of the bluff, and like the original, it can be seen by watercraft at a significant distance from shore. A small garden at the base of the cross is lovingly tended by the town's garden club.

Father John Weikamp played a major role in the development of the area. Weikamp was born in Prussia on April 5, 1818, and became a priest in his early thirties. Soon thereafter, he moved to the United States and was appointed the priest at St. Peter's Church in Chicago. There are differing opinions about whether he was suspended from his duties at St. Peter's over a financial dispute with Bishop Anthony O'Regan, or whether with

O'Regan's approval, he accepted an invitation from Bishop Frederic Baraga to move to the undeveloped area of Cross Village, where he would attend to the spiritual needs of the Native Americans. Either way, Weikamp relocated north in 1855. During his 38 years at Cross Village, Father Weikamp helped the town become self-sufficient. He built a 108-bedroom convent that brought many Catholic brothers and sisters who assisted him in clearing land for farming. They built shops for blacksmithing and established a saw mill, school, and hospital. Weikamp died in a riding accident. He lost control of his horse and was dragged a short distance causing internal injuries that resulted in his death the next day. The convent that he had established lasted for seven more years. It was abandoned due to a lack of residents. A decade later the huge building burned to the ground after being struck by lightning. Weikamp's mausoleum stands near Holy Cross Church in this northern community.

Milo Quaife, in his book, *Lake Michigan*, published in 1945 as part of the American Lake Series, noted that Cross Village was probably the oldest continuous village in Michigan. Its rich history is inextricably entwined with that of the Odawa Native Americans who called the area *Wau-gaw-naw-ke-ze*. As many as 20 tribes of Native Americans populated the region in the late 1780s and came together there around tribal council fires. Because of Father Marquette's cross, they called the area Land of the Cross.

The French called the area *L'Arbre Croche* or Crooked Tree. Like most of the villages and towns of Michigan, Cross Village or L'Arbre Croche went through cycles of fur trading, lumbering, fishing, and farming.

This tiny town, tucked between its interesting neighbors, Harbor Springs to its south and Mackinaw City to its northeast, might not otherwise merit mention in a travel guide, but it is on your route. You may want to stop at an art gallery or take a lunch break as you drive along Lake Michigan's scenic coast. Parts of the Cross Village area are protected nesting grounds for the endangered piping plover.

• MUSEUM

The **L'Arbre Croche Museum** was opened in 1995 by Father Albert Langheim. The museum provides information on Cross Village, beginning with the Odawa and moving to the present day. Separate rooms in the museum are dedicated to the Native Americans, lumber industry, and Father Weikamp, along with a research room containing books about the village. Hours are very limited. In the past, it has only been open two hours on Saturday afternoon. If this is a place that interests you, call first.

• PARK

Wilderness State Park, just north of Cross Village, is a rare natural and uninhabited spot along Lake Michigan. The park runs next to Sturgeon Bay with over 25 miles of shoreline and is revered for its bass fishing near Waugoshance Point. Campsites are available.

• A DRIVE TO ENJOY

The Tunnel of Trees runs for 20 miles on M-119 between Cross Village and Harbor Springs, paralleling Lake Michigan's shoreline. The Tunnel of Trees earned its name because of the canopy formed overhead by the tree branches. This is an especially breathtaking trip during the fall color tour which is at its peak in early October. If you go then, allow yourself plenty of time to enjoy the scenery.

Tunnel of Trees between Cross Village and Harbor Springs.
Courtesy of Pixabay Free Images.

● LIGHTHOUSE

Waugoshance Lighthouse. During its working years, this brave lighthouse protected a stretch of the most treacherous waters in Lake Michigan. In the early 1800s, sailors frequently ran aground in the shallow waters of Waugoshance Shoal. Safety required a lighthouse to mark the danger and guide ships into the Straits of Mackinac. In 1832 a lightship was stationed on the shoal to protect water traffic until a lighthouse could be constructed. The lighthouse had to be built on an underwater crib, and that presented a daunting challenge. It had been tried on the East Coast, but would be more challenging in Northern Lake Michigan battered by fierce storms and daunting winter ice. The project began in 1850, and the lighthouse was completed and put into place in 1851. The 76-foot Waugoshance lighthouse was the first on the Great Lakes to use the Fresnel lens that directed beacons much farther and brighter than lamps alone.

Sixteen years later, weather damage had caused deterioration and the tower was unstable. The lighthouse needed to be rebuilt. The repairs only lasted 24 years before the structure again needed serious repairs.

For many days in 1871, lighthouse keepers around the state rang bells warning sailors of shoals as they crept through the smoke from fires that raged across the state. In spite of valiant efforts, many ships succumbed to the murky gray haze.

Waugoshance was decommissioned in 1912 when the more powerful White Shoals Light a few miles north made the Waugoshance beam redundant.

The lighthouse that had faithfully carried out its duties became a bombing target for pilot training during WWII. A massive fire, likely started by a direct hit, destroyed much of the interior of the tower and the keeper's dwelling. It is considered one of the most at-risk lighthouses on the lakes. There has been interest and a few attempts to restore the lighthouse. At this time, it is not open to the public. You can get there by boat but must maneuver through dangerous waters. Shepler's Ferry Service offers annual tours of lighthouses including one that sails past Waugoshance.

● GHOST STORY

The Ghost of Waugoshance Light. By day, Waugoshance Lighthouse looks like a besieged, worn-down, ancient lighthouse that lacks the strength to harm a soul, as she turns her woebegone countenance to the midday sun. At night, eerily sitting on her crib in dark roiling Lake Michigan waters, far from shore, she is an ominous presence and home to the ghost of John Herman.

Herman was the keeper of the light from about 1885 to October 14, 1900 when the waters around Waugoshance ended his life.

Herman was known to imbibe in spirits—the alcoholic kind—maybe a side effect of his confinement on a distant isolated shoal. He was also a practical joker, a personality trait not always appreciated by his assistant, who one moonless and windy night ascended the tower to light the lanterns and heard a lock click behind him. He was the target of yet another of Herman's jokes. The irritated assistant began rattling the door and yelling, "John, John, stop this nonsense. Let me down."

After he believed the joke had run its course, but before his pal would be angry enough to do him bodily harm, Keeper John Herman drunkenly staggered along the pier intending to unlock the door. Instead, he slipped, lost his footing, and plunged, screaming and flailing, into the churning waves where he drowned.

After several hours of patiently waiting for John to release him, the assistant signaled a nearby lighthouse, and another keeper arrived to investigate the problem. The two men searched for Herman, but his body was never recovered. For the next twelve years, lighthouse keepers contended with Herman's ghost who continued his pranks. During checkers games, Herman tipped keepers over in their chairs, even when they had not been leaning backward. Doors were locked, but not by the hand of a living soul. The lighthouse's reputation and the stories of its many strange occurrences spread, and the haunting kept many keepers from accepting the assignment. Even though Waugoshance is now decommissioned, Keeper John Herman walks the crib and continues to inhabit the lighthouse that squelched his life more than 120 years ago.

2. HARBOR SPRINGS

Harbor Springs enjoyed a 2020 population of 1,222. Predating European arrival, an Odawa village stood on a prominence between Cross Village and Harbor Springs. The coastline between the two points was called *Wau-*

gaw-naw-ke-ze which in the Odawa language meant large crooked tree. The French explorers translated *Wau-gaw-naw-ke-ze* or large crooked tree to *L'Arbre Croche*, and erected the L'Arbre Croche mission nearby. They called the indentation in the shoreline where Harbor Springs now stands *La Petite Traverse*, or the Little Crossing.

In 1823 the Odawa petitioned President James Monroe and the U. S. Congress for a religious teacher to serve their spiritual needs. Their request was honored, and in 1827 Father Peter De Jean visited the mission at L'Arbre Croche and baptized 21. In 1829 or 1830, Father De Jean returned to the area and moved the L'Arbre Croche mission to *Ville Neuve* (New Village). The mission at the new location became known as New L'Arbre Croche, to distinguish it from the earlier L'Arbre Croche on the coast. The New L'Arbre Croche mission in Ville Neuve was the beginning of Harbor Springs.

In 1853 Richard Cooper opened a general store and started commercial development of the little village. On March 27, 1862, postal service came to Little Traverse or Bayfield, yet another name by which the settlement was known. The first postmaster was Chief Andrew Blackbird. In 1881 after many attempts to finalize a name for the village, it was incorporated and became Harbor Springs, a designation that flowed from its natural harbor and many springs. In 1932 it became a city.

The harbor was a tremendous asset to the area's development. Deep and sheltered, it offered giant ships protection from angry storms.

To serve the lumber industry, a branch of the Grand Rapids and Indiana Railroad located in Harbor Springs in 1837. The train depot was a stunning architectural structure intended to gain attention and entice passengers. It succeeded on both counts. Its tall, ornate spire, bay window, and oversize roof brackets were part of the overall package created by architect Stanley

Osgood who also designed the Muskegon Union Station and the Mason County Courthouse.

The third weekend of July, model train and history buffs flock to Harbor Springs for Shay Days. This three-day event celebrates the life and inventions of nineteenth century Harbor Springs resident Ephraim Shay. (See Famous or Infamous with Ties to Harbor Springs.) During the annual event Shay's historic hexagon house at 396 Main Street, one block east of downtown Harbor Springs, is alive with activity.

By the turn of the twentieth century, resorts replaced lumbering. The Northland Limited, a special train serving northern Michigan towns, brought passengers in Pullman cars from Cincinnati, Louisville, St. Louis, and Fort Wayne. Additional cars from Chicago were added at Kalamazoo for the trip north.

In Petoskey passengers transferred to suburban trains traveling to resorts between Petoskey and Harbor Springs. In 1915 the suburban trains ran each direction eight times a day, and over a half million tickets were sold. The trains' popularity ended in the 1930s when automobiles provided an alternate means of transportation.

The depot was eventually sold to private owners and became a dress shop, a dance hall, and even an ice cream parlor before it was restored and became an art gallery where visitors admire current art and old architecture.

Harbor Springs has upscale shopping and a multitude of interesting boutiques.

● MUSEUM

Blackbird Museum, 368 Main Street. This building was the original post office as well as the home of Chief Andrew Blackbird, the first postmaster of Harbor Springs. The museum displays Native American artifacts and crafts. It is listed on the Michigan State Historical

Register. Blackbird lived there from 1858 until his death in 1908. Limited and seasonal hours.

<<>>

Harbor Springs History Museum, 349 East Main Street, located in the historic former city hall, brings the area's past to life in a family-friendly environment. Changing and permanent exhibits.

<<>>

● BEACHES, PARKS, AND TRAILS

City Beach near Zorn Park along the harbor front. Amenities: a bathhouse, restrooms, swimming raft, and a sandy beach with a view.

<<>>

Little Traverse Conservancy Nature Preserve, 3264 Powell Road, is dedicated to protecting 25,000 acres of scenic land but invites you to enjoy and appreciate it. You can wander through hardwood forests, walk sandy beaches, watch the activity of critters in and around the creeks, and delight in the wildlife you are sure to encounter.

<<>>

Thorn Swift Nature Preserve, 6696 Lower Shore Drive. A well-maintained boardwalk (some wood chip areas) through the forest to the edge of Lake Michigan. Also, a little pond and a beach overlook. The path runs along a ridge overlooking the shoreline.

<<>>

Zoll Street Beach. Small beach, close parking, picnic tables, floating raft, small playground area, beach house, and restrooms. Grassy spots and tree-shaded areas from which to watch the boat activity. A fenced area is home to a herd of deer accustomed to people visiting them. There is also a feeding station and a large space for the deer to run free.

● OTHER STOPS TO CONSIDER

Nub's Nob, 500 Nub's Nob Road. Skiing and snowboarding. Well-groomed slopes and varied terrain.

<<>>

Ziplining, wine tasting, breweries, tours, charters, parasailing, birdwatching, hiking, and cruises all await the traveler lucky enough to spend vacation time in Harbor Springs.

● THE FAMOUS OR INFAMOUS WITH TIES TO HARBOR SPRINGS

Andrew Blackbird, Odawa chief and first postmaster of Harbor Springs, was born in 1814 and died in 1908. Blackbird was an Odawa tribal leader and historian. He authored the *History of the Ottawa and Chippewa Indians of Michigan* in 1887.

<<>>

Joe Dart was born in and grew up in Harbor Springs. He began playing bass at age eight and played for Vulfpeck, an American funk band founded in 2011. The group attended and met at the University of Michigan.

<<>>

Robert Klark Graham was born in 1906 in Harbor Springs. He was a businessman who made his fortune creating shatterproof eyeglass lenses. He became interested in eugenics, created a sperm bank for geniuses, and solicited the sperm of Nobel laureates. His desire to create a better world through genetic engineering was highly controversial. His business closed two years after his death with only 218 children born under the program.

<<>>

Ephraim Shay was an inventor, railroad engineer, and entrepreneur born in 1839. He is remembered for designing the Shay locomotive. In 1888 Shay moved his family to Harbor Springs. He built the Shay Hexagon House (396 E. Main Street) with four wings opening off a central space with a tower on top. The house is listed on the National Register of Historic Places and is worth a drive-by. The building is currently owned by the Harbor Springs Historical Society which is in the process of restoring it. Shay died in 1916 and is buried in Harbor View Lakeview Cemetery.

● **Book with a Tie to Harbor Springs**
Kristie Dickinson, ***Devil's Elbow, a Harbor Secret*** is set in Harbor Springs. The title comes from a dangerous curve in the Tunnel of Trees known as the Devil's Elbow. Protagonist Kylie Branson visits idyllic Harbor Springs expecting a quiet day at the beach until her dog runs off, chasing a fawn. Kylie pursues them and finds more than her dog. She discovers what appears to be human remains and is thrust headlong into a secret that has been kept for hundreds of years.

3. Petoskey
Including Bay View
A popular resort town, Petoskey had a 2020 population of 5,810 and offers visitors year-round activities.

Antoine Carre, a descendant of French nobility, visited the Petoskey area in the late 1780s. He joined John Jacob Astor's fur company and married a Native American woman from the Odawa tribe. Carre thoroughly assimilated into his wife's tribe, became a chief, and was given the name Neaatooshing.

In the spring of 1787, after spending the winter near what is now Chicago, Neaatooshing and his family began their trek back to northwest Michigan. One night during this journey, they camped on the banks of the Kalamazoo River. Before daybreak, a son was born to the chief. As the sun rose in the sky, its rays fell on the newborn. Seeing the sunshine on his child's face, the Chief proclaimed, "His name shall be Petosegay, and he shall become an important person." The translation of the name is rising sun, rays of dawn, or sunbeams of promise.

Petosegay became a leader of his people. In the summer of 1873, a few years before his death, a city was founded along the bay at Bear Creek. The site had a few nondescript buildings and a field overgrown with June grass. The population was no more than fifty or sixty. The city was named Petoskey, an English adaptation of Petosegay, in honor of the chief who gave his land, his name, and the heritage of "sunbeams of promise."

Petosegay's son, Ignatius Petoskey, grew up to be a chief in the Bear River Native American Village. Ignatius received a grant of land in accordance with the provisions of the Treaty of 1855. He lived in a log home on this land and bought additional land from the government, ultimately owning much of the acreage on which Petoskey, named in his father's honor, now stands. Ignatius served as a translator during church services, turning the words of the minister into the language of the Native Americans who attended the services along with their English-speaking neighbors.

The Petoskey fossil is found in rock strata called the Gravel Point Formation located in the Traverse City and Petoskey area. However, these interesting stones are found on Lake Huron's shores as surely as they are found on the northern coast of Lake Michigan.

At 5:00 p.m. on November 25, 1873, the first steam locomotive penetrated the wilderness to Little Traverse Bay. It signaled the start of an exciting era in Petoskey history. Aboard was George Gage, a reporter for the *Grand Rapids Times*, who was awed by what he proclaimed the million-dollar sunset. Those words have described Lake Michigan's fabulous sunsets ever since. The Grand Rapids and Indiana Railroad played a major role in transforming Petoskey into a bustling city by the turn of the century.

Change came at a heavy price. In 1874 the railway had land to sell and vigorously promoted settlement in the area. The campaign championed the magnificence of the wilderness—the clear, fresh, health-giving air, the pure, sparkling lakes and streams with abundant fish, and the unspoiled forests of pine and hardwoods. Would-be settlers embraced the dream, and for the next five years impressive numbers of people stepped off the GRI at the last stop in Petoskey.

The claims that induced those early immigrants to relocate were all true, but the city was unequipped to meet their basic needs of food and shelter. Many of the new transplants were looking for a fresh start after losing everything in the Panic of 1873. Others were Civil War veterans seeking a place to pick up the pieces of their lives. These uprooted pioneers sometimes lived in holes dug in river banks until they could erect a suitable cabin. Even with long days toiling in the field, starvation seemed an ever-ominous threat.

By 1877 tales of the deprivation suffered in Petoskey reached Grand Rapids, and that city sent boxcars full of supplies to sustain the populace of this northern outpost until Petoskey could get its fields tilled and producing.

At about the same time the relief train arrived from Grand Rapids, a miracle of sorts took place. Great flocks of passenger pigeons flew across the northern Michigan skies seeking places to nest. They were trapped by the hundreds of thousands and became a desperately needed food source.

In addition to becoming dinner to starving settlers, the birds were hunted and exported by the boatloads to large city markets until the passenger pigeon was extinct.

Martha. Courtesy of Pixabay Free Images.

Martha, the last passenger pigeon died in the Cincinnati Zoo in 1914. She had been named to honor Martha Washington. John Herald, a bluegrass singer, wrote a song dedicated to Martha and the extinction of the passenger pigeon that he titled "Martha, Last of the Passenger Pigeons." In 2019 Greg Benchwick published a children's chapter book, *Martha, the Last Passenger Pigeon.*

Today Petoskey covers an area of approximately four square miles. While summer is its high season, winter sports are also popular. Locals tell you that it is the year-rounder who is truly fortunate. He or she gets to enjoy each beautiful season in its turn.

The **Bay View** area near Petoskey is a census-designated place that enjoyed a 2020 population of 233. In 1875 the Methodist Camp was established there "for scientific and intellectual culture, and for the promotion of the Christian religion and morality." From the tent city of its early camp days, Bay View evolved into a community featuring Victorian cottages. Summer homes sprang up, and the wealthy new residents of Bay View infused the Petoskey economy with their money. Many other summer colonies followed. Situated along five miles of stunningly beautiful Lake Michigan shoreline between Harbor Springs and Petoskey, Bay View is a seasonal community with residence limited to May through October. The Terrace Inn of Bay View is home to resident ghosts.

● MUSEUMS AND GALLERIES

Petoskey has dozens of art galleries dotting its streets and inviting you inside to peruse the merchandise and exhibits.

<<>>

Little Traverse Historical Museum, 100 Depot Court (at Bayfront Park), located in the historic Chicago and West Michigan Railroad Depot. The museum features Native American Cultural Art, Emmet County genealogy, an Ernest Hemingway exhibit, a Petoskey Stone exhibit, and the nautical history of the Little Traverse Bay. Seasonal hours.

Downtown Petoskey. Courtesy of Bob Royce.

● BEACHES, PARKS, AND TRAILS

(At the corner of Petoskey and Bay Streets, there is a tunnel under US 31 from the shopping district to the downtown parks and marina. It allows you to avoid crossing the busy highway.)

Little Traverse Wheelway, a paved 26-mile trail takes you from Charlevoix to Harbor Springs. The Wheelway suffered a massive washout in 2020, and the path has been rerouted for the indefinite future. (See Charlevoix for details.)

<<>>

Magnus City Park Beach, 901 West Lake Street on the Little Traverse Bay in downtown Petoskey. Amenities: playground, restrooms, great views. Perfect place to find Petoskey stones; this is a rocky beach and not the ideal place for swimming or sunbathing. Camping sites accommodate various sized RVs, motor homes, and campers.

<<>>

Pennsylvania Park, downtown. The park gazebo is the site of summer entertainment.

<<>>

Petoskey State Park, 2475 M-119, midway between Petoskey and Harbor Springs. The park has 305 acres along the Grand Traverse Bay. The day-use park offers picnic facilities and a playground, a mile-long sunbathing beach, trails, access to the Little Traverse Wheelway, fishing, and water sports. Lots of Petoskey stones. The park has two separate campgrounds; Tannery Creek offers 98 campsites, and the Dunes has 70 campsites. All sites have electric hookups, and the camps have modern bathroom and shower facilities. Camping facilities are seasonal. There are two rustic mini-cabins with electricity available for rent. There are no boat launches within the park.

Note: The park's day-use area closed in October 2021 for the construction of a new nonmotorized trail to connect the beach house to the campground road. The Tannery Campground, toilet and shower buildings, sanitation station and utilities remain open and functional. The trails are accessible from the parking lot near the camp office.

26

Petoskey. Courtesy of Bob Royce.

• Other Stops to Consider

Harris Gardens, 1515 Howard Street, on the North Central Michigan College campus boasts 25 sculptures making a campus walk an art adventure.

<<>>

Historic Trolley Tours originate at Stafford's Perry Hotel in downtown Petoskey. The seasonal tours last about 90 minutes. The COVID-19 pandemic halted the trolley in 2021. Its future uncertain, it was hoped that the trolley would return in 2022. The trolley is free and takes riders through downtown, south to the Village at Bay Harbor and north to Petoskey State Park. Regular season is June to August. Call for additional information.

<<>>

Hunting for Petoskey Stones

The most easily identifiable rock for collecting purposes is the Petoskey stone. The Petoskey fossil is found in rock strata called the Gravel Point Formation located in the Traverse City and Petoskey area.

Petoskey stones were formed about three hundred and fifty million years ago. What is now Michigan was near the equator, and a warm, shallow sea covered the state. In this sea habitat, trilobites, fish, and many other forms of life, including the coral that is now fossilized as Petoskey stone, developed. The soft living tissue of the coral was called a polyp, and at its center was a mouth for food intake. During the petrification process, this center filled with silt and created the dark spots of the stone. Surrounding the center, you see tentacles that the coral used to gather plankton into its mouth. A Petoskey stone is a colony coral. Each separate chamber of the fossil was a member of the colony.

The derivation of the name Petoskey Stone comes from the city where so many are found. (See city history at the beginning of this section.)

Polishing Petoskey Stones. Often these stones are fairly well polished by the natural action of the wind, waves, and sand. Petoskey stones found inland lack the definition of their beach cousins. Even those along the shore appear more defined with a bit of polishing. If the stones you find are not polished to your satisfaction, a bit of sandpaper, a piece of corduroy, and polishing powder can enhance the finish.

The sanding process should involve three grits of sandpaper: 220, 400, and 600. With the 220 you can remove any scratch marks. The 400 grit should remove any coarse spots. The 600 grit will make the stone smooth. You start with the coarsest grit, and the trick is to sand longer than you think the stone needs. Sprinkle the polishing powder (available at hobby stores) on the corduroy fabric and begin polishing the stone. Rinse and you should see a new luster. If you are unhappy with the finish, you can sand some more and repeat.

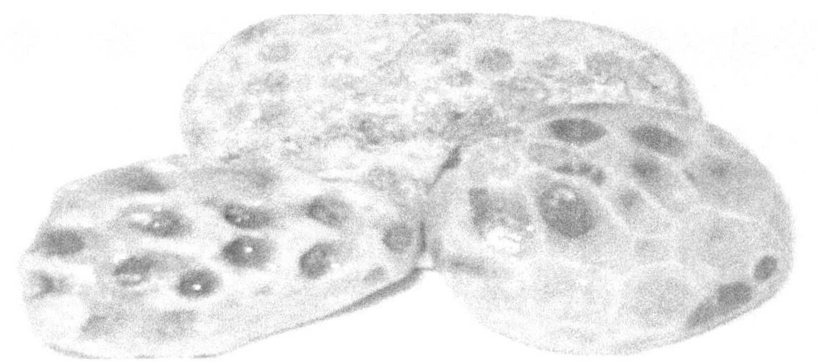

Petoskey Stones. Courtesy of Bob Royce.

<>>>

Petoskey Walking and Bay Tours are available. You can download a walking tour map online. The self-guided tour will take approximately 90 minutes. Boat tours can be arranged locally.

<<>>

Saint Francis Solanus Mission Church, West Lake Street, was built in 1859 and is often referred to as the Little Church by the Lake. The church was constructed under the directive of Bishop Baraga, the Snow Shoe Priest, and was a religious home to Native Americans and early settlers. It was named in honor of St. Francis Solanus, a Franciscan missionary working among the indigenous people of South America. The years took their toll on the little mission church, and it has been restored twice. It still stands at its original location and is the oldest building in the Northern Lower Peninsula.

<<>>

Tri-County Driving Tour, 62 miles and approximately 1½ hours driving time. Depart Petoskey east on Mitchell Street (C-58) to Wolverine. Take a right at the traffic signal onto Straits Highway and continue for seven miles to Thumb Lake Road (C-48), then right to US 131. Turn left on U.S. 131 to Boyne Falls. Turn west on M-75 to Boyne City. Stay on M-75 North through Walloon Lake Village to US 131. Turn left and return to Petoskey. A pretty ride with one of the area's most spectacular views as you crest the hill re-entering Petoskey.

<<>>

Underwater Crucifix, Little Traverse Bay near Petoskey. If you are a tourist to Petoskey, it isn't likely you'll be lucky enough to see the Underwater Crucifix unless you dive the Bay or chance upon the rare winter showing. Still, it seems remiss not to mention it in a travel book. It is the only freshwater underwater crucifix in the world. The 11-foot-tall cross, with a five-foot, five-inch figure of Jesus Christ, is settled at the bottom of the Bay near the breakwall in Bayfront Park. It had been commissioned in the late 1950s by the grieving parents of a 15-year-old boy killed in a shotgun accident on the family farm.

Crafted in Italy of white marble, the cross was significantly damaged during shipping and rejected by the purchasers. It was bought by the Wyandotte dive club at an insurance sale. The crucifix made its way to Little Traverse Bay and was placed by the U.S. Icebreaker *Sundew* 1,200 feet off the Petoskey breakwall on August 12, 1962. Originally intended to honor a diver who had drowned in Torch Lake, the club decided the monument should pay tribute to all who have perished at sea. In 1985 the cross was raised and a new base built. It was decided to hold a winter viewing through a hole in the ice when weather conditions permitted. Underwater lights are used to make the cross visible.

<<>>

White Water Park in Bear River Valley Recreation Area, located in the heart of Petoskey includes a ¼ mile white water course, the only one of its kind in the Lower Peninsula.

<<>>

Petoskey has an abundance of activities from low-key to high adrenalin. There are tours (including the Hemingway tour), produce farms where you can pick up fresh fixings for dinner, a culinary trail, wine and brewery tours, inside water park, and every water activity you can imagine.

● THE FAMOUS OR INFAMOUS WITH TIES TO PETOSKEY

Megan Boone, FBI agent Elizabeth Keen in the TV series *Blacklist,* was born in Petoskey. Before starring in *Blacklist*, Boone had roles in *Law and Order*, *Blue Bloods*, and a variety of other movies and TV shows.

<<>>

Antoine Carre, (See city history at beginning of this section.)

<<>>

William Bruce Catton, American Civil War historian and Pulitzer Prize winner in 1954 for his book, *A Stillness at Appomattox*. Catton was born in Petoskey and died in nearby Frankfort at age 78 in 1978.

<<>>

Ernest Hemingway is the best-known of the notables with a tie to Petoskey. He deserves more space and consideration than can be allocated here. Hemingway spent his early writing days in Northern Michigan. A complex man, he battled his demons using cathartic fictionalization and an alter ego, Nick Adams. His stories drew heavily on his private turmoil and experiences. Hemingway was handsome, strong, and intelligent. He loved hunting and the great outdoors. He was a womanizer and an alcoholic. He was macho and, at the same time, weak, self-destructive, and troubled.

Ernest was a Midwestern boy, born in Chicago in 1899 and raised, at least partially, in the rugged north woods of Michigan. His family owned a rustic cottage at Walloon Lake. To get there, the family boarded a steamer destined for Harbor Springs. At the train station on West

Bay Street near the Municipal Marina, they transferred their baggage onto a Dummy Train to Petoskey and Walloon Lake.

Hemingway's mother Grace often dressed him and his sister Marcelline as twins, sometimes as boys, sometimes as girls. A picture of the two taken at Walloon Lake in August 1900 bears the admiring description, "Two sturdy little chaps in overalls."

In Northern Michigan, Ernest was taught to hunt and fish by his father, Doctor Clarence "Ed" Hemingway. Ernest hiked and camped and explored his north woods, feeling safe and at peace there. This was before he became a famous writer. Those early years provided a backdrop for much of his subsequent writing. In later life, he was consumed by living the legend he had become, enjoying the enormity of his fame. But he never again found the security and serenity he knew in Michigan's North Country. During the 1930s and 1940s, after he stopped summering in Michigan, Ernest's fame landed him in the news almost daily. Peace became elusive.

Gregory Hemingway, called Gig by his famous father, was Ernest's youngest son. After Ernest committed suicide, Gig authored a biography, simply titled *Papa.* In his book, he describes his childhood ordeal in the hospital with polio-like symptoms. Gig writes: "Papa wouldn't allow anyone else in the room except for himself and the doctors, and he took my temperature every four hours, and he brought my meals in himself. He'd lie beside me on the cot at night telling wonderful stories about his life up in Michigan as a boy, how he'd caught his first trout and how beautiful the virgin forests were before the loggers came. He told me about a furry monster that grew taller and taller every night and then, just as it was about to eat him, would jump over the fence. He said fear was perfectly natural and nothing to be ashamed of. The trick to mastering it was controlling your imagination, but he said he knew how hard this was for a boy. Mainly he just told me stories—about how he had fished and hunted in the Michigan north woods, and about how he wished he could have stayed my age and lived there forever—until I fell asleep." Ultimately, Gig recovered from his illness and became a doctor like his grandfather.

Hemingway's work based in, or influenced by, his summers in Michigan include *Up in Michigan, On Writing, Summer People, The Last Good Country, The Torrents of Spring, Sepi Jingan,* and several of the Nick Adams stories, most notably, *Indian Camp, The Doctor and the Doctor's Wife, Ten Indians, The End of Something, The Indians Moved Away, Wedding Day,* and *Fathers and Sons.* Ernest spent time in Petoskey, Harbor Springs, Lake Charlevoix, Horton Bay, and Traverse City. Many of his early stories were inspired by and reflect these locations.

In 1916 Ernest stayed at the well-known Perry Hotel in Petoskey's famous gaslight district after a northwest Lower Michigan camping trip with his friend Lewis Clarahan. Hemingway wrote about Greensky Hill Indian Methodist Church on Old US 31 North Highway. Ernest lived in charming and quaint Petoskey during the winter of 1919-1920. In the cold, bleak months of that season, after he returned from World War I, he rented an upstairs room at Potter's Rooming House at 602 East State Street. He was trying to write fiction but having a hard time staying focused. Billiards with old friends at the City Park Grill proved a tempting distraction. Hemingway frequented the Petoskey Public Library that winter trying to get back on his writing track. Still unable to work, it is believed he fled the genial company of his friends and holed up in a small room in Evelyn Hall, an unoccupied women's dormitory at the Bay View Conservatory.

Jesperson's Restaurant was a place that Ernest and his friend Dutch frequented.

Near the end of 1924, Hemingway sent a lengthy letter to Bill Smith, another northern Michigan friend. In the letter, Hemingway noted that since he and Bill had last been in touch, he had been doing a lot of writing, and of the work he had thus far produced, "almost everything worth a damn" had been about Michigan. He was nostalgic about the country that he and Bill had known in their boyhoods and insisted, "The swell times we used to have with Auntie [Mrs. Dilworth] at the farm, the first swell trips out to the Black and the Sturgeon, and the wonderful times we had with the men and the storms in the fall and potato digging and the whole damn thing."

In a letter to his father he said, "I've written a number of stories about the Michigan country—the country is always true—what happens is always fiction." Ed Hemingway did not approve of his son's writing.

While it is apparent that some of Hemingway's happiest and fondest memories revolve around his time spent in northern Michigan, he never returned to the state in later years. His life took him to Spain, Paris, Africa, and Colorado, all to "find his voice," and yet he abandoned the place where it may have spoken to him the loudest.

During his writing career, which spanned approximately 43 years, Hemingway wrote nine novels, four books of nonfiction, over 100 short stories, nearly 400 articles, poetry, and a play. He participated in five wars, and sustained serious injuries during World War I. He suffered four automobile accidents and two plane crashes. The plane crashes occurred on consecutive days in East Africa in 1954; they prompted untimely obituaries throughout the world. He was married four times and had three sons. In 1954 he won a Nobel Prize for literature and a Pulitzer Prize for *The Old Man and the Sea.*

He suffered grave depression and spent two months in 1960 at the Mayo Clinic undergoing the cure of the day—electric shock treatments. He was tormented by his father's suicide. Two siblings also committed suicide; and the family curse continued after his death when his granddaughter, Margaux, overdosed, killing herself. Hemingway believed the electroshock had addled his brain to the point where he could no longer write, and to him that was worse than death.

In June of 1961, Hemingway attempted suicide and was hospitalized for more electroshock therapy, but he convinced everyone he was well enough to be released. On July 2, 1961, at 7:00 a.m. on an otherwise quite ordinary Sunday morning, still dressed in pajamas and a bathrobe, Ernest Hemingway went to the basement and grabbed a shotgun and a box of ammunition. He carried them upstairs to the foyer where he loaded two shells into the twelve gauge. He put the barrel into his mouth and pulled the trigger.

Today Michigan has a Hemingway Society of devoted fans. They meet each year to discuss his writing in the location where so many of his stories took root. They focus on his happier days.

<<>>

Alan Hewitt is a musician, composer, producer, and recording and performing artist who was born in Petoskey. He played keyboard for The Moody Blues and for several years, produced alongside Maurice White of Earth Wind and Fire.

<<>>

David Robert Malpass was born in Petoskey in 1956. He is an economic analyst and served as Under Secretary of the Treasury for International Affairs under Donald Trump.

<<>>

Herbert Vaughn Orvis was born in 1946 in Petoskey. He played ten years of professional football, five years with the Detroit Lions and then five years with the Baltimore Colts. He was a defensive tackle. He was inducted into the College Football Hall of Fame in 2014. He died in 2020.

<<>>

Hal Smith was born in Petoskey in 1916 and is best remembered as Otis Campbell on the Andy Griffith Show. He was also a voice actor credited with more than 300 film and TV productions.

• BOOKS AND MOVIES WITH TIES TO PETOSKEY
Petoskey and the surrounding cities are the settings for several of the Nick Adams stories by Ernest Hemingway. (See Famous or Infamous with Ties to Petoskey.)

<<>>

Michael R. Federspiel, ***Picturing Hemingway's Michigan***, introduces readers to the Hemingway family whom he says in many ways were typical of those who vacationed in the area. Federspiel paints a picture of life in northern Michigan between 1900 and 1920 and traces the many connections between the area and Hemingway's body of work. The book includes more than 250 photos, many from the Hemingway family's collection.

Gregory Hemingway, ***Papa: A Personal Memoir***. This is the story of the painful and troubled, yet loving relationship between Nobel Prize-winning author, Ernest Hemingway, and his youngest son. Gregory Hemingway's personal account doesn't capture a reader's attention and admiration like his father's eloquent stories did, but the son's recollections and anecdotes make interesting material for any Hemingway fan. Ernest's suicide foretold the tragic ending.

36

• GHOST STORIES

The City Park Grill Ghost roams McCarty Hall, a building constructed in 1875. It is one of Petoskey's oldest buildings and steeped in rich history. A regular haunt of Ernest Hemingway, the City Park Grill performed a stint as a speakeasy selling bootleg booze to thirsty northern Michiganders. Underground tunnels run between connecting buildings, and ghosts reside on the premises. Ghost hunters found the most activity in the basement where they reported five spirits at one time.

<<>>

The Ghost at 326 Mitchell (main shopping street of Petoskey). Several occupants of the upstairs apartment have reported a white-aproned man lurking about as though he owned the place. In an earlier life, the building's street level housed a butcher shop. The ghost is reported to be a butcher who committed suicide in the basement.

<<>>

The Perry Hotel Ghost. In 1899, 20 luxury hotels were built in or near Petoskey. They signaled the advent of the city as an upscale tourist destination. The Perry is the only one of those hotels still standing. In 1902 a young woman committed suicide in the hotel, and her ghost hangs out in the garden overlooking the lake.

<<>>

The Ghosts of the Terrace Inn. The old hotel built in 1911 was originally the site of two boarding houses that were torn down to make way for this Victorian hotel. During construction, two men died when a beam fell on them. After the hotel was finished, it is believed those two men decided to stay. Some visitors report hearing hammering when no remodeling or other work is being done. Speculation suggests the construction workers still ply their trade.

The hotel embraces its gaggle of ghosts and haunted reputation. It hosts paranormal conventions. If you ask at the front desk if ghosts reside in the building, you may be handed a guest book wherein visitors have recorded their sightings. The second and third floor stairwells are described as hubs of ghostly activity. In the lobby, piano music is heard when there is no human hand creating it. Other spirits include an old man and an elderly woman who remain in the hotel, two maids, and a little boy who mostly resides in the basement but sometimes follows people up and down the steps.

The hotel restaurant attracts a lady in gauzy white who has visited guests in their rooms. A man in a tweed suit looks out from the balcony.

The most dubious ghost story is that of Elizabeth Abigail Sweet whose wraith purportedly haunts the hotel. She is alleged to have visited when she was pregnant with twins. During her stay, she fell, miscarried, and died in room 211. The story goes on to say that some years later, Elizabeth's husband returned to the hotel where his wife had died, and he expired there from a broken heart.

4. BAY HARBOR

Bay Harbor does not have census data separate from Petoskey and was indistinguishable from Petoskey from the sixteenth to the nineteenth centuries. The two locations were separated by a couple of miles and shared a history common to nearly every shore community along Lake Michigan. Native Americans inhabited the land, Europeans came when fur became a lucrative business, lumber came on the scene to replace the fur industry when animals became too scarce for profitable hunting, and then the forests too were depleted. The citizenry of these little villages and towns awoke to the splendor of Lake Michigan every morning. There is a saying, *If you are lucky enough to live on Lake Michigan, you are lucky enough.* Unfortunately, that alone did not put food in your stomach or a roof over your head.

The death of lumbering meant drastic changes for shoreline communities. Harbor Springs became a resort community to wealthy families from all over the Midwest, including Chicago. It was the place to have your summer home. Petoskey grew into a bustling business community, but also had hotels and motels that accommodated a growing tourist trade. Bay Harbor's destiny took a different direction. About a century ago, limestone was discovered on the outskirts of Petoskey in Bay Harbor. It drew mining interests and became the site of a large cement manufacturing facility owned by Penn-Dixie.

For more than a century, mining operations defaced about five miles and more than 1,000 acres of Lake Michigan shoreline along the Little Traverse Bay.

When mining operations were abandoned, they left in their tracks scarred acreage pockmarked by asbestos, coal, and two and a half million cubic yards of kiln dust. It was not a benevolent way to treat the natural beauty of the Big Lake.

The scenic magnificence of the Traverse Bay, however, induced creative and enterprising folks to undertake a cleanup effort to reclaim this eyesore and transform it into a first-class resort area with wonderful tourist facilities.

By 1995 the toxic, hideous, and deformed lakeshore became a luxury resort, the rival of any of her pretty older neighbors. Today, instead of the reek of chemicals and carcinogens, Bay Harbor smells of elegance and money.

● SOMETHING TO CONSIDER

Great Lakes Center for the Performing Arts, 800 Bay Harbor Drive. If you travel to the Petoskey area, it is worth looking at what's happening at the Great Lakes Center for the Arts. Secure tickets in advance for this beautiful venue. The seating is comfortable, the acoustics excellent, and the experience worthwhile. The Center presents major talent and varied entertainment including jazz, blues, country, comedy, theatre, dance, pop, and more.

Bay Harbor Marina. Courtesy of Lloyd Pedersen.

• PARKS

Little Traverse Wheelway. This 26-mile trail takes you from Charlevoix to Harbor Springs and can be accessed in Bay Harbor. The Wheelway has been disrupted and rerouted because of a washout. (See Charlevoix for additional details.)

5. CHARLEVOIX

Charlevoix is a modest-sized town with a 2020 population of 2,497. Its size multiplies by ten with the summer tourist invasion. Charlevoix perches on an isthmus straddling Lake Michigan and Round Lake and spreads east to Lake Charlevoix. The Pine River runs through the heart of town.

Charlevoix County was part of the territory acquired in 1836 by the Treaty of Washington, an agreement between representatives of the Odawa and Ojibwe

Nations and the United States Government. By this treaty, Native Americans ceded nearly 14 million acres in the northwest portion of the Lower Peninsula and the eastern portion of the Upper Peninsula to the United States. This area, which represents slightly more than one-third of Michigan's current landmass, was known as Michilimackinac. It is alleged that after the land transfer, many Native Americans who signed the treaty were killed by members of their tribes for participation in ceding their land.

In 1840 the Michilimackinac territory was divided into several regions, and the part today that includes Charlevoix was first called Keskkauko. When parceled into counties, Charlevoix County was originally part of Emmet County. It organized as a separate county in 1869, drawing part of its acreage from Emmet County and part from Antrim County.

The name Charlevoix honors Pierre Francois Xavier de Charlevoix, an explorer and Jesuit missionary, who traveled the Great Lakes seeking the water passageway to the Pacific and China. Father Charlevoix lived from 1682-1761, dying at age 79—an impressive lifespan for an explorer of those days. It is not known if the priest ever set foot in the area of Charlevoix, either the city or county.

Charlevoix County experienced slow growth until 1870, but in the years after the Civil War its economy was sparked by its natural bounty of White Pine. The Grand Rapids and Indiana Railroad brought a station to the area enabling the commercial lumbering of the old-growth forests.

In 1878 H.W. Page, a professor from the University of Chicago, formed the Belvedere Summer Home Association which was the first of many retreats to locate in Charlevoix. Even at that early date, the area was revered as a summer destination, and the city became home to several extravagant summer hotels.

When the forests were exhausted, the town turned to farming, fishing, and tourism for sustenance. Many residents believed that a sugar factory, a cement factory, and a seed warehouse would spell ongoing prosperity. Ultimately, resorts and tourism became the leading economic resource.

Charlevoix was home to Michigan's first nuclear power plant, Big Rock Point, which operated from 1962 to 1997.

The city has had its share of notoriety because of its connection to the Loeb family of the infamous Leopold and Loeb case that involved the kidnap and murder of a 14-year-old boy by two wealthy college students. Charlevoix was also the summer home of John and Patsy Ramsey, parents of Jon-Benet Ramsey, the little girl crowned as "Little Miss Charlevoix" the year before her infamous murder.

Today, Charlevoix is populated by a blend of longtime residents, who often work in the town's industrial park, and summer resorters. Some year-rounders are descendants of early commercial fishermen who lived there.

While in this area that locals call "Charlevoix the Beautiful," you will want to see the Charlevoix South Pier Light Station that marks the opening of the channel, and the railroad depot that serves as a museum and home to the Charlevoix Historical Society.

The State of Michigan purchased the track between Charlevoix and Petoskey from the Chessie Railroad System, and in the 1990s the track was removed and the rail line paved as a bicycle trail between Charlevoix and Harbor Springs. Skaters, walkers, and runners share the path with bicyclists. In the winter, it is a popular cross-country ski path.

It is only a short ferry ride to Beaver Island where you can explore the history of Michigan's only real king—King

James Jesse Strang. (See the Famous or the Infamous with Ties to Charlevoix.)

In addition to dazzling harbors, beaches, and quaint shops, a visit to Charlevoix presents opportunities for hunting, fishing, mushroom picking, wine tastings, brewery tastings, apple festivals, and downhill skiing.

Bridge open for passing ship. Courtesy of Bob Royce.

● MUSEUMS AND GALLERIES

Bier Art Gallery and Pottery, 03500 US 31 South, six miles south of Charlevoix in a turn of the century red and white schoolhouse with a view of Lake Michigan. More than 80 regional and national artists contribute their work to this gallery. You will find stoneware originals, photography, glass, woodcuts, watercolors, sculpture, metal works, baskets, and jewelry to tempt you.

<<>>

The Charlevoix Historical Museum at Harsha House, 103 State Street. Built in 1891 by Charlevoix businessman and community leader Horace Harsha, this lovely Victorian home was donated to the city by Mr. Harsha's granddaughter to be used as a museum. In addition to the museum, the building houses two apartments that provide the funds to maintain the grounds and building. Inside three Victorian period rooms await with their displays of over 9,000 historic photos and negatives along with local historical artifacts and collections including a 1917 working player piano.

<<>>

Railway Depot Museum, east end of Dixon and Chicago Avenue on Lake Charlevoix across from Depot Beach Park Area. The Charlevoix Railroad Station was donated to the Historical Society by Robert Pew in June 1992 on the 100th anniversary of the first train arrival in Charlevoix. The Society has restored and preserved the Depot building which is only open for special exhibits. The Charlevoix Area Garden Club created and maintains the gardens which are always open.

• BEACHES, PARKS, AND TRAILS

Charles Ransom Nature Preserve. Quarterline Road off Boyne City Road to Maple Grove until it dead ends. Treat yourself to a 1½ mile trail system with fabulous views from its 320-foot elevation. You can see Lake Michigan, Leelanau Peninsula, and Fox and Beaver Islands. The preserve is 89 acres of open fields and northern Michigan hardwoods.

<<>>

Depot Park Beach, east end of Dixon and Chicago Avenue on Lake Charlevoix. Great park for children. A historic beach offers a playground, pavilion, and picnic area plus a beautiful place to relax and enjoy views of Lake Charlevoix. Easy access to the water for kayakers or paddleboarders. (Site of the Railway Depot Museum, see above.)

<<>>

Ferry Avenue Beach, 224 Ferry Avenue, on Lake Charlevoix near downtown, provides a gentle slope to the sandy beach. Amenities include playground, pavilion, volleyball nets, basketball courts, horseshoes, restrooms, concessions, and boat launch. There is a swimming area and paddleboard rentals.

<<>>

Fisherman's Island State Park, 16480 Bells Bay Road (just south of Charlevoix). This park is not an island, but rather 2,678-acres with five miles of unspoiled Lake Michigan shoreline. However, tiny Fisherman's Island is encompassed by the park. Rustic campground with some sites nestled into the dunes. Amenities: picnic area, grills, firepits, hunting, cross-country skiing, swimming, fishing, and hiking.

<<>>

Little Traverse Wheelway. This 26-mile route takes you from Charlevoix to Harbor Springs. The trail is paved, and you meander through delightful parks and along spectacular shoreline on the way to your Bay Harbor, Petoskey, or Harbor Springs destination. A ¾ mile boardwalk protects the wetland ecosystem. Many spots offer access to the well-marked trail; one is the Charlevoix Township Hall at 12491 Waller Road where there is also parking. The trail is nonmotorized and open to bikers, skaters, skiers, walkers, and runners. Pick your favorite sport in any season and enjoy the views along the way. (Note: In April 2020, a washout struck the railway, and parts of it have been rerouted. Much of the trail remains open, but a small portion toward Charlevoix is under construction. Hopefully the inconvenience will be short-lived.)

<<>>

Michigan Beach Park, 95 Grant Street on Lake Michigan, is a favorite spot for locals and tourists alike.

45

Much of the beach is rocky so you should wear water shoes. The beach offers some white sand for sunbathers, Petoskey stones, playground, walking trails, basketball court, volleyball net, pavilion, concessions, restrooms, swimming area, fishing off the pier, and amazing sunsets. The Charlevoix Lighthouse is within walking distance.

<<>>

Surf and Turf Driving Tour, a 35-mile tour from Charlevoix that takes about 45 minutes. Drive through rolling hills, typical Michigan farmland, and the south arm of Lake Charlevoix. Depart Charlevoix along US 31 south to the Ellsworth turn in Atwood. Turn left on C-48, continue five miles and turn left on Church, then left again at the next stop, staying on C-48. In east Jordan, turn left on M-66. You pass the Ironton Ferry, highlighted in *Ripley's Believe It or Not.* (See Ironton Ferry under Other Stops to Consider.) Stay on M-66 to US 31. A right on US 31 takes you back into Charlevoix.

<<>>

Young State Park, a 563-acre park situated along Lake Charlevoix. It offers a 4-mile loop with both flat and rolling terrain.

● OTHER STOPS TO CONSIDER

Beaver Island. Enjoy a pleasant day on Beaver Island, the site of the former kingdom of James Jesse Strang. You can book a flight, take one of the commercial ferries from Charlevoix, or sail your own boat the distance of about 32 miles. Beaver Island has the Municipal Yacht Dock and a full-service marina that provides a lounge, modern bathrooms and showers, and a large picnic area. The marina accommodates small boats up to medium size yachts with drafts up to 8 feet. It is open May through September. There are day tours of the island (bus trips are available). You can also rent a car on the island or take off on your own hiking excursion. (See Famous or

Infamous with Ties to Charlevoix for information about King James Jesse Strang.)

<<>>

Castle Farms Historic Landmark, 5052 M-66 North, the site for many local functions including wine tasting, theatre productions, and even local weddings proves a unique stop on your journey along the Sunset Coast. Tours of the castle provide visitors with the opportunity to see the exquisite courtyards and gardens, including a hedge maze and giant chessboard. Castle Farms is one of Northern Michigan's top historic attractions. It provides visitors a pleasant stroll through magnificent stone buildings dating back to 1918.

Alfred Loeb, father of the Richard Loeb of the Leopold and Loeb case, built Castle Farm as an experiment to create the perfect farm. On its 1,600 acres, Mr. Loeb dreamed of raising prize-winning livestock. He hired Arthur Heun, the architect who designed the primary Loeb home in Chicago, to work on the project. The outbuildings were to be modeled after stone barns in Normandy. The house was constructed in the architectural style of a French Renaissance Châteaux. Thirty-five masons were employed for the project. They used local fieldstone as the main building material. The farm was a big enterprise and helped support the local Charlevoix economy by hiring 90 employees.

Today the farm features a variety of museum-quality collections including miniature castles, antique toys, and royalty memorabilia from around the world. The Castle's 1918 Museum showcases items from that era plus World War I memorabilia. Children delight in feeding the huge rainbow trout swimming in the Reflection Pond, participating in a game of giant chess, or playing hide-and-seek with the fairies and gnomes dwelling in the Enchanted Forest.

A self-guided tour or a scavenger hunt for children add to the adventure. There is a Garden Railroad with more than ½ mile of track and a 68 G-scale train. Castle Farms is a world-class historic property listed on both the National and State Historic Registries. It enchants visitors with old-world charm and modern-day elegance.

Castle Farm also has its dark history. Albert Loeb died in 1924 shortly after his son Richard was sentenced for the murder of Bobby Franks (See Leopold and Loeb under The Famous or Infamous.) His oldest son, Ernest, took over the farm and ran it for many additional years. By 1927 the farm no longer operated at a profit, and the livestock was sold. For several decades the property was rented, and many of the buildings were used for storage.

In the mid-1960s, the farm was sold to John Van Haver who charged visitors a fee to walk through the property which he had renamed Castle Van Haver. No doubt part of the appeal was its history of association to the infamous murder.

Van Haver could not make his venture pay and eventually sold the estate in 1969. The plan for the property, by then called simply Castle Farms, was a major arts and crafts center. Later a stage was added for rock concerts, and many performances took place there including Aerosmith, Alabama, Kenny G, Kiss, the Monkeys, Ozzy Osbourne, Rod Stewart, Stevie Nicks, and Sting. The local community, mainly wealthy summer residents, was not happy with the noise, rowdiness, traffic congestion, and general chaos of concert days.

In 1995 there was a failed attempt to purchase the property and turning it into a 4-H camp. The deal lacked adequate funding, and Castle Farms was finally purchased at auction in January 2001, the buyer intending it for public use: weddings, corporate meetings, antique and art shows, and public fundraisers. It appears Castle Farms has finally outlived its infamy.

Courtesy of Castle Farms.

<<>>

The Ironton Ferry, 9800 Ferry Rd (East side) or 10122 Ferry Rd (West side). The four-car Ironton cable ferry crosses a narrow point on the south arm of Lake Charlevoix and remains a piece of the city's history. It connects Ironton (2020 population of 114) to Boyne City. The ferry is located about five miles south of Charlevoix. The ferry began operation in 1876 when the operator took individual passengers across the lake in a rowboat. That worked for about four years before it was replaced by a ferry.

George Hemingway, Ernest's uncle, owned a tree farm in tiny Ironton. Ernest spent time on the farm in what became known as Hemingway Point. In the *Nick Adams Stories*, Nick was camping at this point when he became frightened and fired rifle shots to signal his father and uncle who were out on the lake.

The Ironton Ferry rated mention in *Ripley's Believe it or Not* when Ripley's reported a little story that got worldwide attention. Sam Alexander, who piloted the ferry from 1900 until his death in 1948, had traveled the equivalent of the earth's circumference but had never been more than 1,000 feet from his home.

The ferry ride takes only about ten minutes, but there can be a long line.

<<>>

The Mushroom House Tour lets you visit unique stone structures sometimes called Gnome Homes or Hobbit Houses. You'll learn about the architecture that is found nowhere else in the world and hear stories and history about Charlevoix.

• LIGHTHOUSE

Charlevoix South Pier Light stands a mere hundred feet from shore on a concrete pier. It rests atop a squat tower, the bottom third of which is open steel frame. The first lighthouse was constructed in 1885 and was moved to the pier in 1914. The current federally-owned tower was built in 1948. The light is automated and not open to the public.

Charlevoix South Pier Light. Courtesy of Bob Royce.

• SHIPWRECK

The **_Carl D. Bradley_** went down on November 18, 1958, and remains the largest ship to sink in Lake Michigan. When launched in 1929, she was the most powerful vessel on the Great Lakes. This giant tangled with a November gale and proved no match for the mighty lake. Thirty-three men lost their lives that night; two survived to tell the story. Twenty-five of the crew hailed from the small town of Rogers City. Most were of Polish descent, many knew each other's families, and many were related.

The cook often served the sailors kielbasa purchased from a neighborhood market in the *Polish Town* section of Rogers City.

Ship Captain, Roland Bryan, was an outsider. He still made his off-season home in Loudonville, New York, but he had been sailing with the Bradley Transportation Line for twenty-four years, and even when his crewmen sprinkled their conversation with Polish, he usually understood.

The night the *Bradley* sank, she was returning empty after delivering her last shipment of limestone for the 1958 season to Gary, Indiana. It was a happy day. Captain Bryan had a sweetheart in Port Huron. For the eight-month shipping season, he rarely saw her unless he picked up a load in Lake Huron and could blow his horn in salute as he passed by. In a couple more days, the couple would be reunited. He wished the weather forecast was less ominous, but he had endured many storms in his career. He knew if he delayed leaving Gary his entire crew would be unhappy. They, too, wanted to get back to families and loved ones.

The *Bradley* was in her thirty-first season, and she was due for inspections; inspections that would have revealed she needed work. But that was what winter was for.

Captain Bryan headed northwest, seeking protection from the winds along the west shore of Lake Michigan. The next day the weather worsened and winds reached sixty to sixty-five miles an hour. Waves rose at least twenty-five feet high. It might not have been the worst storm to ever hit Lake Michigan, but it was more than the *Bradley* could endure.

The ship's Mayday signal was picked up at the Charlevoix Coast Guard Station at 5:30 a.m. on November 18. The message described the *Bradley*'s position twelve miles southwest of Gull Island. The radio operator listened to the crewmen shouting, "Run, grab life jackets. Get the jackets." Then came another, "Mayday. The ship is breaking up."

It was the terrified voice of Elmer Fleming sending the Mayday calls. He and Frank Mays, the two survivors, were found the next morning in the life raft they shared. Two additional crewmates had clung to the raft until a huge wave flipped the frail vessel, drowning Dennis Meredith in the brackish water. Fleming, Mays, and Gary Strzelecki managed to climb back aboard. Just after dawn, Strzelecki declared he had enough. The men were sending up flares but had no reason to believe they had been spotted. Strzelecki jumped off the pontoon-like raft and began swimming toward shore.

Fleming, too, doubted his Mayday signals had been heard. He was a relieved man when he saw the Coast Guard rescue ship *Sundew* headed his way an hour after his crewmate had given up and begun swimming to his death. Mays admitted to doing a lot of praying that night, and said he had never been so cold in his life. His numb hands did not want to continue hanging on to the ropes attached to the raft, but his mind did not want to let go. Ice formed on the hair and clothing of the survivors who endured fourteen hours before their rescue.

When news reached Rogers City that two survivors had been found, the city rejoiced, hoping the remaining thirty-three missing were also alive. Instead, search vessels began retrieving bodies. The survivors gave the following accounts: Mays was working below deck when the ship started breaking up. He was thrown into the water as the *Bradley* capsized. He had the good fortune to surface a few feet from the raft and was able to climb aboard. From there he watched the stern of the ship go straight down. An explosion followed as the *Bradley* slipped under, and water hit the boilers.

Fleming had been in the pilothouse with the ship's captain when he was first alerted to trouble by a loud thud and an alarm. When he saw the stern sagging, he knew it was bad. Instinctively, he realized the vessel was going down. He stepped out on deck as the *Bradley* rolled to its side, throwing both him and a raft into the water.

While many casualties on shipwrecks from the 1800s and early 1900s were attributed to lack of lifeboats, lack of life jackets, and the lack of radio communication—all of which were no doubt important in saving lives—Lake Michigan made it very clear there were times when even those were not enough.

• THE FAMOUS OR INFAMOUS WITH TIES TO CHARLEVOIX

Leopold and Loeb. The Loeb family owned Castle Farms in Charlevoix. (See Castle Farms under Other Things to See and Do.) It was built as their prestigious summer home. Richard Loeb partnered with Nathan F. Leopold to become half of the most notorious killing duo of the twentieth century. These two near-genius college kids were rich, privileged, and bored when they murdered Bobby Franks for sport on May 24, 1924. Franks was small for his age and unable to put up much of a struggle. Like his murderers, he also came from an extremely wealthy Chicago family. His naked corpse was stuffed into a culvert near Wolf Lake. His father, Jacob Franks, was ready to pay a ransom when the body was discovered.

Dickie Loeb (as Leopold called his accomplice) was the handsome, eighteen-year-old son of retired Sears-Roebuck vice-president and attorney, Albert Loeb. Richard was the youngest graduate ever at the University of Michigan but spent much of his time reading detective stories and planning crimes. It was a game to him. The ultimate challenge was to contrive the perfect crime for no other reason than to see if he could get away with it. He needed an escape from the mundane aspects of his life, and he sought a way to establish his superiority.

Nathan Leopold, Loeb's nineteen-year-old partner in the vicious crime, was interested in ornithology and had already achieved recognition as the nation's leading authority on the Kirtland Warbler, an endangered songbird native to the Lake Michigan shoreline. Leopold was the son of a millionaire box manufacturer. At the time of the Franks killing, he was a law student at the University of Chicago and planned to begin studies at Harvard Law School after a family trip to Europe in the summer.

In the 1920s, Chicago was a violent city where the citizenry continually questioned whether it was safe to walk the streets. For Bobbie Franks it was not. But fears raged over the likes of Al Capone and John Dillinger, not well-dressed, wealthy college boys. Even with crime running rampant, the heinous act of Leopold and Loeb drew special attention. It was easy to identify the enemy if they were bootleggers, mobsters, and pimps. Such unsavory sorts generally left the average folks alone. Sometimes they even offered a few crumbs to them. But how could you protect yourself against someone as innocuous in looks and background, someone so seemingly unlikely to commit a crime as these two well-heeled boys? Clarence Darrow represented the accused in one of the first criminal cases dubbed "the Crime of the Century," a killing for fun that outraged the public conscience.

Leopold, after his conviction, acknowledged, "For some reason, back in 1924, the newspapers found in our particular case apparently something that would sell, something that would interest the public, whether it was our youth, the position of our families, the fact that we were college students, a combination of these things, I really don't know." In Chicago the Loeb family lived down the street from the Franks, and it is believed that Richard Loeb may have been a distant cousin of Bobby Franks. Loeb would later bristle at the suggestion that it was he, who led Leopold in committing the crime; Loeb insisted Leopold was the leader because Nathan was able to achieve a more subtle dominance by his force of will and his superior intellect. Yet psychologists believed Loeb was more of a natural leader with a dominant social presence.

The psychiatrists, hired to examine the boys for the defense, insisted the Loeb parents were not responsible for their son's transgressions. The experts offered the following conclusions: "The father, Albert H. Loeb, is fair and just. He is opposed to the boys' drinking and often spoke of it; he is not strict, although the boys may have thought he was. He never used corporal punishment. In early childhood, he was not a play-fellow with the boys." Of Loeb's mother, the psychiatrists concluded, "A woman in good health, with excellent poise, keen, alert, interested."

The psychiatric reports provided information that Loeb had been a sickly child until four-and-a-half years old. The problem, it seemed, was his tonsils, and once they were removed his health improved. At age fifteen, at his parent's summer estate in Charlevoix, Michigan, he suffered a concussion in an automobile accident. Stories spread that Loeb had killed someone in that accident, that he purposely caused it by ramming a buggy that blocked his automobile, and that his family was able to avoid any publicity about it through bribery. Those rumors were never substantiated, and the more official story is simply that Richard had an accident that involved a collision with a horse and buggy on a dark street corner. A woman might have been injured, but Loeb, slightly injured himself, helped take the woman to the hospital.

He visited her in the hospital and persuaded his father to pay all the hospital bills and to pay off a mortgage on the woman's house and send her on a trip that winter to mend her shattered nerves.

In an interesting aside, Carl Sandburg (See Carl Sandburg under The Famous or Infamous with Ties to Harbert.) testified at Leopold's parole hearing in 1958 and said, "He was in darkness when he came here, but he has made a magnificent struggle toward the light." Sandburg had not testified at two earlier parole hearings, and he was a new voice in proceedings that included Leopold's friends and family. Sandburg became interested in the case partly through the intercession of Gene Lovitz, who had written a biography of the great poet after Lovitz was released from prison. Sandburg said, "I never thought it would get to the time I would make a winter morning journey to Joliet to face the Board of Parole, to plead for a Chicago Jewish boy who at nineteen was out of his mind." Of Sandburg's plea, it was said he rambled some (he was by this time 80 years old), but in the overall content of his discourse, there was still something unbelievably magnificent. Two weeks later Leopold was released after serving 33 years in prison.

Loeb did not fare as well in prison. He died with at least fifty-six razor cuts to his body, killed by fellow inmate, James Day. There were no witnesses other than Day, so the exact circumstances will never be known. Day alleged that Loeb attacked him and made homosexual advances. There were no cuts on Day's body which somewhat refutes his version of the story. Loeb gushed blood and attempts to save him, by suturing the gashes and stopping the spurting blood, failed. He died on January 28, 1936. Richard Loeb had spent his last morning of his life in prison with his friend, Nathan Leopold. In *Life Plus 99 Years*, Nathan Leopold wrote about his friend's death. "We covered him at last with a sheet, but after a moment I folded the sheet back from his face and sat down on a stool by the table where he lay. I wanted a long last look at him. For, strange as it may sound, he had been my best pal. In one sense, he was also the greatest enemy I have ever had. For my friendship with him had cost me my life." Richard Loeb was thirty-three years old.

<<>>

Jon-Benet Patricia Ramsey, a six-year-old former Little Miss Charlevoix, was the daughter of John and Patsy Ramsey who owned a summer home in Charlevoix. On Christmas night, 1996, Jon-Benet was strangled and bludgeoned, her body found the next day in the basement of the family home in Boulder, Colorado. Like the Leopold and Loeb case above, this was a crime that shocked the conscience of the country. The investigation, arguably badly bungled, made headlines for weeks. It had all the elements of titillating journalism—a strange ransom note, speculation of family member involvement, and a child whose young life revolved around beauty pageants and dress-up that made her look glamorous far beyond her tender years. The murder was never solved and remains a cold case.

<<>>

James Jesse Strang was the King of Beaver Island. By proclaiming himself king, he defied his country that swore it would never have a monarch. Strang was born in 1813 in New York State, joined the Baptist Church at twelve, and began the study of law at twenty-one. He was admitted to the Bar, married, worked as a lawyer, minister, and postmaster.

In 1844 he met Joseph Smith, founder of the Mormon Church, and converted to the Mormon faith. That appears to have been the major turning point in his otherwise seemingly normal life. Within a month, he was made an elder of the church. When Smith was assassinated three months later, while serving a jail term for destroying the office of a newspaper that angered him, Strang claimed succession to Smith's position, insisting that Smith had told him the leadership was to be his.

Brigham Young contested Strang's claim and eventually won the battle for leadership. Young excommunicated Strang, who with his dissident followers, went to Voree, Wisconsin. Strang was strict about his Mormon religious observances and when non-Mormon settlers located to the area, he moved his group to Beaver Island off the northwest coast of Michigan's Lower Peninsula not far from Charlevoix. Sitting smack dab in the middle of Lake Michigan, Strang declared himself king of "The Kingdom of God on Earth."

As king, he collected tithes from all residents of the island, Mormon or not. Eventually non-Mormons were forced off the island. Strang built a temple, theater, sawmill, school, and other businesses on the island. Church was compulsory. He levied taxes, published books, and founded a newspaper. He initially denounced polygamy but eventually, when he wanted another wife, embraced it and decreed every elder of the church must have two wives. For a while, living up to the decree was difficult—even for the king. When Strang took his second wife, a former school teacher from Eaton Rapids, his first wife was displeased and left him. Strang remedied the situation by taking wife number three. Eventually, he had five wives and twelve children.

As bizarre as he sounds, Strang was no laughing matter. By 1851 he controlled all the political offices of Mackinac Island. Beaver Island was attached to Mackinac Island for judicial and elective purposes. Governor Kinsley Bingham was careful to cultivate the 700 votes of Strang's followers.

Strang's detractors were successful in getting attention to his misdeeds, and Stephen A. Douglas advised President Millard Fillmore that the U.S. Attorney General should issue orders for the U.S. District Attorney of Michigan to begin prosecuting Strang. Strang's alleged list of offenses was long: cutting timber on public lands, tax irregularities, counterfeiting, and interfering with the U.S. mail among the charges. Strang and his followers were taken by a U.S. Marshal and deputies to Detroit for a three-week trial. Everyone believed Strang would be convicted, and there was an air of incredulity when the self-appointed monarch emerged from the trial victorious. He returned to Beaver Island stronger than ever.

On June 16, 1856, Strang was ambushed, shot, and mortally wounded. He lingered until July 8, giving him time to return to Voree where he died in the arms of his first wife who apparently had forgiven him. A drunken mob of Mackinac Islanders and Irish fishermen burned and looted Beaver Island and drove out all of Strang's followers. There is a legend that Strang sunk a huge trove of gold in Fox Lake on the island before his flight. The gold, if it exists, has not been recovered.

<<>>

Earl Young was a real estate developer in Charlevoix. Before that, he was a dropout from the University of Michigan's School of Architecture. He built several stone houses in the city over a span of 57 years. His structures continue to amaze and delight visitors. A local writer once described his three clusters of homes—26 in all—as looking like something from J.R.R. Tolkien's Hobbiton.

● BOOKS WITH TIES TO CHARLEVOIX

Mike Barton, ***The Mushroom Houses of Charlevoix***. Mike Barton is a photographer who created an intimate portrait of Charlevoix with over 190 full-color photographs. The images range from colorful Bridge Street to the legendary Earl Young stone houses to the spectacular sunsets over Lake Michigan.

59

Nathan Leopold Jr., **Life Plus 99 Years** is the autobiographical account of one of Bobby Frank's killers. (See The Famous or Infamous with Ties to Charlevoix.) This grim account is nonetheless a fascinating saga of a crime for sport and the subsequent legal machinations that put the young perpetrators away for life. With a famous attorney (Clarence Darrow), who took the case in part to attack the death penalty, the book says as much about the judicial system as the crime. Several other books have been written about the crime including *For the Thrill of It: Leopold, Loeb, and the Murder that Shocked Jazz Age Chicago, The Leopold and Loeb Files: An Intimate Look at One of America's Most Infamous Crimes,* and *Leopold and Loeb: The Crime of the Century.*

• GHOST STORIES

No ghost stories surfaced in Charlevoix. That seems a strange happenstance considering the brutal deaths connected with the small city. If Bobbie Franks, Richard Loeb, King James Jesse Strang, or Jon-Benet Ramsey remain unsettled dead, they are keeping quiet.

6. ELK RAPIDS

Elk Rapids had a 2020 population of 1,644. Located in southwest Antrim County and bordered on the west by Grand Traverse Bay, on the east by Elk Lake, on the north by Bass Lake, and with the Elk River running through it, picturesque Elk Rapids explodes with opportunities for day-trippers, boaters, anglers, and water enthusiasts. Whether you paddle or motor about, absorb the tranquil expanse of natural scenery, or cast your line in the hope of catching dinner, you will not lack for something to do.

The first people in Elk Rapids were Anishinaabek of Algonquin origin, primarily the three brother tribes of Ojibwe, Odawa, and Pottawatomie. They migrated to the Great Lakes area from the East Coast. It is impossible to hike a Northern Michigan trail or paddle a Northern Michigan waterway and not follow a path taken by Native Americans hundreds of years ago. Until the early 1800s, the Original People enjoyed the vast unbroken woodland around Elk Rapids without European interference.

Europeans brought inevitable change. The first immigrants to test the Elk River waters were the missionaries and the surveyors. The agenda of the former was saving souls, and that of the latter was claiming new lands for their respective governments.

The first documented surveyor to the area was Abram Scranton Wadsworth, who in 1847, according to local legend, discovered a pair of elk horns in the rapids near the mouth of the river and considered that an appropriate sign for naming it Elk River.

Wadsworth brought with him his family: wife Martha, their three children, and brother-in-law, Samuel Northam. Assisted by local Native Americans, the Wadsworth clan spent their first winter at Old Mission Peninsula. Abram's thoughts, however, returned to the pleasant little river across the bay. He was a millwright and the river seemed the perfect place to construct a mill.

Wadsworth returned to the location he admired along the Elk River and built a log cabin near the present site of the Town Hall. The family established a friendly relationship with their Native American neighbors who taught Wadsworth to strip the bark from trees; he then sold the bark for enough profit to build his lathe mill where operations began in 1850. Wadsworth platted the village in 1852 and sold lots for $25 each. Originally, the village was called Stevens, but it was later renamed for the rapids of its beautiful river. In 1853 a post office came to Elk Rapids, and the first school opened. In 1863 the first issue of the *Elk Rapids Eagle* was printed. In 1864 the village boasted seven churches and seven saloons.

Geographically, Elk Rapid's growth was somewhat constrained. Wedged between the Grand Traverse Bay and Elk Lake, there was little room for expansion. Farmers were limited to utilizing acreage to the north and south, and although water travel was a blessing, land travel was impeded by the unbroken 75-mile chain of lakes north and east. The pathways that eventually became roads twisted and contorted, and even Traverse City seemed far away. Early residents of Elk Rapids must have felt isolated in their lovely countryside.

In 1872 the logging company of Dexter and Noble constructed a charcoal blast furnace forty-seven feet in diameter to produce pig iron. The vast hardwood forests surrounding Elk Rapids provided lumber that was converted to charcoal for firing the furnace. Iron ore for use in the process was imported from the Upper Peninsula by freighter. Dexter and Noble built a dock for ships bringing the ore. During its heyday, the furnace turned out 24 tons of pig iron a day and employed 365 people. It closed in the early 1900s because the forests were depleted, and cheaper smelting processes were developed.

Several plants and factories helped sustain Elk Rapids after the iron company closed. By the mid-1900s, agriculture and orchards aided the economy, and Elk Rapids relied for support on cherry packing plants, but economic decline continued to grip the village until Grace Memorial Harbor and tourism brought needed revitalization.

Today, Elk Rapids is a tiny gem, often overshadowed by the glitz of neighboring Traverse City and Charlevoix. Elk Rapids, however, beguiles with her own special charm and slower, more peaceful pace. Fast food restaurants and chain motels have not made an appearance. Even in the heart of summer, you can find a quiet patch of paradise along vast stretches of sandy Lake Michigan beach. Your eyes can feast on well-manicured flower gardens maintained by dedicated garden club volunteers. One place to view the results of their green thumbs is around the local library, a building worth a peek, and if you wander inside you can grab beach reading from their ongoing sale of used books.

Local stores offer any tourist trinket you may need— from T-shirts to fudge to collectibles. Elk Rapids galleries, like the Twisted Fish, are special and feature some of the finest artwork you will find along Lake Michigan's coast.

Visit Elk Rapids during your summer vacation, and you will leave with your spirit rejuvenated.

• MUSEUMS

The Elk Rapids Historical Museum, 401 River Street (in the old Town Hall), inspires people to explore the past, understand the present, and envision the future through varied exhibits that include a replica of the Township Hall's 1883 jail. The old Town Hall building was designed by Charles H. Peale and built near the spot where Adam Wadsworth, the earliest white settler, had lived. The hall provided a social and political center for over 120 years and served the need of citizens for a place to meet. There is a replica of the Elk Rapids ironworks as well as exhibits of vintage clothing, antique tools, local art, and a history of how the Chain of Lakes region changed the face of Northern Michigan. The hall faces the city's park and the beach on East Grand Traverse Bay. The building also houses the Elk Rapids Historical Society. Limited hours.

<<>>

Elk Rapids History Museum, 301 Traverse Street, offers materials about the history of Elk Rapids including displays from a bygone era. Very limited hours.

<<>>

Guntzviller's Spirit of the Woods Museum, US 31, two miles south of Elk Rapids. Native American artifacts, history, hunting and fishing gear, and hundreds of preserved animals including bear, bison, deer, and mink.

<<>>

Twisted Fish Gallery, 10443 South Bayshore Drive. One of the loveliest and most interesting galleries in West Michigan. Twisted Fish Gallery was voted Best Fine Art Gallery in Northern Michigan two years running by *Traverse*, the region's lifestyle magazine. Featured art covers the spectrum of fine art for serious collectors to fun pieces for the casual art lover. You'll find oils, watercolors, pottery, glass, metal, jewelry, wood, yard art, paper art, kaleidoscopes, flowers, and sculptures, along with representational and abstract paintings by a diverse group of artists. Many regional and some national artists display works reflecting the northern spirit.

● BEACHES, PARKS, AND TRAILS

Elk Rapids Day Park/The Walk of Art Sculpture Park, 920 South Bay Shore Drive at the village limits. Great trails, hiking, Lake Michigan beach, picnic area, pavilion, and art. The sculptures are scattered along the trails and the beach. Plaques list the artist (most from Northern Michigan), date, and city of origin. Art and natural beauty. What more could anyone want? This park may be less crowded than beaches in other tourist towns, at least during the week.

<<>>

Veterans Memorial Park, River and Pine, on Lake Michigan. Tennis courts, picnic tables, grills, playground, slides, volleyball on the beach, and great view of Old Mission Peninsula.

● OTHER STOPS TO CONSIDER

Elk Rapids Farmers Market, at Rotary Park, 305 US 31. Fridays at 8:00 a.m. Vendors from 13 counties bring seasonal fruits and vegetables, baked goods, dairy products, plants, honey, and more, sold directly to you from the producer. On the bank of the Elk River, the farmers market is the perfect way to taste what Northern Michigan has to offer without leaving the beauty of Elk Rapids.

<<>>

Elk Rapids District Library, 300 Isle of Pines. The library resides in the Island House, a designated Michigan Historic Site, built in the1860s. As the name suggests, the house was constructed on an island. At that time, the only access to the property was by footbridge or boat. Since then, land access has been established, although the footbridge still provides a connection to the village. Island House became a library in 1949. Homey, charming, and with a fireplace to warm you on cold or rainy days, this is an appealing place to spend a couple of hours. You can pick up used books to take with you, and there are computers if you didn't bring your laptop or iPad and are experiencing withdrawal.

<<>>

Stone Circle Theatre, ten minutes north of Elk Rapids. Turn right from US 31 onto Stone Circle Drive to the end (look for sign on the east side of US 31). Enjoy a night of poetry readings, music, and storytelling in a unique setting around a campfire. Weekend nights, summer only.

<<>>

(Restaurants aren't included in this guide, but Appendix One includes a pecan pie recipe that is a favorite of both locals and tourists at Pearl's New Orlean's Kitchen.)

7. ACME

The Township of Acme is a county subdivision of Grand Traverse County. No separate population data is available.

Acme was originally part of Whitewater Township and became a station stop for the Pere Marquette Railroad. With no clear evidence of how Acme got its name, it seems reasonable to assume the word origin itself provides a clue: Acme in Greek, means the peak, zenith, prime, or best of something. That may be how the first settlers viewed this lovely area.

The village of Acme was established by L.S. Hoxsie in 1855 when he moved upstate from Lenawee County. Three years after moving to Acme, Hoxsie built a sawmill that became part of the region's booming lumber craze. Acme soon had a hotel, a shingle mill, and several stores to provide for the needs of its growing population.

John Pulsipher organized the area as a township and became the supervisor in 1891—a position he held for nearly three decades. During his tenure, he saw the depletion of the virgin timber in the area and bank foreclosures on many farms because the owners could not grow enough on the nutrient-deficient land to pay their taxes.

Hoxsie tried to make a go of a woolen mill in the area, but in spite of his efforts, it failed. Eventually, the few small stores closed, and the hotel was razed. Acme's economy barely limped along. The government consolidated state lands, and many farmers relocated. Those who remained turned to fruit farming because cherry and apple trees flourished in the poor, sandy soil.

In the first part of the twentieth century, railroads expanded, and highways were built. The country's population moved into cities and away from farms. This new trend fueled a desire for resorts where weary city-dwellers could get away and relax. Acme capitalized on the need this created. Relying on its spectacular location on the East Grand Traverse Bay and its proximity to Traverse City which was rapidly becoming a significant tourist area, it became a major playground.

Today, Acme's claim to fame is its major resort and golf courses. It is the gateway to fun. It is often considered part of the Greater Traverse City area. (See Traverse City in this guide for additional background. Traverse City chronicles a similar history to Acme.)

● MUSEUM

Music House Museum, 7377 US 31 North. Guests get a private tour during which instruments are explained, and some are played. The museum houses an extensive collection of fine, rare automatic musical instruments, antique radios, phonographs, nickelodeons, organs, and music boxes. Seasonal.

Theophilus Mortier Band Organ at the Music House in Acme.
Courtesy of Pixabay Free Images.

The **Grand Traverse Resort** has shows, a dinner theatre, dining, and golf.

<<>>

The Wolverine, designed by Gary Player. Par 72 course with a 73.9 rating and a 144 slope rating.

The Wolverine Golf Course. Courtesy of Pixabay Free Images.

<<>>

The Bear, perhaps Michigan's best-known course named for its famous architect, Jack Nicklaus, is a challenge. A par 72 course with a 76.8 rating and a 146 slope rating.

<<>>

Showcase Dinner Theatre, M-72 East, located in the Old Acme Cinema. (Also called the Williamsburg Showcase Theatre.) Dinner and Stage Shows.

8. TRAVERSE CITY
INCLUDING MISSION PENINSULA
AND OLD MISSION

Traverse City, 2020 population 15,785, is a spectacular and vibrant city with a personality shaped by its location and intriguing past. Like all of Michigan, this area was originally inhabited by Native Americans, specifically the

Ojibwe (Chippewa). Its recorded history starts in 1838 when Protestant missionary, Reverend Peter Dougherty, was sent to the region to establish Old Mission, where he built a school and provided an education and religious training to the Native American population. By 1841 Dougherty was joined by John Johnson, and together they created a small village consisting of five buildings at Mission Harbor. On the heels of the missionaries came the settlers, some intending to live in the area, and others merely following the money to be made in timber.

Until 1845 Native Americans remained in the Grand Traverse Area, holding a considerable portion of the land. However, in that year, a government treaty expired and the Native Americans were forced to surrender the land if there was a demand for it by "whites." Property on the west shore of the bay, in what is now Leelanau County, was settled by homesteaders in 1846. In 1852 Reverend Dougherty moved his settlement from Old Mission to New Mission (now Omena). In 1847 the village of Traverse City at the west end of the bay began to grow. Traverse City was incorporated as a city in 1895.

Logging defined the area in the 1800s. Traverse City forests provided wood to the prairie states where the need for building materials was great. White Pine first caught the attention of lumbermen because it was light, cheap, and easily worked and crafted. Finding the timber to harvest was only half of the equation; it was also necessary to have access to shipping so lumber could be transported to the intended market. Grand Traverse Bay provided an excellent spot for schooners and other freighters to anchor. At this location, they took on the pine boards and planks and sailed them to Chicago, Racine, and other ports for shipment south and west.

The area's first sawmill was built at the head of the West Bay by Horace Boardman in 1847. His name reflected perfectly his occupation, and today a river, a park, and a street are named in his honor.

By 1893, 14 sawmills operated in the county, and shingle mills had also gained importance. This was the high point of lumbering in the area. Timber continued to be cut in enormous quantities for two decades, but the number of mills and men involved in the lumbering operations slowly dwindled as forests disappeared.

By 1915 Traverse City boasted 14 churches and 21 saloons among its downtown buildings. The city readied for significant change. Lumber no longer maintained the economy, and another means to support the populace was needed. Attention turned to agriculture. The land that had been cleared of trees offered new soil that was particularly good for potato growth. In the early years of the twentieth century, the Grand Traverse potato farmers found their niche.

Traverse City soon began producing diversified crops; hay and grain flourished. Fruit became a particular boon to the area. Back when Reverend Dougherty came to Old Mission, he found fruit-bearing apple trees. Pioneer farmers planted orchards experimenting with a variety of fruits. Apples and cherries thrived and remain the important orchards of the region. Vineyards also do well on the Mission and Leelanau Peninsulas.

The cycle of the cherry crop made orchards a tremendous gamble; growers endured winterkill and early spring frosts. If their trees survived both, they still faced the bugs and other pests. By 1923 the cherry industry became so important, it attracted more than local attention. That year the combined churches of the Grand Traverse Region were asked to pray for the success of the harvest. From that request came the "Blessing of the Blossoms" ceremony held in the orchards on a Sunday in May when the cherry blossoms are at their peak. By 1926 that simple religious ceremony grew into a full-fledged National Cherry Festival that is celebrated each July. A queen is crowned and a parade marches through the city. Thousands of spectators attend the week-long celebration.

Traverse City is now a resort town. In the frenzied summer months, its numbers swell as harried big-city dwellers crowd in to take advantage of the natural beauty and water activities the lake and bay offer.

In your travels along the Sunset Coast, you will not find better dining with more variety than in the epicurean center of Traverse City.

• MUSEUMS AND GALLERIES

Bella Galleria and Sculpture Studio, 17015 Center Road, (same building as the Old Mission Tavern on Old Mission Peninsula). Showcases the works of over 75 artists, some well-known in the area and beyond. Bronzes, oils, watercolors, batiks, fiber art, blown glass, fused glass, direct metal, acrylics, and prints.

<<>>

Dennos Museum Center, 1701 East Front Street (on the campus of Northwestern Michigan College), seeks to engage, enlighten, and entertain its audiences through the collection of art, and the presentation of exhibitions and programs in the visual arts, sciences, and performing arts. The museum has a permanent collection that is one of the largest and most historically complete displays of sculptures, prints, and drawings of the Inuit artists from the Canadian Arctic. They also have changing exhibits of historical and contemporary art and a hands-on Discovery Gallery that children love. From September to May the museum presents more than 25 concerts in the 367 seat Milliken Auditorium. The gift shop carries the works of many local artists.

<<>>

The Dougherty House, 18 miles north of Traverse City, at 18459 Mission Road, Old Mission Peninsula. Built in 1842 by Reverend Peter Dougherty, it is the first frame building in the region. It is a restored log house used as a church and school for the Ojibwe Native Americans. The house was the focus of religious observances, schooling, farming, trading, and medical care for Native Americans in the area.

<<>>

Gallery 50, 800 Cottageview Drive, Suite 50, is located in the original Building 50 of the former Traverse City Regional Psychiatric Facility. (See Traverse City Ghost Stories.) In the expanded 2,200 square foot galleries, the work of 150 regional and North American artists and designers is displayed showing original fine art, fun and funky objects, contemporary craft, jewelry, photography, ceramics, glass, wood, metal, and handcrafted gifts.

<<>>

Grand Traverse Heritage Center, 322 Sixth Street, showcases the history of the area with emphasis on Native Americans, local pioneers, railroads, the lumber era, and the shipping industry. During the past 70 years, the collection has grown to over 10,000 artifacts.

<<>>

Great Lakes Children's Museum, 13240 South West Bay Shore Drive, (M-22 in Greilickville just north of Traverse City limits), was created to provide hands-on, interactive, and informal educational environments for children and the adults in their lives. The museum invites curiosity, allows exploration, encourages participation, and celebrates the child-like wonder in all of us. A variety of games, activities, and interesting exhibits challenge children. Little ones love the weather cart, the water table area, and the art room.

● BEACHES, PARKS, AND TRAILS

Bowers Harbor Beach, tucked in Bowers Harbor on Old Mission Peninsula, 15 miles north of Traverse City. Amenities: swimming beach, picnic facilities, restrooms, and boat launch.

<<>>

Brown Bridge Pond Natural Area and Nature Preserve, Garfield Avenue south to Hobbs Highway, left to Ranch Rudolf Road. Owned by the city, this is a local secret that most travelers miss. Easy hiking trails take you past a small lake created by a dam on the Boardman River. You will also pass two platforms that jut out over a steep slope affording spectacular views of the lake and the Boardman Valley. Swans and even eagles often delight hikers by making appearances.

<<>>

Bryant Park, Peninsula Drive where Garfield and Front Streets intersect at the base of Old Mission Peninsula. Broad, sandy swimming beach. Amenities: play area, picnic area, charcoal grills, and restrooms.

<<>>

Clinch Park, 161 East Grandview Parkway, offers 1,500 feet of sandy beach along West Grand Traverse Bay in downtown Traverse City. The park is a hub of activity. Amenities: swimming beach, picnic tables, biking path, playground, restrooms, kayak rental, and volleyball courts. Spectacular views. Adjacent to the park is the Bijou by the Bay. (See Other Things to See and Do.)

<<>>

East Bay Park, located at the foot of Front Street. A popular beach for families with children because of shallow water and gradual slopes. The park has playgrounds and restrooms.

<<>>

Elmwood Township Park, one mile north of the M-72 junction in Traverse City. Beach, shady picnic area, playground, and restrooms.

<<>>

Grand Traverse Commons, 1200 West 11th Street. In 1885 this became the site of the State Psychiatric Hospital. In 1989, a century later, the hospital was converted to a restaurant and gallery. The grounds, referred to as the Commons, remain open and are a favorite place for runners, walkers, cross-country skiers, and bird-watchers.

<<>>

Haserot Beach Park, 20 miles north of Traverse City on Old Mission Peninsula. Amenities: protected bay of Lake Michigan with sandy beaches, playground, picnic facilities, restrooms, and boat launch.

<<>>

Muncie Lakes Pathway, southeast of Traverse City. Follow Supply Road to Remote Lake Road, turn right and continue to Ranch Rudolf Road intersection, turn left, drive about a half-mile to the trail parking lot on the left. This trail has rolling hills covered with a variety of hardwoods and evergreens and is moderately difficult, but perfect for either hiking or biking if you are up to it.

<<>>

Peninsula Township Park, Center Road to the end of Old Mission Peninsula. This lovely little park located on the 45th Parallel offers three miles of developed trails and another 500 acres of woodlands, old abandoned orchards, and open highlands. You will be able to see both East and West Bay as you look out over the orchards. The sandy farm lanes provide a couple of invigorating climbs to get to higher land, but you will appreciate the effort when the magnificent view stretches out before you.

<<>>

Power Island, accessible only by boat, located on West Grand Traverse Bay's Power Island off Bowers Harbor on Old Mission Peninsula. Amenities: picnic facilities, restrooms, and hiking trails.

<<>>

Pyatt Lake Nature Area, Neahtawanta Road, Old Mission Peninsula. This peaceful nature preserve provides hiking trails, boardwalks, wetlands, botanical diversity, and observation points.

<<>>

Sand Lake Quiet Area, M-72 to Broomhead Road then right about four miles to parking on the left. This 3,500-acre tract is perfect for a number of outdoor activities including mountain biking, fishing, hiking (7.4-mile loop), cross-country skiing, or walking. It is called a quiet area because no motorized vehicles are allowed. It is considered a moderately difficult trail through scenic small lakes and woods brimming with wildlife.

<<>>

TART (Traverse City Area Recreation Trail). Many access points throughout Traverse City. This 10-mile, non-motorized trail is a popular cross-city route for walkers, runners, in-line skaters, and bicyclers. It stretches from M-72 on the West side of Traverse City to Bunker Hill Road in Acme winding through several popular parks along the way. You also pass restaurants, ice-cream shops, and a number of attractions.

<<>>

Traverse City State Park, 1132 US 31 North. Amenities: quarter of a mile of sandy beach along the east arm of the Grand Traverse Bay. Swimming, sunbathing, boating, fishing, camping, picnic tables, grills, beach house, children's playground, and 342 campsites.

Even the seagulls enjoy the Traverse City beaches.
Courtesy of Bob Royce.

• OTHER STOPS TO CONSIDER

Traverse City has many temptations vying for your attention. Among them are balloon rides, paintball, an adventure park, and a casino in addition to theatre, farmers markets, wineries, upscale boutique shopping, and plenty of winter activities including downhill skiing, cross country skiing, and tubing.

<<>>

Sarah Hardy Downtown Farmers Market, between Cass and Union Streets (across from Clinch Park). The market started with fewer than ten vendors and has grown to one of the largest markets in the state. It holds title as the largest growers-only market in Michigan. Shoppers find produce from more than 115 area farmers. Arrive early for the best fruits, vegetables, plants, flowers, and baked goods. Seasonal and open Saturday and Wednesday mornings.

<<>>

Wineries dot the peninsula. Chateau Chantal Winery and Inn, 15900 Rue de Vin, Old Mission Peninsula, Chateau Grand Traverse, 12239 Center Road, and Peninsula Cellars Tasting Room, 11480 Center Road, Old Mission Peninsula are all places to consider.

Theatre is alive and well in Traverse City. If you are planning to visit, check the following for performance schedules.

Bijou by the Bay, is a 150-seat nonprofit movie theater in Clinch Park on Grand Traverse Bay next to the TART Trail. It is one of the venues for the Traverse City Film Festival. It occupies the Con Foster Museum Building and is worth a stop to see the amazing murals that grace its walls. The murals feature views of the shores of Lake Michigan and hidden in the paintings are eggs that reference classic films and Michigan artifacts.

<<>>

The **City Opera House**, 112½ East Front Street. Constructed in 1891, the Opera House seats 720 people and offers a variety of performances and events.

<<>>

The **Milliken Auditorium**, 1701 East Front Street (Dennos Museum Center), has more than 350 seats and is one of the larger stages in the region. The auditorium is fully accessible and hosts campus events and touring productions.

<<>>

The **Open Space Theatre**, corner of Union Street and Grandview Parkway, is a beautiful gathering place with views of the West Grand Traverse Bay. One of the sites of the Traverse City Film Festival.

<<>>

The **Old Town Playhouse**, 148 East 8th Street, is home to the Traverse City Civic Players that came into existence in 1960 to bring amateur theatre to Traverse City. The productions range from Broadway musicals to avant-garde, one-act plays. The season runs from fall to summer. The mainstage theatre can seat 358, and there is also an 80-seat studio theatre.

• LIGHTHOUSE

Old Mission Lighthouse, Mission Point 20500 Center Road. The lighthouse has been a Traverse City and Old Mission Peninsula icon for decades. Located at the north end of a picturesque drive along M-37 through cherry orchards and vineyards, Mission Point Lighthouse stands as a classic piece of Michigan history. It no longer guides mariners through West Grand Traverse Bay as it did from September 10, 1870, until it was decommissioned in 1933. However, it now offers visitors a peek into what life was like around the turn of the century for lighthouse keepers and for others who lived and worked in the area at the time.

Self-guided tours of the lighthouse museum are available May-October, and weekends in November. There is also a large, wide beach with shallow water ideal for wading, a picnic area, a reconstructed early settler's cabin, and an outhouse.

• SHIPWRECKS

The Grand Traverse Bay Underwater Preserve is the resting place for several shipwrecks as well as evidence of businesses that once existed along the waterfront. Divers can explore the Clinch Park Woodpile that contains the remains of lumbering activities, the pipeline that holds the detritus of piping from the power plant, several small boats, and a Ford Pinto. The Junk Pile, located near Haserot Beach at the tip of Old Mission Peninsula, was created by teenagers in the 1950s when they tried to establish an artificial island.

The shipwrecks in this preserve are not generally the storied wrecks like those that went down in the storm of 1913, or the *Edmund Fitzgerald*, nor even the *Daniel Morell* where we are captivated by tales that stir and horrify our imaginations with feats of bravery and danger.

For most of the preserve's wrecks, the cargo was salvaged, and no lives were lost. Still, they make interesting dive sites for those inclined to underwater exploration.

- The ***Elmwood*** is a partially intact wood fishing tug resting in 20 to 40 feet of water. She was found in deeper water and relocated to her current spot. Many training dives take place at this site because it is close to shore with easy access.
- The ***Metropolis*** was a 125-foot schooner whose captain became disoriented in a November 1886 snowstorm. He ran his ship aground south of Old Mission Point. She leaves divers a shallow debris field just offshore and a deeper dive site where the hull can be seen.
- The ***A. J. Rogers***, a schooner, was built in 1862. On October 8, 1898, she was headed for Sandusky, Ohio, with a cargo of pig iron when she began leaking. Unable to make port, her captain attempted to beach his ship on Old Mission Point, but she sank before reaching land. Her final resting place is in 53 feet of water.
- The ***Tramp*** was a 55-foot tug built in 1926. She sank in the 1970s. Her wreck is semi-intact in 44 feet of water near Power Island. She is sometimes buoyed and has become a popular dive site.
- The ***Yuba***, a schooner, sank in 1894 and lies in a shallow dive site in approximately 15 feet of water.

● THE FAMOUS OR INFAMOUS WITH TIES TO TRAVERSE CITY

Daniel Lewis Majerle, known as Thunder Dan to his fans, was born in 1965 in Traverse City. Majerle played 14 years in the National Basketball Association, primarily for the Phoenix Suns, with a stint for the Miami Heat, and briefly for the Cleveland Cavaliers. He was named to the All-Star team three times.

<<>>

William Grawn Milliken was born on March 26, 1922, in Traverse City. He is the longest-serving governor in Michigan history. In 1965 he became governor when George W. Romney left office to join President Richard Nixon's cabinet. Milliken served three additional, elected, four-year terms in 1970, 1974, and 1978. Although a Republican, he endorsed John Kerry against George W. Bush in the presidential election of 2004.

<<>>

Carter Oosterhouse, was born on September 19, 1976, in Traverse City, and returned often to enjoy sailing—one of his leisure time passions. He was a carpenter on the reality TV shows *Trading Spaces* and *Three Wishes* and has appeared on the Tony Danza and Oprah Winfrey shows.

<<>>

Craig Thompson, a graphic cartoonist from Traverse City, is best known for his 2003 *Blankets*. He has contributed many short works to *Nickelodeon Magazine* under the name Craigory Thompson. In 1999 he created the graphic novella *Good-Bye, Chunky Rice* and in 2000 the mini-comic *Bible Doodles*. (For more info about Craig Thompson see Marquette in *Exploring Michigan's Upper Peninsula Coasts* of this travel series.)

<<>>

Martha Teichner, CBS News Correspondent and journalist, was born in Traverse City. She covered the Cuban boat lift and the Shah of Iran's exile to Panama. She had two London assignments and was based for a period in Johannesburg, South Africa, during the struggle against Apartheid. She reported on Bosnia and the fall of Communism in Central and Eastern Europe.

<<>>

80

Barry Watson was born in Traverse City in 1974. As an actor, he is best known for his role as Matt Camden in the television series *7th Heaven*. He also appeared as the title character in the series *What About Brian*.

● BOOKS AND MOVIES WITH TIES TO TRAVERSE CITY

Richard Fidler authored ***Traverse City, Michigan: A Historical Narrative, 1850–2013*** documenting the history surrounding Traverse City.

<<>>

Emily St. John Mandel, ***Station Eleven***. A dark, apocalyptic book set along the Great Lakes coastlines, primarily Lake Michigan. While many of the cities aren't named, Traverse City is one of the identified places a small troupe of actors and musicians wander offering their performances to give humanity purpose and rekindle a love of the arts after destruction that ended the world as it had been known.

<<>>

Chris Miller, ***Traverse City State Hospital*** traces the history of this psychiatric facility called The Asylum, beginning with the mental health context in which it was founded. The journey takes the reader through its growth, development, decline, and finally to its renovation and preservation as a vital part of the Traverse City community.

<<>>

Earle E. Steele and Kristen M. Hains authored ***Beauty is Therapy: Memories of the Traverse City State Hospital.*** This book, in its fifth printing, contains the memoirs of Earle Steele, a fifty-year employee of the Traverse City State Hospital. The book contains historical black and white photos and illustrations by Steele.

<<>>

Dave Vizard, **A Place for Murder** (4th in the Nick Steele Series). An undocumented worker is murdered; her body discovered in the back of a truck in Northern Michigan. News reporter Nick Steele is drawn into the case that takes him from the Straits of Mackinac to dairy farms in the Thumb to a Traverse City den of pleasure and the underlying crime of human trafficking.

• GHOST STORIES

The Ghosts of the Traverse City Regional Psychiatric Facility. Mental Health Facilities are the perfect setting for horror stories that make our skin crawl. Just the thought of Jack Nicholson in *One Flew over the Cuckoo's Nest* sends chills down our spines. Old psychiatric hospitals are even more frightening. They existed at a time when shock therapy, brain tissue manipulation, implants, drug experimentation, and lobotomies were treatments de jour.

Also known as the Northern Michigan Asylum, Traverse City State Hospital opened in 1885 surrounded by rolling meadows and steep wooded slopes. Wetlands ringed a central building area. Mules hauled yellow-gold bricks to the site on special flat cars that ran on wooden two-by-four tracks. The bricks were used in the construction of Building 50. Michigan quarries provided the slate needed for the roof. Building 50, the main, and eventually most haunted building of the complex, boasted three floors, a basement, and an attic. Every horror movie fan knows that basements and attics are the scariest parts of haunted buildings. Building 50 was designed by Gordon Lloyd, the architect of many churches and cathedrals during this period. The off-white walls and large windows presented a pleasant façade to all manner of mayhem that resided within.

The building had two wings separated by a central staff and office area. The south wing housed male patients, and the north housed female patients. At the back of the building were two infirmary wings that were originally separate buildings but later attached to Building 50. A chapel was added behind the center section of the building, and it stood as a place of prayer and hope until the 1960s when fire destroyed it. It was replaced by a new section referred to as Building 50-A. This strictly utilitarian structure was typical of mid-1900s construction and cheapened the beauty of the original Building 50.

From the time it opened its doors, the population of the asylum grew until it became necessary to build cottages to accommodate the need; each addition housed 60 to 125 more patients.

Within a few years of construction, attention turned to beautifying the grounds. The first superintendent of the hospital, Dr. James Decker Munson, contributed trees from his worldwide travels. He determined where the trees should be placed, and the farm manager saw that they were properly planted. One of Munson's trees became known as the Hippie Tree and supposedly near its trunk was an open portal gate to hell.

The hospital carried out large farming operations during its early history. The resultant crops provided much of the food the patients ate. Championship cows were raised from the quality herd of Holsteins kept on the farm. The agricultural operation was discontinued in 1957, in part due to the high cost of labor, and in part due to a lack of suitable patients to carry out the work.

To outward appearances, especially during the daylight hours, the lovely buildings and grounds were not creepy—at least not if you could avoid thinking of the misery of the residents therein. An estimated 30,000 people died during the facility's century-long history. That is likely a misleading number. Many of the residents/inmates were there for their natural (or perhaps unnaturally shortened?) lives and would be expected to die there. Rumors of torture surfaced, but yesterday's treatment is often considered torture by today's standards. Many ghosts of the pathetic souls who resided at the Asylum roamed the grounds. The presence of evil was described as so great that it caused holy relics such as Bibles, holy water flasks, or crosses to be destroyed or harmed as people tried to enter the premises with them. The only place that was considered safe was the chapel, but in that holiest of spots, a spirit was said to be present—that of a priest who committed suicide there. One can speculate what manner of evil caused a priest to yield to that most unpardonable of sins.

Lights went on and off even when there was no electricity connected in the buildings. Voices and screams were commonplace and suggested the presence of those from the nether regions. Abnormal sightings included a small baby left in one of the rooms, elderly patients shuffling inside the vacant buildings on various floors after the facility closed, a ghostly figure that chased anyone brave enough to enter, and disfigured creatures roaming the basements and tunnels.

In the late 1970s, the hospital closed. It has been recreated to house several businesses including an upscale restaurant with the best Italian food in Traverse City and a gallery offering local art. Plans continue to unfold for Building 50's new life. A few ghosts feel it should have been razed and covered with twenty feet of hallowed ground.

Building 50 today. Courtesy of Bob Royce.

Genevive, the Ghost of Bowers Harbor Inn. Old Mission Peninsula is an incredibly beautiful strip of land north of Traverse City. Chicago millionaire J. W. "Charles" Stickney and his wife Genevive chose this spot to build their dream home. Stickney made his fortune in lumber and steel, although one account also described him as a captain of a Great Lakes shipping liner. The mansion the Stickneys built was befitting a queen, and Genevive Stickney was known to act the part. She attempted to capture the feeling of grace and leisure of the era as she chose expensive furnishings for her fabulous new dwelling. One piece that she treasured until her death was a gilded mirror that made her look thinner. She stood in front of the magical looking glass and saw herself as she wanted to be.

Genevive was an eccentric character—if not downright weird. In her kitchen, she preserved fruits and made jams, wines, and brandies that she buried about the estate to prevent them from being stolen. She was a vain and jealous woman, an unpleasant combination in a wife who was both frumpy and plump. Adding to, or perhaps causing, her other character flaws was a lack of self-confidence in matters of the heart. The years merely added more pounds and additional layers of self-doubt. Poor Genevive Stickney also suffered from a host of medical ailments. Her physical health deteriorated to the point that her husband hired a nurse to care for her. He installed an elevator so his spouse could reach the upper floors of her beloved home.

Instead of gratitude, Genevive grew paranoid, convinced her husband was having an affair with the nurse. Genevive obsessed that Charles would leave everything they owned to this tart—his lover. Time bore out the truth hidden in Genevive's fears of her husband's infidelity. Charles predeceased Genevive by only a few months, and he left his entire fortune, with the exception of their Mission Point residence, to his mistress. Genevive was heartbroken as she contemplated the evidence of her husband's cruel betrayal. She slipped into a severe depression, quite possibly accompanied by a unhealthy dose of madness.

Genevive shuffled her corpulent self to the elevator rafters, tied a noose about her neck, and hung herself in the shaft. Ever since her ghastly death, she has been reported haunting the inn, opening windows, blowing out candles, and preening in front of her special mirror in the second floor ladies' room where her image nearly frightened one customer to death. Other visitors have reported a blurry female figure appearing in their vacation photographs.

Employees of the Inn have seen Genevive on the second floor, standing in front of the mirror. They confirm stories about lights switched on and off without human assistance. The elevator takes restless trips up and down, at no one's beck and call.

An inn manager says that he closed the inn for the evening as was his routine. He locked the freezer door, turned the lights off, and secured the front door when he walked out. He arrived the next morning to find the lights blazing and the freezer door not only unlocked, but standing open. Patrons insist they watched the fireplaces lighting themselves. Pictures fall from walls. During one of Genevive's temper tantrums, guests gathered in the dining room witnessed her fury firsthand. No one was near the salad bar, but a bowl of food flew off the table and shattered as though it had been deliberately hurled to gain attention.

Another manager, a nonbeliever in ghosts, reported checking the ladies' room as he prepared to close for the evening. He flipped off the light, and the door banged shut in his face. That seemed strange since he had experienced difficulty opening the newly installed door because insufficient space had been left for the carpet. The door also had a self-adjusting arm that prevented it from slamming. In spite of the manager's skepticism regarding the spirit of Genevive Stickney, he said the door could not have slammed without help.

Genevive is one of the more active ghosts chronicled in this guide. Her antics earned her a segment on *Unsolved Mysteries* and paragraphs in several books.

9. SUTTONS BAY

Suttons Bay had a population of 611 as of July 1, 2020. In 1854 Harry C. Sutton founded a small village at the site of his wooding station in the Leelanau Peninsula near Traverse City. The efforts of Harry and his crew of woodsmen supplied fuel to wood-burning steamboats. Before the first road connecting Traverse City to Suttons Bay was built in 1862, mail was delivered by boat every two weeks.

Harry named his little settlement Suttonsburg, but in spite of honoring himself in that manner, the village was renamed Pleasant City shortly thereafter. In the end, Sutton prevailed, and the village was named Suttons Bay in 1861.

The second enterprise to locate in Suttonsburg, after Harry's wooding station, was a sawmill built in 1870. It was operated by Sutton's son-in-law, George Carr. By 1876 a railroad ran through the center of town behind Lars Bahle's Drygoods & Clothing Store. The railway provided a means to transport lumber from inland to the deep-water harbor. The population grew to 250 residents by 1880, and the small village enjoyed the services of four stores, three docks, two hotels, a brick schoolhouse, the sawmill, and a brand-new Catholic church.

Voters of Leelanau County approved moving the county seat to Suttons Bay from Leland, but the move never materialized. The mill run by George Carr changed hands and was managed by the Greilick brothers until 1902 when E. R. Dailey purchased the business and operated it as a stave and heading mill. A stave is part of a wooden keg or barrel; generally, the thin, narrow-shaped pieces of wood that form the sides of a cask or keg, and the ends of a barrel were called the heads. The factory burned in 1907.

Olaf Olson and Charles Chadsey disassembled a large building in nearby Thompsonville and moved it by rail to Suttons Bay in 1914. When reconstructed, they operated it as a planing mill for the next 30 years. A planing tool is used to shape wood by flattening, reducing the thickness, or smoothing the surface of a rough piece of lumber. Gerald Selby purchased the business in 1944 and named it Northern Lumber Company which operates today as a lumber company and hardware.

Time brings changes, but in the small village of Suttons Bay, time's touch has been gentle. Suttons Bay is still a safe harbor serving boats and ships that dock there. It also attracts tourists and visitors to its old-fashioned allure—a slow-paced, charming corner of Michigan away from it all.

● MUSEUMS AND THEATRE

The Bay Community Theatre, established in 1946, has brought entertainment to the community for over 70 years. Located at 214 North St. Joseph Avenue, the Bay Theatre began operating as a nonprofit community theater in 2019. Over the decades the venue has filled the screen with countless films, hosted dozens of fine musicians and live theatre on stage, and featured special events. It is one of the original arthouse theatres providing a selection of mainstream, Indie, and foreign films to satisfy the discriminating film buff.

The theatre is proud of its role as the place where art and community come together. It bills itself as world class cinema and small town theatre, a venue where you will enjoy the atmosphere and architecture almost as much as the entertainment. The sophisticated sound system enhances viewing and listening pleasure. The Bay Theatre is a local gem.

<<>>

Eyaawing Museum and Cultural Center, 2304 North West Bay Shore Drive, Peshawbestown, four miles north of Suttons Bay. Museum volunteers share stories from Anishinaabe culture and belief systems. Exhibits include canoes, a life-size wigwam, and fishing and trapping artifacts that present a picture of the lives of local Native Americans. There is also an amazing taxidermied eagle and a small gift shop with Native American music, jewelry, books, and dream catchers made by local tribal members. Closed during Covid-19, you should check current hours.

<<>>

The Painted Bird, 216 North St. Joseph Avenue. This gallery has offered its customers treasures for more than 14 years. The emphasis is on contemporary art with displays from over 100 area and American artists: jewelry, candle holders, decorative and functional art for the home, mirrors, tiles, glass sculpture, clothing, leather, furniture, and rugs.

● BEACHES, PARKS, AND TRAILS

Bahle Park, north end of West Street. Thirty acres of walking trails, skiing, sledding hill, and a warming house that can be rented and holds up to 41 guests. The warming house has a refrigerator and restrooms. The hill is used by residents and visitors throughout the winter.

<<>>

Suttons Bay Marina Park, off Front Street, just east of town on Lake Michigan. Sandy public beach, playground, volleyball nets, picnic areas, tables, grills, boat launch, and 30 transient slips.

● OTHER STOPS TO CONSIDER

Suttons Bay Farmers Market, St. Joseph Street, north end of the village. If you are in town on a Saturday morning between May and October, it is worth a stop at this fresh produce market. You will also find gourmet items and crafts. Open Saturday 9:00 a.m. to 1:00 p.m.

<<>>

Visit a Winery. Mawby Sparkling Wines, Shady Lane Cellars, Willow Vineyards, Big Little Wines, and Longview Winery, among others, are located around Suttons Bay. Spend a couple of hours of your vacation sampling the area wines.

10. NORTHPORT AND OMENA

Northport is a village with a 2020 population of 531. Omena is a census-designated place with a 2020 population of 288. Before there was a Northport, there was Waukazooville where in 1840, Reverend George Smith established a Native American mission. Originally located in Southwestern Michigan, the mission was moved to the Leelanau Peninsula so the parishioners could escape a smallpox epidemic. The mission served the Odawa and Ojibwe and was named in honor of Chief Peter Waukazoo.

The move did not end the struggles endured by the plagued first settlers. Trying to produce enough food was a life-and-death battle that required enormous labor. The planting and growing season was short; crop failure often left the tribes and early settlers threatened by starvation.

If there was a silver lining, food preservation was aided by large chunks of ice that could be chopped from the lake.

In 1852 or 1854, depending upon the historical account you read, Deacon Joseph Dame and his son Eusebius, platted the land just north of Waukazooville. They named their plat Northport because it was the northernmost port on the Leelanau Peninsula. The availability of land brought more settlers to the area and soon the mission village became a bustling center of activity, and Northport annexed Waukazooville.

When the United States recognized the Grand Traverse Odawa and Ojibwe reservation on the Leelanau Peninsula in 1855, Northport was excluded from the boundaries.

William Voice built the first sawmill in the area in 1856. As with most small Michigan harbor towns, Northport lumbering supported the population. Northport's location as the first harbor in the Grand Traverse Bay gave it strategic importance.

Northport served as the original county seat of Leelanau County from 1863 to 1883. It was incorporated as a village in 1903. Today the hills around Northport are dotted with cherry and apple orchards. Hotels and motels fill with seasonal visitors transforming the quiet village into a summer tourist haven.

Tiny Omena lies in sheltered Omena Bay about six miles south of Northport. Credit goes to Chief Shab-we-sung for establishing the village and to his tribe for the name, Omena. According to legend, in 1852, Reverend Peter Daugherty started a small mission/Presbyterian Church in the area, and many of the Ojibwe became friends with the minister. They shared their news and problems with him. When told of a recent happening he always asked, "Is that so?" and O-me-nah translates to "Oh, is that so?" in the Ojibwe native tongue. The

Presbyterian Church is a historical building in Omena. (See Other Things to See or Do.)

Another possible explanation for the name is that omena means apple in Finnish and apple trees are plentiful in the area. There is no evidence, however, that Finns were early settlers in Omena. A post office with that name—whatever its origin—opened in February 1858.

You have to appreciate Omena's sense of humor and creativity. Every three years, the tiny village elects a mayor. It's all to raise money for the historical society. For more than a decade, only candidates clothed in fur, fleece, or feathers have been permitted on the ballot. As you may have guessed, this isn't humans wearing animal clothing, but rather members of the canine, feline, equine, or other animal species. Each dollar contributed in a candidate's name constitutes one vote. The winner is announced after a parade. The community is invited to join in the revelry.

In the 2018 election, Sweet Tart (McKee), a beautiful long-haired calico defeated 13 dogs, a peacock, and a goat to be announced purr-fect for the position. Sweet Tart, so named because she was rescued along the Tart Trail on Sweetest Day (and the Omena area raises so many sweet and tart cherries), had a mohair goat as press secretary, and a special assistant appointed to handle fowl issues— a chicken won that position. Tart's is an all-American success story—from foundling to city mayor.

In the 2021 election, Ms. Tart demonstrated she wasn't done with pawlitics. Although sympathetic to term limits, she ran for reelection. She was unseated by her best friend, a beautiful yellow lab named Rosie Disch. Ms. Tart wasn't upset by the loss and will support Rosie in any way she can. Tart came in a respectable third and will be the Second Vice Mayor (behind First Vice Mayor, Penny the Chicken). Maybe in 2024, Ms. Tart will run again.

Ms. Sweet Tart.
Courtesy of Omena Historical Society and Kanda McKee.

• MUSEUMS

Grand Traverse Lighthouse and Museum, 15500 North Lighthouse Point Road. You can tour the keeper's home, climb to the tower and visit the gift shop. (For more information about the lighthouse, see Lighthouse.)

<<>>

Tamarack Craftsman Art Gallery, 5039 North West Bay Shore Drive, Omena. A special shop where you will find an amazing assortment of merchandise including art of contemporary American artists working in glass, wood, porcelain, oil paintings, and folk art. Tamarack Gallery moved from Sugarloaf to historic Omena in 1976. What began as a small fine crafts gallery featuring ten artists is now a showcase for fine art, crafts, and folk art. The gallery represents over sixty-five artists from all over the country.

Haserot Park, Third Street, downtown Northport. This municipal beach is sheltered by a cove. It provides a grassy park with plenty of room for children to play. The view of Grand Traverse Bay's sparkling waters adds to your enjoyment. Amenities: swimming, playground, picnic facilities, and restrooms.

<<>>

Leelanau Conservancy's Kehl Lake Preserve, Kehl Road north of Northport. The 279-acre natural area features 2,500 feet of undeveloped shoreline along the 74-acre lake. Paths meander through hardwood-conifer swamps. Birders spot blue-headed vireo, blackburnian warblers, herons, kingfishers, and loons. You may share your walk with deer, opossum, porcupines, and raccoons. At certain points, you will be surrounded by old-growth white pines and hemlock with branches reaching for the clouds.

<<>>

Leelanau State Park, 15310 North Lighthouse Point Road. This 1,350-acre park at the top of the Leelanau Peninsula includes coastal dunes and beaches where Petoskey stones are prevalent. The park is filled with wildlife and provides an 8½-mile hiking and cross-country ski trail winding to the beach. The Grand Traverse Lighthouse, built in 1852, now a museum, is in this park. Camping is available.

<<>>

Peterson Park, 10001 East Peterson Park Road outside of Northport. The Lake Michigan Coastline in West Michigan is generally known for its sugar sand beaches, but this is a rocky beach. You can find Petoskey stones as you walk the shore, and the sunset is beautiful. Amenities: playground equipment, picnic tables, grills, a volleyball area, viewing platform, stairway to the beach, and a paved parking lot.

● OTHER STOPS TO CONSIDER
Theatre
The Northport Community Arts Center and Theatre Company. Check online for tickets and information about what is playing. Local citizens raised a million dollars and built the auditorium and gave it to the school. The school gets to use it whenever they need it, but the theatre company performances are remarkable and a pleasant surprise in such a tiny town. Usually, a banner at the blinking light in town describes what is playing.

<<>>

Wineries. Spend a relaxing afternoon at a local winery or tasting room. Consider Gill's Pier Vineyard and Winery, 5620 North Manitou Trail, Northport or Leelanau Wine Sellers Tasting Room, 5019 North West Bayshore Drive M-22, Omena.

<<>>

Drive by the Frank Lloyd Wright-designed **Amy Alpaugh Studio Residence** at 71 North Peterson Park Road. This home, built in 1946, is a private residence so be respectful—just quietly enjoy the structure as you drive past.

Amy Alpaugh Studio Residence. Courtesy of Pixabay Free Images.

Omena Presbyterian Church, (On the National Historic Register as Grove Hill New Mission Church), 5098 North West Bay Shore Drive, Omena. A white clapboard church with an attached shed resting on a foundation

Grove Hill New Mission Church. Courtesy of Pixabay Free Images

constructed of pine lumber. Originally the church had two front doors but no front windows. The bell is original. The manse (a Presbyterian minister's home) is a Sears-Roebuck home.

<<>>

Northport U.S. Post Office, 117 East Nagonaba, Northport. Not a tourist site, but something to look at as you are walking about. The unique architecture is a local treasure.

● LIGHTHOUSE

The Grand Traverse Lighthouse, 15500 North Lighthouse Point Road, Northport. The lighthouse sits inside Leelanau State Park, has been restored, and is open to the public. The Grand Traverse Lighthouse marks the Manitou shipping passage on Lake Michigan and the entrance to Grand Traverse Bay. It was built by the U.S. Lighthouse Service in 1858. The fog signal building was built in 1899. Later a modernized kitchen was added. In the mid-1950s, additional modernization took place including electricity to the porch wings and an automated light tower built nearby. The lighthouse was deactivated in 1972.

● The Famous or Infamous with Ties to Northport and Omena

George Armstrong Custer reportedly had a summer home or other residence in the Suttons Bay or Omena area. Biographies about the man best known for his catastrophic defeat at Little Big Horn do not substantiate that story, but the chain of ownership of the building that houses the Omena Historical Society can be traced to Custer's father-in-law and Custer.

<<>>

Captain Clint F. Woolsey, one of the pilots who led the inaugural Pan American Goodwill Flight to Central and South America in 1926-1927, was born and raised in Northport. He died in a crash over the Amazon. The local airport is named to honor him. Woolsey was one of the last pilots to instruct Charles Lindbergh, and it was Lindbergh who, three months after his instructor's death, fulfilled Woolsey's vision of flying over the Atlantic.

<<>>

You may see faces that look familiar as you explore Northport. The tiny town attracts the rich and famous who try to live or vacation quietly and anonymously in the area. Among them, Mario Batali, celebrity chef; Tim Allen who reportedly spends summers at Northport; Mark

Spitznagel, a multi-billion-dollar hedge fund manager; Olympic silver medalist and speedskater, Jonathon Kuck; and War hero, Frederic W. Galbraith. Another persistent local rumor says that Kevin Costner has an interest somewhere in Leelanau county.

11. LELAND

INCLUDING HISTORIC FISHTOWN

Leland, 2020 population of 2055, was born of the lumbering era, but fishing was always an integral part of its economy. Its name originated from the nautical term lee ward, lee land, or lee shore which refers to the side of a ship or bay sheltered from the wind. You might move to the leeward side of a vessel so you don't have the wind in your face. Leland offers protection from the north winds of stormy Lake Michigan. Leelanau, the peninsula on which Leland sits, is believed to mean "delight of life" in the Odawa language.

Not far from the Carp River (now the Leland River) that flows into Lake Michigan, bark-covered shelters, gardens, and fishing sites marked the settlement of *Mishi-me-go-bing* or the "place where canoes run up into the river to land because they have no harbor." Today Leland is the site of the oldest and largest Odawa village on the Leelanau Peninsula. It is also the site of a manmade harbor.

In 1853 Antoine Manseau brought his family from North Manitou Island to the Leland area. Manseau, his son, Antoine Jr., and John Miller built a dam near the outlet of the Carp River. Next to the dam, they erected a water-powered sawmill to cut timber to construct a small city. After building the settlement, they used the mill for commercial lumbering. Docks were established as wooding stations. Steamers and schooners tied up at these docks, bringing with them more and more settlers.

In 1882 Leland became the county seat of Leelanau County, and by 1887, it boasted 200 residents.

As the area grew, hotels and other businesses came, and resort clientele made the trek to the charming village and countryside. Some tourists returned summer after summer; others made Leland their permanent home. By 1900 the county population was over 10,500, and today it is twice that number.

Historic Fishtown. Courtesy of Rick Lahmann.

Fishtown, an integral part of Leland, is a 140-year-old commercial fishing complex on the river's edge. Its weathered, cedar-shingled shanties, fishing tugs, and docks create a living legacy to the area's maritime culture and provide a glimpse of early fishing life. The shanties remain intact and look much as they did when first built. Today, Fishtown is one of the few thriving fishing districts on the Great Lakes. Initially home to Native Americans, who worked and fished in the area, European settlers arrived in the 1850s and created the current fishing center. As you walk the streets, you'll see functioning smokehouses, overhanging docks lined with fish tugs, and charter fishing boats. Many of the shanties have been repurposed as small gift shops and galleries. Each year, thousands of visitors flock to the area that remains a crucial part of Lake Michigan's fishing heritage.

Carlson's Fishery, a family business passed down through five generations, opened in 1906 in one of the shanties along the docks. Nels Carlson moved from his home on North Manitou Island, where he endured ferocious winters, to Leland. Carlson, a farmer, turned to fishing, and along with his four sons opened Carlson's Fisheries. Today, you can watch as salmon and whitefish are removed from smoker racks at the same spot the family began its business more than a century ago. If you are lucky, you might be offered a sample.

Before refrigeration, fishermen chopped and hauled mammoth chunks of ice from the solidly frozen lake and dragged those blocks to shore where they were covered with sawdust in a large ice house. During the summer, workers chipped ice to cool the daily catch of whitefish and lake trout.

By the 1940s, many commercial fishers abandoned fishing. They could not support families with the empty nets they brought up each day from the chilly Lake Michigan waters. The lamprey eel extracted a huge price from the industry. The Carlsons survived a decade when most others abandoned their shanties. The family weathered many changes besides the invasive lamprey— from government policy change, revisions in fishing territories, adjustments in quotas, fish population dynamics, and contaminants—and still Carlson's remained a viable business. In 2004 they sold their Fishtown property, fishing licenses, tugs, and gear to the nonprofit Fishtown Preservation Society, with the provision that they be allowed to continue operating their retail business at the dock.

The Fishtown Preservation Society manages and maintains Fishtown where you can still find the best smoked fish, whitefish sausage, fish pâté, and fish jerky in the region.

The endearing fishing tugs, the *Janice Sue* and the *Joy*, Fishtown icons—integral to Leland's continued fishing culture—remain in service. Visit Fishtown, and enjoy the unique shops and galleries. Relish the best fish sandwich you have ever had the pleasure to taste and contemplate how to fill the hours of the beautiful day that looms ahead.

• MUSEUMS

Leelanau Historical Museum, 203 East Cedar Street. The museum exhibits reflect the cultural history of the Leelanau Peninsula and the nearby islands from the time man first stepped foot in this area. Collections and archives contain more than 20,000 items including a collection of Anishinaabek traditional arts. The museum is the recipient of the 2014 State History Award for Outstanding Local Society.

<<>>

Reflections Art Gallery, 199 West River Street, Fishtown. An intriguing gallery with a nautical flair. The space brims with local artwork, boat replicas, CD music, jewelry, sculpture, framed photographs, and accent pieces. Treasures peek out from every nook and cranny.

Downtown Leland (above and next page). Courtesy of Rick Lahmann.

• Beaches, Parks, and Trails

Bartholomew Park (Nedow's Beach), at the end of Pearl Street, seven blocks east of Main Street, is a public park and beach on North Lake Leelanau. Amenities include swimming beach, boat launch, picnic area, and dock.

<<>>

Schneider's Beach and Park, is a public beach on North Lake Leelanau at the end of Popp Road (off M-204), 1½ miles west of the village of Lake Leelanau. The park offers a picnic area, grills, firepit, parking, dock, and boat launch.

<<>>

North Manitou Island Camping has low impact, open camping. 15,000 acres of wilderness with the emphasis on self-reliance. Leave-no-trace camping is the rule. The primary visitor activities include hiking, swimming, backcountry camping, and backpacking. The island is home to a large whitetail deer herd and is the summer range for a variety of raptors including the bald eagle.

<<>>

South Manitou Island Camping. Camping is permitted at three locations on the island: the Bay, the Weather Station, and the Popple Campgrounds. Low impact camping is the rule to prevent damage to the fragile ecosystem. Remember to store all food in hard containers to avoid thievery from the Northern Miniature Tiger (chipmunk). There is no transportation from the lakeshore to the campgrounds, and all gear must be trekked in and out.

<<>>

Van's Beach. Favorite local public beach. The trailhead to the beach is downtown just beyond Van's Garage and the end of Cedar Street. Often secluded, lovely beach.

<<>>

Charter Boats. More than a dozen charter boats in Leland are waiting to take you on a fishing or sightseeing adventure.

● OTHER STOPS TO CONSIDER

South Manitou Island is part of an island chain that extends north to the Straits of Mackinac. The 8.2 square mile island is a ridge of limestone buried under glacial debris. A grove of white cedars more than 500 years old, ten miles of rocky beach, dunes, and a campground await your arrival. A visitor center helps you get your bearings and acquaints you with the island's history.

South Manitou Island, now uninhabited, was originally a settlement founded by William Burton who built a dock that offered the only natural deep-water harbor between Chicago and Buffalo. At its peak in the mid-1800s, the village had a blacksmith shop, grocery store, barn, and a railroad track that extended inland to haul wood for steamers. Farming developed on the island

and crops—rye, beans, and peas—that exceeded local need were sold to passing ships and mainland markets. South Manitou Island has a lighthouse. (See Beaches, Parks, and Trails, and Lighthouses.)

Tours of the island are offered, or you can blaze your own trail to areas that can't be reached by vehicle. The views that await the intrepid hiker are a suiting reward for the effort.

<<>>

North Manitou Island is approximately eight miles long and slightly over four miles wide. It boasts 20 miles of shoreline and has a land area of more than 22 square miles. It has been called "fifteen thousand acres of wilderness floating in the sparkling waters of Lake Michigan," which seems an apt description. Campers seeking a rugged experience, solitude, and a challenge to their self-reliance will love North Manitou Island. You can book a ride to the island from Leland.

<<>>

St. Wenceslaus Church and Cemetery are located a few miles north of Leland, where the community of Gill's Pier once stood, at County roads 626 and 637 in Leelanau Township. In the 1860s and 1870s, Bohemian settlers came to the area. In 1890 they built the St. Wenceslaus Catholic Church and established the cemetery. The membership increased, and in 1914 an additional brick church was constructed to provide for the needs of the larger congregation. The two churches, old and new, stood side-by-side for many years. Now only the 1914 church survives, and it is about all that remains of Gill's Pier. A walk through the cemetery with tranquil views of the surrounding farmlands can be a refreshingly quiet moment in otherwise hectic travels. The original settlers to the area worked at the Leland Lake Superior Iron Foundry and the Gill sawmill. When one of their own died, to mark the grave, they handcrafted an ornate metal

104

grave marker, reminiscent of their Bohemian heritage. The church is a designated Michigan Historic Site.

<<>>

Wineries. Gill's Pier Winery, 5620 North Manitou Trail, a few miles north of Leland and Good Harbor Vineyards and Winery, 34 South Manitou Trail, Lake Leelanau, a few miles south of Leland, both promise a pleasantly relaxing afternoon.

• LIGHTHOUSE

South Manitou Island Light. South Manitou Island was popular in the nineteenth and twentieth centuries as a harbor and fueling station. With the completion of the Erie Canal in 1826, the development of commercial navigation on the Great Lakes increased rapidly. The Manitou Passage was the most important route for schooners and steamers traveling the length of Lake Michigan. The island was a stop for early mariners between Chicago and the Straits of Mackinac.

Congress appropriated $5,000 in 1838 to establish a lighthouse to increase the safety of the 300-mile stretch of Lake Michigan between Chicago and the Straits of Mackinac. The original lighthouse is no longer standing. In 1858 the original lighthouse was replaced with a two-story brick residence and a 35-foot tower. A fog signal building was added. Both structures still stand today.

In 1901 the United States Lifesaving Service built a station on the island. The USLSS became part of the United States Coast Guard in 1915. The station was permanently closed by the Coast Guard in 1958 and became the island's ranger station. It is not open to the public. Once considered the most beautiful lighthouse on the lakes, the South Manitou Light was deactivated the same year the lifesaving station closed. The building is now a museum, open to the public.

• SHIPWRECKS

The *W.C. Kimball* may be the most interesting ship to go down near the Manitou Islands because she went down over a century ago and was found by chance in 2018. The identity of the wreck, discovered by Shipwreck Hunter Ross Richardson, was a mystery. With a bit of sleuthing, the remains were identified and videos were taken. Richardson spotted the wreckage by sonar a year before he identified her.

The *W.C. Kimball* was built and launched from Manitowoc, Wisconsin in 1888. The schooner operated out of Northport, and often sailed along the coastline of Lake Michigan to Chicago and back, delivering salt, roofing shingles, and potatoes.

The *Kimball* was headed north in the early morning of May 8, 1891, when a gale swept in and riled Lake Michigan. Later, vessels following the *Kimball*'s course came to a wreckage field and spotted shingles floating off North Manitou Island and washing up at the tip of the Leelanau Peninsula. Search efforts failed to locate the ship or bodies of the crew.

<<>>

The **Manitou Passage Underwater Preserve** allows divers to explore historic docks and shipwrecks that date back two centuries. The preserve surrounds the North and South Manitou Islands and lies next to Michigan's Sleeping Bear Dunes National Lakeshore.

▪ The **Alva Bradley**, a three-masted schooner, was lost in a gale on October 13, 1894. Her wreckage was discovered in 1990 in about 20 to 27 feet of water between North and South Manitou Islands. She remains largely intact. Like the *Kimball* described above, the *Bradley* remained in an unknown grave for nearly a century.

▪ The **Congress**, a wooden steamer, caught fire at South Manitou Island on October 4, 1904. The stern was engulfed in flames when she sank in about 165 feet of water.

• The ***Francisco Morazon***, a freighter that ran aground in December 1960, is the most popular wreck in the preserve. It is an easy dive, resting in 15 feet of water. The *Morazan* was an ocean-going vessel built in 1922. Her crew became disoriented in a November snowstorm and ran aground on the rocks off the south end of South Manitou Island.

• The ***Walter L. Frost*** was a wooden steamer lost in blinding snow. She ran aground on November 4, 1903, on South Manitou Island. Her remains broke up years later when the *Morazan* ran aground on top of her. The *Frost* allows divers an excellent view of the remains of her hull and boilers.

• The ***Three Brothers***, a wooden steamer, was beached on September 27, 1911, on the lee side of South Manitou Island where she was abandoned due to treacherous weather and shifting sands that buried her. In 1996 the sands that had quickly buried her, shifted again exposing her in nearly perfect condition and easily accessible from the beach. Her bow is broken, the stern is intact, and as might be expected, the hull is filled with sand. She presents an easy novice exploration.

• The ***Montauk***, a schooner, was stranded on North Manitou Island on November 23, 1882. Her remains rest in about 35 feet of water.

• The ***H.D. Moore***, a schooner, was stranded at Gull Point, South Manitou Island on September 10, 1907. Her wreckage is scattered in 10 to 12 feet of shallow water.

• The ***James McBride***, a brig, a small sailing vessel with two square-rigged masts, ran aground during a storm on October 19, 1857. Her remains lie in 5 to 15 feet of water near Sleeping Bear Point.

• The ***Rising Sun***, a wooden steamer, was stranded just north of Pyramid Point on October 29, 1917. She crashed into pieces, and her wreckage rests in shallow 6 to 12 feet of water.

• THE FAMOUS OR INFAMOUS WITH TIES TO LELAND

Thomas W. L. Ashley was a democratic U.S. representative from Ohio who died in 2010, at age 87, in Leland.

<<>>

Barbara Ninde Byfield was an author and illustrator who died in Leland in 1988. Her first book was *The Eating in Bed Cook Book* about which she said, "There is a secret, wholesome indulgence to eating in bed which perhaps explains why it has not received the uniformly good press of other things which go on in bed." Byfield wrote several children's books.

<<>>

James Harrison was a prolific American poet, novelist, and essayist. He published more than three dozen books in several genres and wrote screenplays, book reviews, and also published essays on a variety of subjects. Harrison described his versatile writing career as the result of a fall from a cliff while birdwatching. He suffered serious injuries and required a significant convalescence. A friend suggested that with nothing else to do, he should write a book. The result was *Wolf: A False Memoir.* Harrison maintained a residence in Leland for more than thirty years.

<<>>

Keewaydinoquay Pakawakuk Peschel's mother gave birth to her daughter in a fishing boat while on her way from the Manitou Islands to a mainland hospital. The boat capsized; Keewaydinoquay's survival deemed a miracle. Her adult name Giiwedinokwe, recorded

Keewaydinoquay, was given to her after her vision quest and is interpreted as Woman of the North(west) Wind.

Starting at age nine, Kee apprenticed with Anishinaabeg medicine woman Nodjimahkwe. Kee's higher education started late in life. At the age of 57, she studied anthropology, believing people would be more willing to listen to her if she had a degree. She received a Master of Education Degree from Wayne State University, and finished all course work for a Ph.D. in ethnobotany at the University of Michigan. She was honored with the Michigan Conservation Teacher of the Year Award in 1975 for "Outstanding Work in the Field of Conservation." She was a professor at the University of Wisconsin-Milwaukee where she taught classes in ethnobotany and philosophy. She lived in Ann Arbor, Milwaukee, Leland, and Garden Island[1].

She died on July 21, 1999, and was honored with a traditional Midewiwin ceremony on Garden Island. In March 2002, the Holy Hill Trust of Leland was awarded a Michigan Humanities Council grant to write a book about Keewaydinoquay's life. *The Life Story of Keewaydinoquay* was published in 2006 and named one of the 2007 Notable Books of Michigan.

<<>>

Emilia Christine Schaub was born in a log cabin in 1891 in Centerville Township near Leland. She attended law school, was the first female prosecutor in the state, and the first woman to successfully defend a murder trial. While serving as Leelanau County Prosecutor, she

---

[1] Garden Island is part of the Beaver Island archipelago. (See Beaver Island under Charlevoix, Other Stops to Consider.) It currently has no year-round residents. The Garden Island Indian Cemetery, continues in active use and contains more than 3,500 burials, most of them unmarked, however, spirit houses, also known as grave shelters, adorn many burial sites. The cemetery land is owned by a nonprofit organization that keeps the site protected and open to all native peoples.

arranged for the return of the Odawa and Ojibwe lands from the state to Leelanau County, creating a de facto reservation. For her efforts, she was made an honorary member of the tribe. She was elected to the Michigan Women's Hall of Fame in 1990. Among other honors, she was named a champion of justice of the state bar of Michigan in 1901. A granite boulder outside the county building in Leland bears her name.

● BOOKS AND MOVIES WITH TIES TO LELAND
Bill Crandell's, **Fishtown**, is 112 pages that recount the history, humor, and tragedy of Fishtown.

<<>>

James Harrison, **Wolf: A False Memoir** is the story of a young man disillusioned with New York City who travels to the wilderness of northern Michigan. He wanders the woods hoping to spot one of the wild wolves that prowl the area. His hunt pauses often for retrospection making this a coming-of-age story. (See The Famous or the Infamous with Ties to Leland.)

<<>>

Mardi Link, **Isador's Secret**. The author shines a journalist's spotlight on this tragic dark story buried in the Leelanau Peninsula's history. Sister Mary Janina Mezek's bones were exhumed in 1918 from a shallow grave underneath the parish church in Isador. The former parish priest, Father Andrew Bieniawski, was rumored to be the father of the pregnant woman's unborn child, but he had an ironclad alibi. The book contains illustrations and photos. One picture is of suspect Stella Lipezynski in the Leelanau County Jail in Leland.

<<>>

Keewaydinoquay Pakawakuk Peschel and Lee Boisvert, **Keewaydinoquay, Stories from My Youth**. In the tradition of oral storytellers, this book describes the life and childhood of Keewaydinoquay who is influenced both by her Native American and white roots. The stories span generations and cultures and provide insight into the way of life of Native Americans in Michigan. Peschel also authored **Cedar Songs**. In the 1900s, most Native American children were removed from their homes and sent to schools to teach them white ways. Keewaydinoquay escaped that fate and enjoyed the amazing gift of growing up able to learn from and value her mixed-race heritage, religious diversity, and her insatiable curiosity. She lived the lessons she shares from her childhood on Garden Island and in Leland.

12. GLEN ARBOR AND GLEN HAVEN

Glen Arbor had a 2020 population of 861. Glen Haven had a 2020 population of 407. Like nearly all Michigan coastal communities, Glen Arbor and Glen Haven followed the pattern: fur, lumber, farming, and resort/tourism. However, the current status of these two villages, located a few miles from each other, diverges significantly. Glen Arbor is a quaint and busy little village known for its annual art fair and galleries, friendly people, and lack of chain restaurants and motels. Glen Haven, situated within Sleeping Bear Dunes National Lakeshore exists only as a historical village with an operational blacksmith shop, an inn, and a general store where you can purchase souvenirs and hear about Glen Haven's earlier days.

John LaRue, a fur trader from South Manitou Island, moved to the Glen Haven/Glen Arbor area in 1848 to establish a trading post at Sleeping Bear Bay. From his post, he traded with Native Americans who camped in the area. Gradually, settlers followed and in 1854, Mrs. John E. Fisher named the area Glen Arbor because she felt it was a pleasant glen surrounded by beautiful Michigan forests.

Also in 1854, John Dorsey set up a cooper shop where he made fish barrels to ship to fishermen along the coast. About the same time, John Fisher purchased 1,000 acres of land on the north side of Glen Lake, and with his brother-in-law, C.C. McCarty, built the Sleeping Bear Inn which was originally a residence for lumbermen.

George Ray built a dock in 1856 so the small villages could connect to the shipping highway. Ray later became the tiny settlement's first postmaster.

W.D. Burdick established a sawmill and a grist mill southeast of Glen Arbor in 1864. He gave the location his name, and it became known as Burdickville. In 1878 David Henry Day, a land developer and agent for the Northern Transportation Company, moved into Glen Arbor, which by then had about 200 residents, three docks, two hotels, four stores, a blacksmith shop, and a cooper. Wood products from the surrounding forests became the area's primary source of revenue. Both Glen Arbor and Glen Haven provided fuel for the schooners and steamers that traveled Lake Michigan carrying cargos of lumber.

In 1983 Glen Haven was added to the National Register of Historic Places. During its heyday in the logging era (late 1800s and early 1900s), Glen Haven was a bustling community, but the tiny village had a hardscrabble existence—starting when it was burned in the fire of 1871. It fought to remain alive, but most of the residents moved when logging suffered its death blow in the 1900s. The village shuffled along trying to survive on agriculture and tourism but slipped into a state of disrepair with no one to watch out for its health. The Department of the Interior bought the land on which Glen Haven sits for the Sleeping Bear Dunes National Lakeshore (See listing under Empire for information about the Visitor Center to Sleeping Bear Dunes National Lakeshore) and required the few remaining residents to sell after twenty-five years or, if they died before twenty-five years, their estate would have to sell the property to the park. By that time the village had lost many of its historic points of interest including the dock, sawmill, and railroad. Still, the Park Service acquired a remarkably intact 1920s-era village which brings the ghost harbor back to life.

Sleeping Bear Sand Dunes. Courtesy of Jon Royce.

The National Park Service is committed to restoring and maintaining Glen Haven. The buildings provide a fascinating stroll back in history. The maritime museum is worth a stop. In 1901 the Coast Guard established a lifesaving station at Sleeping Bear Point. In 1931 it was moved east to its present location near Glen Haven. It closed in 1944 and now is part of the Maritime Museum.

Glen Arbor survived the setbacks that turned Glen Haven into a ghost town. Today the year-round residents welcome the summer tourists and the boost they bring to the local economy. They also relish the advent of fall and an opportunity to reclaim their quiet village and the relative solitude of winter's cross-country skiing and snowmobiling.

Lake Street Studios, 6023 Lake Street, showcases four galleries featuring the art of many talented Northern Michigan artists. Lake Street Studios is the name of the property housing the individual galleries which include Glen Lake Artists' Gallery, Forest Gallery, North Gallery, and the Center Gallery. Each gallery features different merchandise and artwork.

<<>>

Glen Haven Historic Village is a small village on the Lake Michigan shoreline that invites you to step back in time to when little villages and docks awaited the arrival of steamers along the Great Lakes. Glen Haven is the best-preserved cordwood station on the eastern shore of Lake Michigan. It was a company town and eventually diversified into farming, fruit canning, and tourism. In the village, you will find much to explore.

▪ **Glen Haven Cannery Boathouse Museum**. Sleeping Bear Dunes National Lakeshore. The cannery was first built as a warehouse and converted to a state-of-the-art cannery for cherries in the early 1920s. In recent years, the cannery has housed the largest public exhibit of Great Lakes small craft and historic boats used around Glen Haven and the Manitou Islands.

▪ **Glen Haven General Store**. While in the village you can peruse shelves at the General Store and browse merchandise related to the history of Glen Haven including kitchenware, toys, maritime items, and books. The Leelanau Ranger Station is located upstairs.

▪ **The Blacksmith Shop** is a fully restored 1920s blacksmith shop. Watch the smithy heat a piece of iron in the forge and pound out intriguing and useful shapes. The exhibit is interactive, so feel free to ask questions. You can see some of the parts they have made in the shop and ask the blacksmith questions about his trade or the history of the local area. While you are watching, you will learn about D. H. Day and his role in developing Glen Haven.

▪ **Sleeping Bear Point Coast Guard Station Maritime Museum** is located just west of Glen Haven Village in Sleeping Bear Dunes National Lakeshore. It is the original Sleeping Bear Point U.S. Lifesaving Station which was moved to its present location because of the encroaching dunes. During the summer there are reenactments of the breeches buoy rescue drill using a Lyle Gun.[2]

<<>>

Synchronicity Gallery of Michigan Art, 6671 Western Avenue, displays the original work of 95 Michigan artists in a wide variety of media including contemporary paintings, original prints, pottery, photography, sculpture, and jewelry. This large gallery is seasonal from May-October.

● BEACHES, PARKS, AND TRAILS

Glen Arbor Municipal Beach. Amenities: beach with picnic facilities, restrooms, and a playground.

<<>>

Glen Haven Beach in Sleeping Bear Dunes National Lakeshore. This may seem like your own private Lake Michigan beach when there are not many others around—a refreshing and relaxed change of pace.

<<>>

---

[2] In the 1870s, the U.S. Lifesaving Services began operations in Michigan. Each station was responsible for a section of coastline, and the crews regularly walked the beach checking for signs of trouble or, in some cases, the wreckage of ships that had gone down. When a ship was sighted too close to land, flares were fired to warn the captain of the danger. If a ship foundered near shore, a Lyle gun (similar to a small cannon) fired a thin rope across the water to the stranded ship. The mates on the ship used the rope to haul over a much thicker line. A sling called a "breeches buoy" could then be attached to the sturdier line. The buoy rode above the water and hauled the ship's crew to shore. Demonstrations of the breeches buoy are offered during the summer at Sleeping Bear Point Lifesaving Museum. If disabled ships were not within reach of the Lyle gun, the crew of the lifesaving station had to consider whether the conditions would permit rescue by a small motor boat.

115

Old Settlers Park. On the east shore of Glen Lake off Interstate 675. Amenities: playground, restrooms, and picnic facilities.

<<>>

The Lake Michigan Beach can be accessed at the site of the Cannery Boat Museum. Park your car in the lot and walk over the dune to the beach. From this spot, you can get a good view of the Manitou Islands, and you can see the pilings remaining from the old Glen Haven dock. Take a few moments to read the interpretive sign under the shade tree by the parking lot. It shows a picture of the dock as it was in the early 1900s with a passenger ship docking.

● OTHER STOPS TO CONSIDER

The Beach Bards, on the Lake Michigan shore near Glen Arbor. A venue for Michigan's home-grown poets who light a campfire on the sand and invite everyone to gather and listen. The hearty blow of the conch shell wails into the warm summer evening. When the last sound fades, the show starts. The various bards proclaim stories of love lost, or mother bear and her cubs, or a soulful ballad, or maybe a tale of a demon/ghost or two. Verse after verse fills the air until the last words fade, leaving only Lake Michigan waves to break the night's silence.

<<>>

Farmers Market, 6394 Western Avenue, behind the township hall, Tuesday mornings 9 a.m. to 1 p.m.

13. EMPIRE

The little village of Empire, with a 2020 population of 306, was named for the steamboat, *Empire State*, which ran ashore on its sandy beaches more than a century ago. The *Empire State* was one of the largest ships on the Great Lakes and provided its passengers with luxurious accommodations on its route from Buffalo to Chicago. It carried immigrants bound for the western farmlands. On August 9, 1849, the *Empire State* was caught in a sudden, violent squall on Lake Michigan. She sprang a leak and was deliberately beached three miles south of Sleeping Bear. While beached and out of service, it is believed she served as the area's first school. After repairs, the *Empire State* sailed until 1857.

Like many cities along the Manitou Passage and the northern part of Lower Michigan, the village of Empire was founded by lumber entrepreneurs. From 1870 to 1910, small villages and towns grew up around local sawmills.

In 1885 a small steam-powered sawmill was built on Empire's shore. Twelve miles south of the village, two docks stretched into Platte Bay. Railway cars from inland brought hemlock bark, white pine, and the other lumber products to load onto ships at these docks.

In 1887 the T. Wilce Company established the Empire Lumber Company. With one of the largest mills in the state, it supported the Empire economy. Many Norwegian mill workers settled in the area near the Wilce Company, and the spot became known as Norway Town.

The Empire Lumber Company's sawmill burned twice and the second time, in 1916, there was no need to rebuild it. The forests were depleted, and the lumbering era had ended. A historic monument marks the remains (a piece of the foundation) of the mill in Empire Village Park.

Empire, once a bustling town with hotels, a newspaper, seven stores, and a bank, shrank into near obscurity. After the lumber boom fizzled, small dots-on-a-map villages like Empire turned to agriculture. Farmers finished clearing the land that had already been stripped of trees and started growing potatoes and grain crops.

These early forays into farming were supplemented, and eventually overtaken, by fruit orchards.

A white ball sits on a hill above the village to remind Empire of the United States Air Force surveillance radar system that operated there for 30 years beginning in the 1950s. The Federal Aviation Authority (FAA) maintains it today for air traffic control at the Cherry Capital Airport that services Traverse City, 20 miles away.

Tiny Empire's main claim to fame is its Visitor Center to the Sleeping Bear Dunes National Lakeshore. (See Glen Haven for additional information about the Sleeping Bear Dunes.) Thousands of visitors pass through the center annually. From this origination point, they travel north soaking up the beautiful parklands which occupy much of the shoreline of the Manitou Passage.

• MUSEUMS

Empire Area Museum, 11544 Lacore. Four buildings reveal area history: turn of the century living is displayed in the main building, but there are also a one-room schoolhouse, a 1911 Fire House, a barn housing horse-drawn farm equipment, and an audio-visual center. Seasonal.

<<>>

Secret Garden, 10206 West Front Street. A gallery that features the works of more than 200 artists working in varied media. Merchandise includes wall art, pottery, watercolors, oils, vases, wearables, chimes, accents, lamps, and coasters. More than 200 artists are represented.

• BEACHES, PARKS, AND TRAILS

Empire Township Campground, 7264 West Osborn, has 60 rustic campsites, nine with electricity. The campground is divided into a hardwoods section and a pine tree section. Amenities: coin-operated showers, one flush toilet, ice, wood, and a dump station as well as outhouses and drinking water throughout the campground.

<<>>

Empire Village Park, tucked behind the village at the intersection of M-72 and M-22. Crashing surf and sugar-sand beaches lure tourists to this marvelous little park. Amenities: playground, restrooms, picnic tables, free boat ramp, benches, and basketball hoops. Historic marker of the Empire Lumber Company which operated from 1887-1916.

<<>>

Sleeping Bear Dunes National Lakeshore. Dunes have been described as Glacier Created Wonders. They are that and more. Sleeping Bear National Lakeshore, established by an Act of Congress in 1970, stretches 35 miles along Lake Michigan. It covers 70,000 acres. Dunes rise a towering 460 feet. The Sleeping Bear Dunes National Lakeshore provides more than a million travelers a year with an abundance of sights, sounds, and experiences. You may climb the well-marked trails and dune paths or venture out on your own in a secluded wonderland sparsely

Endangered Piping Plover.
Courtesy of Pixabay Free Images.

trafficked, rich with unexpected overlooks, quiet lakes, uncrowded beaches, and perhaps a glimpse of a doe with her fawn. Wildlife is abundant; you may stumble upon a species or two that you have never seen before. The rare

Piping Plover,[3] an endangered bird, nests on these beaches.

Within the park are 20 inland lakes, beech and maple forests, two islands, and the remains of more than 50 shipwrecks.

The dunes along the eastern shore of Lake Michigan are the longest assemblage of freshwater dunes in the world. They are Michigan's magnificent sand playground. But they are also a complex and unique ecosystem worth exploring.

We all see the images: A toddler packs his or her red plastic pail with wet sand and tips it over to make a sand cake. A ten-year-old, advanced in sand construction, builds castles complete with water filled moats. A thirteen-year-old picks up a handful of dry sand and lets it slip mindlessly and slowly through her fingers, as she worries about how she looks in her first bikini. An eighteen-year-old couple sits on a beach towel; he reaches forward and with a stick draws R.L. loves J.K. in the damp sand. A young mother contemplates the grains of sparkling color on the palm of her hand—an absentminded distraction in her otherwise furiously paced life. An elderly couple walks hand and hand at the water's edge, feeling the sand massage the bottoms of

---

[3] A small, sand-colored North American shorebird that blends with the beaches which are its primary habitat. It generally weighs only an ounce or two and is between six to six-and-a-half inches long. During the breeding season the legs are bright orange, and the short bill is orange with a black tip. The plover has two single dark bands: one around its neck and one across its forehead between the eyes. In the winter the bill turns black, the legs are a paler orange, and the black bands are lost. The female's neck band is thinner and less complete than the male's. The Michigan population of Piping Plovers has decreased significantly in the last hundred years. They are still spotted along Lake Michigan's coastal shoreline but were declared endangered in Michigan in 1985. Because Piping Plovers nest on beaches where there is heavy human traffic, their eggs get stepped on, and the presence of people causes the birds to abandon their nests. Pets, especially dogs, are also a threat to these tiny birds. Much of their nesting territory has been lost to industrialization, and they fall prey to raccoon, skunk, and fox.

their wrinkled feet. Precious moments of life all washed away with the evening waves. They leave behind memories and a certainty that the sand will be there for a repeat performance the next day, and all the days after, for each stage of our lives.

Sleeping Bear is the best known of the dunes that run the length of Lake Michigan's Sunset Coast. The story of the Sleeping Bear is familiar to Michigan school children even today. It is an integral part of the dunes' history.

According to Ojibwe legend, a long, long time ago in the land that is now Wisconsin, there lived a mother bear and her two precious cubs. A raging forest fire forced the mother and cubs into Lake Michigan. The cubs were brave and swam strongly toward the Michigan shore. The distance and the swirling water proved too much for them, and they fell farther and farther behind their mother. Eventually they slipped beneath the waves and drowned. Mother Bear reached safety on the Michigan shore and climbed atop a bluff to peer back across the water in search of her cubs. They were nowhere to be seen. The Great Spirit saw her grieving and pitied her devastating loss. He raised North and South Manitou Islands to mark the spot where the cubs vanished and laid a slumber upon Mother Bear. (The Mother Bear was a tree-covered bump in the shape of a bear on the dune. It was eroded away by wind and water in the mid-1900s.)

Michigan boasts 275,000 acres of dune formations, and half of them are parks or preserves managed by governmental entities or land conservancies. They are there for the public to enjoy.

The ancient bedrock that produced the dunes was buried beneath mile-thick glaciers for a million or so years. About 12,000 years ago, the ice began melting and over time the glacial waters broke down the bedrock turning it into the sugar-like sand that covers the lake shore today. As glaciers melted, they acted as mammoth steam shovels dredging the huge holes in the earth that would eventually become the Great Lakes.

About 5,000 years ago, Lake Michigan's water level was twenty feet higher. Water levels rose and then slowly dissipated, causing erosion and flooding. This activity and the resultant currents carried the sand to the gouged-out areas of our five Great Lakes. Dunes formed where the sand could collect, and the lakes offered the perfect place for it to accumulate. Loose sand with no receptacle scattered. Waves on the lakes moved the sand toward the shore. Breezes, even the gentle ones, whisked the sand into steep dunes. Wind activity caused migrating dunes. Movable dunes are not found much farther than a mile from the lakeshore because the lake breezes die down by that point, allowing plant life to take hold and cover the dune, anchoring it in place.

From the naked sand at the shoreline to the forest inland, you can see the four zones of the dunes: beach, foredune, trough, and backdune.

The first dune zone is the **beach zone** where the sand is simply an infinitesimal number of tiny granules of crushed rock at the water's edge. The waves and the foot traffic of the beach worshipers prevent vegetation from growing. This zone is easily identified. It is the area scattered with beach towels on any hot summer day. Lake Michigan is famous worldwide for its vast beaches or dune beach zone.

The second dune zone, the **foredune**, is the next area you come to as you walk away from the lake. In these low-ridge areas, beach grass or marram grass sprouts bravely on the sand. This sharp plant, although unpleasant to walk through barefoot, is extremely important to the ecosystem because it provides some protection from the wind, allowing sand accumulation and additional vegetation. After the beach grass has gained a foothold, the juniper, dune willow, sand reed, milkweed, Pitcher's

Thistle, and other plants take root. With the growth of plant life, the spiders and other burrowing animals, like toads and snakes, begin crawling forth. To survive on this extremely hot patch of land, these creatures tunnel deep into the sand where the moisture keeps the inside of the dune cool.

The third dune zone, the **trough**, is the next area you encounter as you walk away from the lake. The troughs are depressions in the land. They become gullies and small ponds for the part of the year when they are filled with water. The trough area is also called swale or wetland. Here you find rushes, and in the more protected areas poplar, cottonwoods, and even oak trees. Animal life becomes more abundant in this dune zone. It draws birds and, if the pond remains filled with enough water, muskrats find it a suitable habitat. Fox, weasels, and other forest mammals slink into the trough to hunt.

The fourth and final dune zone, the **backdune**, has less accumulated sand because of the decreasing winds. The backdunes prove a suitable place for trees to become a forest. On the edge of the backdunes, closer to the water where the soil is less rich, oaks and aspens grow. Further inland, with less exposure to the harsh winter winds and with the benefit of richer soil, magnificent deciduous forests develop. Here the sugar maple, hemlock, beech, and the famous Michigan white pine create beautiful woodlands.

In addition to zones, dunes can also be described by type: linear, perched, parabolic, transverse, and falling dunes.

Linear dunes are the low area that parallels the water's edge. These are the beach dunes or the dune/swale areas. This type of dune is generally less than fifteen feet high. In Sleeping Bear Dunes National Lakeshore, however, these linear dunes reach more than 100 feet.

Perched dunes exist where the glacier has left behind moraines, areas that look as though the waves have cut steep, jagged edges into the land. Winds carry sand against these bluffs, and while the dunes themselves may be less than 100 feet in height, when they lie perched atop these glacier-created moraines or cliffs, they may tower more than 400 feet above the water's edge.

Parabolic dunes are u-shaped dune formations common along the eastern side of Lake Michigan. Periods of high water destroyed the plant cover of a linear dune and left the sand exposed to west winds. This destabilized dune ends up in a crescent shape called a blowout. Strong winds blow the sand inland often eroding the next dune. Marram grass takes root along the edges and on the crest causing the sand to accumulate vertically. Mt. Baldy in P. J. Hoffmaster State Park, more than 200 feet high, is a parabolic dune.

A **transverse dune** is linear or scalloped in shape and formed in shallow bays along the edge of the ancient glaciers. They are found mostly in the Upper Peninsula.

Falling dunes are migrating dunes of sand that spill from perched dunes into neighboring lowlands. The Dune Climb at Sleeping Bear Dunes National Lakeshore is a falling dune. When these falling dunes drift completely beyond the plateau to the lowland, they are called deperched dunes. Sleeping Bear Point is a deperched dune. Twice in the last century, sandslides at Sleeping Bear Point have sent large land masses plunging into Lake Michigan. In June 1998, a large slide at Pyramid Point took thousands of tons into the water. In their movements, the dunes can cover and kill trees forming ghost forests such as the one on North Manitou Island.

Lake Michigan's great treasure, these famed dunes, are not impervious to wanton disregard and abuse. Just as Michigan's forests were felled, and its animals hunted to near extinction, the cherished dunes can be damaged and destroyed. The dunes are beloved as a recreational area for hikers, climbers, and walkers. Visitors should be environmentally conscious and leave vegetation intact, keep pets in check, and pick up the trash they bring with them.

The bigger threat to the dunes has come, however, from sand mining. Up to one-third of the dunes are at risk from mining. During the rise of the Industrial Age in the early 1900s, various industries discovered Lake Michigan's dunes were a perfect source of high-quality sand. Foundries used the sand in castings to make metal car parts. Railroads used the sand in laying tracks. The dunes provided accessible, cheap, and easily transported sand, and there were no legal barriers to its removal. At that time, some people naively believed that ridding the landscape of the dunes would make the land more accessible and therefore more valuable for future development of homes and other projects.

Pigeon Hill in Muskegon vanished. Creeping Joe, near the Manistee River, disappeared—gone forever because the railroads hauled away all of his sand. Maggie Thorpe, an immense dune system located north of the Manistee River from what is now Harbor Village, lay close enough to watch her brother dune, Creeping Joe, vanish. Maggie's own demise came soon after. Although these dunes may have looked barren and desolate to the casual observer, life thrived. Maggie was home to many plants and animals including sandpipers, gulls, and the endangered Piping Plover that hopped about her surface. In earlier days, she was covered with Passenger Pigeons that like Maggie, are now extinct. Maggie's foredune contained sea rockets and the endangered Pitcher's Thistle which in turn provided food and shade to snakes, turtles, ladybugs, butterflies, and mice. The trough was home to toads, heron, raccoon, and the dwarf lake iris, another endangered species. Finally, her backdune was a mixed forest perched on a rich layer of soil with sand underneath.

Sand mining destroys the ecosystem for any aquatic or terrestrial organism living in the mined area. Ultimately, the dune itself disappears. As a result of sand mining and other industrial use, many of Lake Michigan's dunes vanished.

By the 1960s, it became apparent that mining the dunes was negatively impacting the shoreline. As the dunes took on an important role in drawing tourists (two million visitors annually to the Sleeping Bear Dunes National Lakeshore and more than half a million to P. J. Hoffmaster State Park), it became imperative to make efforts to save them. A 1991 study by the National Park Service calculated the economic benefit of the Sleeping Bear Dunes National Lakeshore over the years at a total of $38,910,000 in tourist revenue and the creation and support of a thousand jobs. It was estimated that each visitor to the park spent $64 a day, creating a regional cash flow of about $128 million annually.

Those numbers drew serious attention to dune preservation. In response, the State of Michigan passed the Sand Dune Protection and Management Act in 1976. However, even when efforts at reclamation are successful, they cannot bring back the dunes that have been lost. The forces of nature that created them can never be duplicated. The loss is irreparable.

Nowhere else on earth will you find the unique beauty or majesty you can experience in Michigan's dunes. The iridescent water shining its many hues of blue, murky gray, and even black provide a dramatic backdrop for the dunes while the delicate and brightly colored flowers receding into forests are a visual feast. Hopefully, this beauty will be preserved for future generations to enjoy.

<<>>

The Phillips A. Hart Visitor Center, located on M-72 just east of the intersection with M-22 in Empire, is the place to start your Dune Adventure. Take a minute to talk to the knowledgeable rangers who share their expertise. The Center has models of the park to help you get your bearings. You can watch a short orientation film for a perspective of the area, its history, and what you are likely to discover. The rangers will help you decide where to begin your exploration based upon your interests and their experience.

You can meander trails that were first walked by the early Native Americans who enjoyed the tranquility and beauty of the area thousands of years before you. The Dunes are a living museum and tribute to the factors that shaped this area of Northern Michigan. You will find the remains of sawmills, fueling docks, and old barns; each symbolic of the economy of its era. You are likely to encounter a scattering of fruit trees, early orchards planted in another time, representative of an industry that is still very much alive and vibrant in the newer orchards throughout Michigan's northwest.

In addition to walking or hiking the area you will find the following activities: camping, boating, cross-country skiing, swimming, fishing, picnicking, horseback riding, scenic drives, nature studies, birdwatching, and canoeing. Restrooms and picnic tables are available throughout the park. No mountain bikes allowed.

<<>>

Sleeping Bear Dune Trails

 • **Duneside Accessible Trail**. A flat trail through a field and woods. A little less than two miles round trip, it is accessible to all visitors including those using wheelchairs or with visual impairments. The trail is marked with signs denoting species of trees and other spots of scenic interest. Rated an easy trail.

- **Good Harbor Bay Trail** is a flat trail mostly through a wooded section of the park. Approximately three miles, this loop can be wet in sections. Rated an easy trail.

- **Old Indian Trail** includes two scenic loops (each loop about 2½ miles) winding through evergreen and hardwood forests with majestic views of Lake Michigan. The start of the trail is off M-22 just north of Sutter Road. Rated an easy trail.

- **Alligator Hill Trail** consists of three loops and is about nine miles through hilly old hardwood forests. The view of Lake Michigan and the Manitou Islands from one of its hills is perhaps the best in the area. Rated a moderate trail.

- **Bay View Trail**. Several short loops through hardwood forests, farm fields, and pine trees to a view of Lake Michigan. Rated a moderate trail.

- **Cottonwood Trail**, a short 1½ mile loop through moderately hilly dunes. A self-guided tour allows you to examine the grasses, shrubs, and wildflowers that make up the dunes' ecosystem. Rated a moderate trail.

- **Dunes Trail**, a 3½ mile round trip hike to Lake Michigan that goes up and over a 140-foot wall of loose sand making this a strenuous hike that can take several hours in spite of its short distance. Rated a challenging trail.

- **Empire Bluff Trail** is a two-mile, round-trip route through hardwood forests with views of nearby Empire, Lake Michigan, and the Sleeping Bear Dunes. The trail takes you across old farm fields and orchards and climbs to a perch of more than 400 feet on a dune that is used as the launch for hang-gliding. Rated a moderate trail.

- **Pyramid Point Trail**. A short but relatively steep trail that leads to an expansive view of Lake Michigan, Manitou Passage, and the countryside. Rated a moderate trail.

▪ **Sleeping Bear Point Trail** is a three-mile trail that loops through rolling dunes. The path is adorned with grasses, shrubs, and wildflowers. The trail includes Devil's Soup Bowl and a ghost forest. Because of the loose sand, this is a difficult, challenging trail.

▪ **Windy Moraine Trail**. A short, hilly loop, only about 1½ miles, but relatively steep. You pass beautiful old trees and at the trail's highpoint you see Glen Lake, Lake Michigan, and the Sleeping Bear Dunes. At the start of the trail, you can pick up a self-guided tour brochure that identifies natural plant life in the area. Rated a moderate trail.

You can book charters and rent kayaks, tubes, and canoes in Empire.

● BOOKS AND MOVIES WITH TIES TO EMPIRE AND THE SLEEPING BEAR DUNES

Charles Cutter, ***Bear Bones: Murder at Sleeping Bear Dunes***. Helen Lockwood's body is found in a shallow grave a year after her boat was discovered drifting with no one aboard. Helen had been embroiled in a legal battle with the Park Service to keep her family's four-hundred-acre orchard. The lawsuit had lasted seven years at the time of Helen's disappearance. Helen's husband, Tommy, is arrested for her murder. A less than model husband, Tommy's motive appears to be his desire to sell the property over Helen's objections. But Helen had many enemies, and Tommy may be innocent. Burr Lafayette, a lawyer with a past, represents Tommy in this mystery set in the Sleeping Bear Dunes.

<<>>

Anne Margaret Lewis and Nancy Cote, ***Goodnight Sleeping Bear***, is a children's bedtime book that tells a simple story but imbues it with the important message that we all need to take care of our environment.

Jeffery P. Sandman and Peter R. Sandman, *Soaring and Gliding: The Sleeping Bear Dunes National Lakeshore Area*. To fly as the hawk and eagle has been mankind's dream for centuries. With modern sailplanes and a spot from which to launch, man can now make that dream come true. Michigan-based glider pilots and designers found their soaring paradise in the early 1930s when they ventured north to the Sleeping Bear Dunes area.

Kathy-Jo Wargin (Author) and Gijsbert Van Frankenhuyzen (Illustrator), *The Legend of Sleeping Bear*, named the 1998 Official Children's Book of Michigan. It recounts the legend of the Sleeping Bear Dunes.

14. FRANKFORT
INCLUDING ELBERTA, ARCADIA, AND ONEKAMA

Frankfort enjoyed a 2020 population of 1,302. Elberta's population was estimated at 370. Arcadia is a census-designated place with a 2020 population of 299. Onekama's 2020 population was 399.

Frankfort extends small-town charm and friendliness and invites you to visit Benzie County—Michigan's smallest county. Gently rolling hills provide a scenic backdrop to the area's maritime beauty.

Frankfort has an ongoing dispute with Ludington over which is the site of the death and original grave of Father Jacques Marquette. A plaque in his honor stands in each city.

The first European settler to the area was Joseph Oliver who arrived in 1850. Early residents named the settlement Frankfort because it reminded them of

Frankfurt, Germany. The small Michigan city was originally part of Leelanau County.

1864 saw an influx of Norwegian immigrants drawn to the area by the fishing opportunities. Initially the fishery provided the most important economic support for residents; they later turned to agriculture. Frankfort was incorporated as a village in 1874.

Pastor Rasmus Bull established Michigan's first Norwegian congregation of the Evangelical Lutheran Church in Frankfort in 1873. The actual structure to accommodate his flock was built in 1884.

Elberta was first settled in 1855 just south of Frankfort and was incorporated as South Frankfort in 1894. The village was renamed Elberta because Elberta peaches were grown there.

The Frankfort-Elberta port was opened in 1867, and by 1870 the channel was 200 feet wide with both a south and north pier. In 1873 the United States Lighthouse Service established the first pier head light to mark the entrance to the harbor. Point Betsie Light (See Lighthouses.) was also established to make shipping safer.

While the Great Lakes have long been considered a huge natural asset for shipping and transportation, they were also a detriment and barrier to overland transportation. A train at a station in Manistee or Frankfort had to go south to Chicago, round the Lake's southern end, and head north again. A distance of fewer than 100 miles as the crow flies became a land distance of four times that. The railroads deemed that unacceptable and enterprising minds considered alternatives. On November 24, 1892, a bold experiment began at South Frankfort. Loaded freight cars were carried across the open waters of Lake Michigan on a train car ferry. After that initial experiment, a car ferry fleet was built for this service and operated for a century out of the Frankfort-Elberta port.

Historian author Bruce Catton, who won a Pulitzer Prize for *A Stillness at Appomattox*, died at his summer home in Frankfort in 1978.

Any history of Frankfort, no matter how abbreviated, must mention gliding. In the 1930s, Frankfort was the site of the sailplane company selected to manufacture the first designated military training glider. The area has remained a soaring site ever since. It has hosted two national soaring meets and many Midwest gliding contests. A National Soaring Landmark stands in Frankfort reminding everyone of the popularity of soaring and gliding on the Sleeping Bear Dunes and Frankfort Beach.

A few miles south of Frankfort is the small village of Arcadia. Henry Starke, a German immigrant living in Milwaukee, became attracted to the Arcadia area while he was overseeing the Manistee Pier construction. He was drawn to the lush hardwood forests and by 1883, he had purchased about 2,000 acres of land and established the Starke Land and Lumber Company. Starke built a sawmill and a 1,000-foot pier into Lake Michigan. A jack-of-all-trades, he built a railroad to the timberlands, operated a general store, and ran his own ship, the *Arcadia*. In 1906 his sawmill burned, and Starke made a decision to use the remaining local hardwoods to build furniture. He opened the Arcadia Furniture Company which made bedroom furniture and remained in business until 1952.

Harriet Quimby, the first female aviatrix to cross the Atlantic, lived part of her childhood in Arcadia. Today tourists enjoy the relaxed pace of this small village with its beautiful sunsets and peaceful way of life.

● Museums

Arcadia History Museum, 3340 Lake Street, is located in a restored Victorian-style home built in 1884 by H. E. Gilbert and originally located on Norman Road. The exhibit hall has several displays. One introduces the earliest sawmills in the Arcadia area, the process involved in lumbering, how the business was practiced in the area, and three key sawmills in Arcadia. Others present the history of the railroads and shipping.

<<>>

Gibb Museum of Arcadia History, 380 West Huntington Drive. The museum has various displays ranging from the early history of the area to some of the more recent people who were native to the area and other who moved there.

<<>>

Harriet Quimby State Historical Site, M-22 south of Arcadia to right on Erdman Road, Arcadia Township. Historical marker and the remains of the Quimby home stand at this location.

● Beaches, Parks, and Trails

Bellows Park, across the street from Crystal Lake. Covered pavilion, barbeque grills, and a public beach.

<<>>

Betsie Valley Trail. The bed of the former Ann Arbor Railroad winds through the countryside from Elberta on Lake Michigan into Thompsonville 27 miles to the southeast. Hikers, bikers, and leisure walkers all experience the panoply of visually stimulating scenes.

<<>>

Father Charlevoix (Cannon) Park, west end of Main Street across from Lake Michigan, Frankfort. Civil War cannon located on the edge of the park. Picnic tables and benches available. Close to the beach.

<<>>

Frankfort Beach. It's a clean, fun, sandy, Lake Michigan beach with shallow waters for wading. The views are incredible, especially at sunset. There are benches for sitting and swings for the kids. It's an easy walk out on the breakwater to the pier lighthouse. The lighthouse is both a scenic backdrop to the beach and functional protection warning ships away from any rough water on Lake Michigan.

<<>>

Elberta Historic Waterfront Park, shores of Betsie Bay, Elberta. Amenities: performance pavilion, picnic pavilion, restored lifesaving station, large barbeque grill, and a playscape for children.

<<>>

Market Square Park, M-22, three blocks from downtown Frankfort. Playground equipment, tennis and basketball courts.

<<>>

Mineral Springs Park, 630 Main Street, between Main Street and Betsie Bay across from the post office, Frankfort. Flowing well of mineral water, supposedly healthy but expect a strong taste. Covered pavilion.

<<>>

East Shore Marina, 324 Lake Street. Seventy lighted boat slips, fish cleaning pavilion, picnic area. Slips are rented on annual basis, and only those not rented are available as transient slips.

<<>>

Frankfort Municipal Marina, 412 Main Street. Thirty-five transient slips.

<<>>

Charter Boats are available locally to take you fishing for Chinook, Rainbow, Coho, and Brown Trout. Most places will also clean and package your catch.

● OTHER STOPS OR ACTIVITIES TO CONSIDER

Birdwatching. Elberta Marsh and Betsie Bay are good areas to see waterfowl and shorebirds. The Betsie Valley Trail stretches 22 miles from Frankfort to Thompsonville. The lookout platform adjacent to the Betsie River Bridge is a popular vantage point for birdwatching. You can spot cranes and a variety of shorebirds that frequent the Betsie River delta and marsh area. You can also see wading birds. Birds spotted in the area include sandhill cranes, American bitterns, sedge wrens, willow flycatchers, peregrine falcons, red knots, and whimbrels.

<<>>

Post Office, 615 Main Street, across from Mineral Springs Park in Frankfort. If you need to mail a postcard, take the extra steps to do it at the post office. While you are there check out the murals.

● LIGHTHOUSES

Point Betsie Lighthouse, 3791 Point Betsie Road, Frankfort. Built in 1858, Betsie was not fully automated until 1983. The name, Betsie, did not come from a desire to honor someone's wife or mother. Instead, it came from the French name *Pointe Aux Becs Scies* meaning Saw Beak Point. The English-speaking settlers in the area shortened and ran the words together so Becs Scies became Betsie.

Betsie was the last manned lighthouse on Lake Michigan, and she marked the end of an era. After automation, Betsie became a coast guard residence until 1996 when her boiler failed, and the families living there were forced to abandon her.

Point Betsie Lighthouse. Courtesy of Pixabay Free Images.

The two-story white keeper's house sits on a slight knoll and offers an expansive view of the area. The red-shingled hip roof with dormers add an element of drama to the 3,000 square foot dwelling that accommodated two families. Covered porches add a homey touch. A three-story tower, tall enough to let someone look out from the parapet and see over the house, is attached to Betsie's side. At 37 feet, she is one of the shorter lighthouses on the lake. Steel breakwaters were constructed from the base of the tower toward the lake in an attempt to minimize damage from the power of angry waves. Surrounded by shifting dunes, the tranquility of the location makes it one of the more scenic and peaceful lights on the lake. Betsie remains active today.

<<>>

Frankfort North Breakwater Lighthouse, Main Street, Frankfort. This pierhead light, accessed by an elevated walkway, was built at the outer end of the south pier and commenced operation on October 15, 1873. You have to walk a long concrete pier to reach it. On a nice day, it is worth the walk. If the winds are strong, be careful. Waves will splash up on the pier and the short walk becomes a slippery and dangerous trek.

Keeper Joseph Wilmot died on duty at the lighthouse in August 1911. Keeper Wilmot's wife insisted on rowing with him to start the fog signal because he was ill, and she was worried about him. The evening did not end well. A local paper described it this way:

> "Spurred by his sense of duty the keeper managed to get out to the end of the pier and dragged himself through the task of starting the mechanism of the fog signal. Then with a groan, he turned to his wife. 'I'm sick," said he, "I'm deathly sick.' Mrs. Wilmot ran down the steps of the light and started for the mainland to get help. Finding a couple of boys on the pier she sent them for help and returned to her husband's side. In a few minutes, Captain Morency had reached them. Picking up his old comrade, he carried him like a baby down the stairs and out upon the pier hoping that the fresh night air would revive him. And there, in a hastily contrived bed of blankets, the keeper of the light breathed his last a few minutes later."

A notice of availability, dated June 28, 2010, declared the Frankfort North Breakwater Lighthouse was excess to the needs of the United States Coast Guard and would be "made available at no cost to eligible entities." Ownership was transferred to the City of Frankfort.

• SHIPWRECKS

The **_J.H. Hartzell_** shipwreck wasn't extraordinary when compared to the thousands of her sister ships that have succumbed to the Great Lakes—at least not if you look only at the facts reported by government agencies. The _Hartzell_ was a wood schooner, built in 1863, and sunk on October 16, 1880, one mile south of Frankfort. She was carrying iron ore bound for Frankfort from L'Anse.

All but one of her crew of eight was rescued from the rigging. That one fatality is the story that makes this wreck tantalizingly wicked.

The tragedy occurred nearly a century and a half ago, but the tale is still told, and the ship's remains still litter the lake's bottom near Frankfort. It's rarely a warm, balmy summer night when violence strikes. The lake stores up her anger to vent when the weather turns blustery cold. On that particular night, the sole victim was a woman who died lashed to the sinking ship's mast.

Townspeople and surfmen from the nearby lifesaving station labored under punishing conditions for more than 12 hours. In that time, they saved the seven men aboard. The solitary woman, cook Lydia Dale, remained beyond the rescuers' reach. The men, as they were dragged ashore, told the rescuers that Lydia was already dead. The mystery that remains is, was she?

The *Hartzell* arrived at Frankfort at around 3:00 a.m. Captain William A. Jones explained that he decided to anchor offshore and wait until daylight to enter Frankfort's harbor. That was a mistake. At dawn the winds shifted and the pleasant, late fall weather turned nasty. Hail, snow, and rain whipped across the water and tormented the crew. Captain Jones and the six men with him let both anchors go and tried to turn the *Hartzell* away from the gale, "but in the growing fury of the wind and sea, the vessel would not obey her helm and began to drift in."

The vessel broke up. The cook was reported to be seriously ill. The crew climbed 50 feet, and with four men boosting the heavyset woman to a platform they created, they said they wrapped her in blankets covered in wet canvas cut from the topsail. The ship's perilous situation was noted, and local citizens built a big fire on the beach. Using driftwood, they spelled out "Life Boat Coming."

By the time the lifesaving crew reached the shoreline, only half of the schooner was above water. Local farmers and other townspeople helped as the surfmen started rescue attempts. A surf car was sent to the ship, and the first of the crewmen reached shore. They were asked about the woman and gave evasive answers, saying she'd be in the next run of the surf car. She wasn't. That trip carried the second mate and captain. The third and final time the car went out, the rescuers gave it plenty of time in case loading the woman was a difficult task. It was growing dark, and they finally gave the order to bring the car back.

A dozen men went into the surf to haul in the car. When they opened the hatch, the last two men were inside. But not Lydia Dale. The two men aboard insisted the cook was dead—stiff as a board. It was too dark to attempt another trip out, and the lifesaving station team decided they'd wait until morning before undertaking further rescue attempts.

The next day, the schooner's mast was gone. And with it, any evidence of Lydia Dale's fate. The town engaged in heated arguments of whether Lydia Dale was already dead when the men deserted her and climbed into the rescue car, or whether they mercilessly left her to die alone. The coroner settled the argument when he reported that Lydia Dale died of drowning—she had been left aboard while she was still alive and died later when the ship's mast fell into the lake. The *Hartzell*'s crew was not there for the inquest. They had already left town.

<<>>

The **Minnehaha** was a four-masted, 200-foot, wooden schooner built in 1880. She always seemed to operate under a dark cloud. She wrecked in Detour and remained on the rocks in the winter waters until rescued the next spring and sold.

In October of 1893, Captain Benniteau, operating the steam barge *Henry J. Johnson*, was towing the *Minnehaha* from Chicago bound for Point Edward at the south end of Lake Huron. The *Minnehaha*, captained by William Parker, carried a cargo of 58,000 bushels of corn when 90 miles an hour gale winds bore down on the ships. Benniteau sought shelter behind the Manitou Islands, but at dawn the next day, he and his crew were still south of Sleeping Bear Point fighting high winds and waves to stay out of shallow water.

Benniteau decided the best course of action was to turn the ships south to Frankfort, the nearest refuge. Near Frankfort, high waves crashed over the *Minnehaha's* deck, smashed two hatch covers, began filling the hold with water, and separated the ships. The *Minnehaha* sent up distress signals and headed for the beach. She ran aground near Arcadia. The crew climbed the ship's rigging to avoid the punishing waves. One man jumped overboard and began swimming to shore. He drowned before reaching safety. The ship broke up, and the crew grabbed anything that would float. There were no life preservers aboard. Only the captain made it to shore safely. One crew member got as far as the pier, but exhaustion forced him to let go of the pole used to try to pull him to safety. Five crewmen and cook Mary Keefe perished. Keefe's body was found on the beach the next day.

• THE FAMOUS OR INFAMOUS WITH TIES TO FRANKFORT AND ARCADIA

Father Jacques Marquette was a French missionary and explorer, born in 1637. He died in 1675 either in Ludington or Frankfort. His name is synonymous with the history of Western Michigan. His exploits are covered in the individual histories of many towns in this guide.

His remains, regardless of the place of his death, were taken to St. Ignace and buried at the mission he started there.

<<>>

Harriet Quimby was a superstitious woman. She had her favorite lucky jewelry, and she refused to fly on Sundays. In 1911 she became the first licensed female pilot in the United States, and a year later the first woman to fly across the English Channel. She was beautiful with a strong sense of style that made her a marketable commodity to the press. She designed her trademark purple satin flight suit. There is no record of Harriet ever marrying or having children. She kept her private life very much to herself.

She was born in 1875 in Coldwater, Michigan, but spent her early childhood in a modest home in Arcadia Township on M-22 in Manistee County. The site is identified today by a Michigan Historical Marker. Between 1887 and 1890, the family moved to California and Quimby later claimed Arroyo Grande, California, as her birthplace. But evidence of the family's ties to Michigan is uncontroverted in spite of Quimby's failure to recognize them. Her mother, Ursula Quimby produced and sold patent medicines including *Quimby's Liver Invigorator*, which she advertised in the *Manistee Daily News*. The ads presented testimonials from satisfied customers.

After moving to California, Quimby was an aspiring actress, but in spite of her physical beauty and flair for the theatrical, she became a journalist. An independent woman with strong views, she wrote articles about child neglect, preserving endangered species, and corrupt politics.

Quimby became interested in flying in late October 1910 when she attended the Belmont Park International Aviation Tournament on Long Island. At that event, she

141

came into contact with the aviator, John Moisant, and decided to take flight lessons from John's brother, Alfred, who operated a flight school on Long Island. Being the private person she was, Quimby had no intention of revealing to anyone her ambition of learning to fly. Somehow the press discovered her intentions, and since a woman aviatrix was a big story, she capitalized on it herself and authored a series of articles about her experiences.

Flying the English Channel, in spite of its unpredictable weather and dangers, became Quimby's goal. One of her male aviator friends, Gustav Hamel, offered to don her purple suit and make the flight for her so she would not have to face the risk. He planned it out, insisting that he would land in a remote spot of France and quickly trade places with her so she could take the credit. She refused his offer, regardless of how well-intentioned it may have been.

On April 16, 1912, Harriet left Dover, England, flew across the Channel, and landed about 25 miles from her target of Calais, France. It was a foggy day, and she maintained altitudes between 1,000 and 2,000 feet. The flight lasted a minute short of an hour. Her feat did not receive the press coverage it might have otherwise garnered because the *Titanic* had sunk two days earlier.

On July 1, 1912, Quimby flew her new 70 horsepower, two-seat, Bleriot monoplane in the Third Annual Boston Aviation Meet in Massachusetts. Prior to the meet, William Willard, the event's organizer, and his son, Charles, flipped a coin to see who got the honor of being Harriet's passenger.

Quimby Airmail Stamp.
Courtesy of Pixabay Free Images.

William won. In flight, the monoplane unexpectedly lurched forward ejecting both Quimby and Willard, plunging them to their deaths before more than 5,000 horrified spectators. The plane survived, gliding to the ground and banking in a muddy field. The exact cause of the plane's lurch will never be known, although several theories were proposed, one that Willard, a very large man, had leaned forward to ask his pilot a question, and his great weight threw off the plane's sensitive balance. Whatever the cause, Harriet Quimby was dead at age 37, less than a year after she had learned to fly.

Her legacy inspired Amelia Earhart, and Quimby was a role model to women who dreamed of venturing beyond the day's stereotypical female roles. In 1991 her picture, sitting in her Bleriot, graced a 50 cent U.S. Airmail stamp.

• BOOKS AND MOVIES WITH TIES TO FRANKFORT

Rachel Gilmore (with the Frankfort Area Historical Society), ***Frankfort***. A village known for its 1890s charm, Frankfort is home to people and places that have woven a vibrant fabric for a century and a half—uniting the community for over 150 years. This is Frankfort's story.

<<>>

Leslie Kerr, ***Harriet Quimby: Flying Fair Lady***. Harriet Quimby rejected commonly accepted women's roles. She sought new adventures, but they ultimately claimed her life. This book recognizes her legacy. (See Famous or Infamous with Ties to Frankfort and Arcadia for additional background on Quimby.)

<<>>

The Wreck & Rescue of the Schooner J.H. Hartzell, DVD, a dramatic reenactment of the shipwreck that remains a part of Frankfort History a century and a half after her demise. (See Shipwrecks for more details of the wreck.)

15. MANISTEE

The 2020 population of Manistee was 6,234. Manistee is a Native American word, but while its origin is clear, its meaning is not. It may mean "river at whose mouth there are islands." It may refer to the reddish/brown ochre used for ceremonial decoration of the face and body. Or, it may have a more symbolic meaning and refer to the spirit of the wind blowing through the trees. The Historical Society of Manistee supports the last and more poetic interpretation.

Native Americans placed a high value on the Manistee River and attempted to keep European settlers away from the river's mouth where it met Lake Michigan. However, by the Treaty of Washington in 1836, the land was ceded to the United States, and settlers began arriving.

In 1840 John Joseph and Adam Stronach explored the site of what is now Manistee and built the first permanent sawmill there one year later. The sawmill was the first foundational building block of the village that would soon thrive on the shores of Lake Michigan. Manistee was incorporated as a city in 1869.

On October 8, 1871, the same day as the infamous Chicago fire, flames of biblical fire-and-brimstone proportions also showered down on the small town of Manistee. The loss of property was devastating.

The *Grand Rapids Eagle* carried stories of how the inferno started and chronicled the rampage. Within the city limits lay a twenty-acre hemlock forest; many of its trees were only partially standing, and some were toppling in various stages of decay. Still more were already dead and littering the ground. This timber was as combustible as gun powder, the perfect tinder to start a major conflagration.

At 9:00 a.m. the fire department responded to a dangerous fire burning an old chopping area. The firefighters spent the day battling the flames, and by evening they were exhausted but congratulated themselves for subduing the menace.

At 9:30 p.m., devout congregants returned to their homes from evening worship and prayers of thanks that their city had been spared.

Then the fire alarm rang for a second time. Monstrous gale-force winds raged, and the fire department again rushed to the scene and tried to contain the blaze. The fire threatened the mill of John Canfield, along with his boarding house and about 30 other buildings. The surrounding area, as part of Canfield's milling operation, was covered with pine dust and cords of dry pine slabs—all of which became additional fuel for the flames.

An unidentified reporter described it.

"Down from the circling hills on the lake shore pounced the devouring monster. The burning sawdust, whirled by the gale in fiery clouds, filled the air. Hundreds of dry, pitchy slabs sent up great columns of red flame, that swayed in the air like mighty banners of fire, swept across Manistee, two hundred feet wide, and almost instantly, like great fiery tongues, licked up the government lighthouse, built at a cost of nearly $10,000, and situated a hundred and fifty feet from the north bank of the river."

Soon the winds carried the inferno to other sites and the blaze turned on the city from all directions. Pandemonium broke out. With Herculean, but futile efforts, families tried to stave off the spread.

When the sun rose on Monday morning the city smoldered in ruins. More than 1,000 people were homeless and many of them penniless as well. In spite of the damage, the city had reason to be grateful; there was no loss of life and little serious injury. Cities along the west side of the state pitched in to help Manistee rebuild;

they provided aid and supplies to help victims survive the next year.

Less than two years later in 1873, the city had 5,000 residents, 20 sawmills, a daily line of steamers connecting to Milwaukee and Chicago, three telegraph lines, three schools, five churches, hotels, railroads in the planning stages, and nearly every type of merchandising establishment imaginable—including a candy store. The effort to rebuild Manistee seemed more intense than that for her initial growth before the fire. In 1880 lumberman Charles Rietz helped rejuvenate the local economy when he successfully drilled for salt. Freighters soon hauled salt brine out of the port.

Victorian buildings, many that remain today, graced the downtown. Like the mythological Phoenix that rose from the ashes of a funeral pyre, Manistee again became a great place to live. Current residents will tell you it still is.

It is also a perfect place for a tourist to visit. Wander back in time; take a stroll down River Street. Manistee's central business district shows off lovingly restored Victorians alive with activity from cafes, boutiques, restaurants, and an eclectic mix of other shops.

• MUSEUMS

Manistee Art Institute, 437 River Street, strives to inspire artists and encourage a love of the arts through classes and exhibits. It offers a place for artists to display and sell their work. The MAI also has a permanent collection of watercolor, oil, and acrylic paintings, sculpture, photography, fiber art, collage, and other art mediums. The MAI displays noncommercial exhibits from museums and private and corporate collections. The MAI was established in 1994, but it took the institute until 2019 to find a more permanent home which they believe will allow them to expand and explore how they serve the public.

<<>>

The Manistee County Historical Museum, A.H. Lyman Drug Company Building, 425 River Street. Collection of vintage artifacts, newspaper articles, and photographs depicting the early days of Manistee County. A special pharmacy exhibit pays tribute to the building's origin. The museum collects and displays exhibits that bridge the past to the present and provides an understanding of Manistee's history.

<<>>

Old Kirke Museum/Our Savior's Historical Museum, 304 Walnut Street. A Michigan Historical Site listed on the National Register of Historical Places, this church is the oldest Danish American Evangelical Lutheran Church in America. It is one of the few buildings that escaped the fire of 1871. Call for tour schedules.

<<>>

River Street Gallery (See Manistee Art Institute.)

<<>>

S.S. City of Milwaukee. Manitowoc Shipbuilding constructed six sister ships in the 1920s to serve as railroad car ferries. The *Milwaukee* is the last of those ships to survive. She is moored in Manistee and open for tours that provide a glimpse of the rails across the water legacy. In its day, it carried an entire freight train and 300 passengers across Lake Michigan, year-round, through ice and storms.

<<>>

Ramsdell Theatre, 101 Maple Street. The place where James Earl Jones began his career, the Ramsdell is both a theatre with live performances and a fascinating architectural delight. The Greek Revival edifice is a century-old, ornate structure that houses theatrical and symphony productions. It features regional and local talent.

The Theatre opened on September 4, 1903, with a performance of *A Chinese Honeymoon* which had been a big hit on Broadway. Over the years, the Ramsdell continued as a successful theatre, although during some periods, it resorted to showing movies. Currently, it provides a stage for the Manistee Civic Players.

The theatre was named for Thomas Jefferson Ramsdell who throughout his adult life worked for the continuing improvement of Manistee. In 1883 the city had a large building on the corner of First and Greenbush that met the theatre and cultural needs of the local population. When this building burned, Ramsdell replaced the city's loss.

His new theatre opened three years later at a cost of nearly four times the original projected price. Detractors called it "Ramsdell's Folly" partly in recognition of the outrageous cost and partly because of its artwork. Ramsdell's son, Frederick, was an accomplished artist, and he is believed to have painted the semi-nude Aphrodite adorning the auditorium's dome in the image of his wife. Even more scandalous at the time were the lobby's murals of two nude goddesses frolicking in pastoral fields. Allegedly, these goddesses have the faces of local 1800s gossips and were Frederick's way of getting even with Ramsdell detractors.

Check out what is happening at the Ramsdell during the time you plan to visit.

● Beaches, Parks, and Trails

Douglas Park and First Street Beach. Amenities: municipal boat launch, fish cleaning station, tennis, volleyball, basketball courts, baseball field, one of the area's largest beaches, beach house, picnic area, three playground areas, separate dog area, restrooms, and the Lighthouse Park.

<<>>

Fifth Avenue Beach, on the north side of Manistee at the west end of Fifth Avenue. A place to begin a walk to the lighthouse and catwalk. Amenities: bike racks, parking, playground, beach house, volleyball and tennis courts, fishing from the pier, picnic area, grills, concessions, and restrooms. On the Lake Michigan waterfront with an accessible beach. A Coast Guard facility is adjacent to the park.

<<>>

Hodenpyl Dam, Hodenpyl Dam Road. A tranquil place to paddle your canoe in the wilderness and feel like you own the place. For some visitors, this spot may lack pizzazz, but for others, it offers the best hiking, canoeing, kayaking, fishing, and camping in the area.

<<>>

Lake Bluff Bird Sanctuary, 2890 Lakeshore Road, provides 76 acres and 1,500 feet of lake frontage. Landscaped as an arboretum, the sanctuary surrounds you with beautiful trees and the opportunity to watch nesting and migrating birds.

<<>>

Manistee National Forest. A small part of the Manistee National Forest borders the eastern shore of Lake Michigan. The forest is 540,187 acres and contains trees, rivers, miles of trails, two small lakes (Nichols and Benton), and 18 developed campgrounds—one located on Lake Michigan's shores. The forest is not continuous but is broken by private residences and other structures. Activities include fishing, boating, biking, canoeing, hiking, tubing, swimming, and birdwatching.

There is a semi-primitive motorized area featuring sites for car, tent, RV, and motor home camping. (See also Nordhouse Dunes Wilderness Area under Ludington.)

Three rivers wind through the Manistee National Forest to Lake Michigan: the Pine, Manistee, and Pere Marquette. The smallest is the Pine River, a fast-flowing waterway to the Manistee River. The Pine is recommended only for experienced canoeists who do not mind taking an unplanned dip. The Manistee River is a wider, slower-moving river. Anglers claim the Pere Marquette River provides the best fishing in the forest.

Several hundred miles of trails wind through the Manistee National Forest. Some are designated for mountain bikes while others are specifically designed for off-road-vehicles. Many are reserved for foot traffic only. The highest point in the Lower Peninsula, Briar Hill (1,706 feet), is located in the forest.

<<>>

Manistee Riverwalk follows the Manistee River for 1½ miles along Lake Michigan. Accessible at the First Street Beach near the river outlet to Lake Michigan, or you can walk the full length by parking at the end of Jones Street and entering at that point. Stairs adjacent to the Riverwalk allow you to connect with the shops and restaurants of downtown Manistee. If you need a morning walk to start your day, this is a place to get it. Signs mark every tenth of a mile. The Riverwalk is accessible.

Cruise Ship *Niagara Prince* docked on the Manistee River Riverwalk. Courtesy of the Manistee Area Chamber of Commerce.

<<>>

The Manistee Municipal Marina borders the Riverwalk connecting the historic downtown district to Lake Michigan. Amenities include 24 transient slips, gas and diesel, pump-out, dock attendants, electricity, water, RV 50-amp service, monitor Channel 9, dayroom, snacks, restrooms, showers, and laundry.

<<>>

Magoon Creek Park, 3414 Red Apple Road, sits high on a bluff with a picnic area that overlooks Lake Michigan and trails that lead to the lake and beaches. Restrooms available. Views are perfect, and you can spot the dunes to the south and the lighthouse to the north.

<<>>

Orchard Beach State Park, 2064 North Lakeshore Road. Several short trail loops that can be combined for a longer hike. Situated on a ridge overlooking miles of sandy Lake Michigan shoreline and sparkling water, this 201-acre park has 176 campsites. Amenities include a picnic table at each site, fire rings, electrical hookup, sanitation station, two bathhouses, playground, fish cleaning facility, mini-cabin, and self-guided nature trail.

<<>>

Fishing charters and cruises are available in Manistee.

• ANOTHER STOP TO CONSIDER AND OTHER THINGS TO DO

Oak Grove Cemetery, 1040 Veterans Oak Grove Drive. Sometimes (check calendar) a local expert gives historical tours through this lovely cemetery close to Lake Michigan. Beautifully kept with trees and greenery and enjoyed by local wildlife as much as by humans. Not unusual to spot a white-tailed deer nibbling grass.

<<>>

Summertime brings free music to the parks and local wineries. Additional activities include brewery tours, an

151

alpaca farm, historical tours, shoreline jazz, and shopping.

● LIGHTHOUSE

Manistee North Pierhead Lighthouse. Stroll the pier and enjoy the visual reminder of Manistee's maritime past. The lighthouse welcomes boaters as it continues its task of keeping them safe. The lighthouse was constructed in 1869 but was part of the fire loss that destroyed Manistee in 1871. A new lighthouse, constructed of cast iron, was built in 1872. It stands 39 feet tall and remains an active light. Although the interior is not accessible to the public, the exterior provides a perfect photo op.

● THE FAMOUS OR INFAMOUS WITH TIES TO MANISTEE

Dave "Soup" Campbell, born on January 14, 1942, in Manistee, was an infielder for the San Diego Padres.

<<>>

Fred Warren Green, the 31st Governor of Michigan (1927 to 1931), was born in Manistee on October 20, 1871. He earned a law degree from the University of Michigan in 1898.

<<>>

James Earl Jones' first performance was at the Ramsdell Theatre in Manistee. During his high school years at Brethren Michigan High School, he was an outstanding student and excelled in forensics and track. While still in high school, Jones worked as a carpenter for local productions at the Ramsdell Theatre. There he developed a passion for acting and proved to be a natural. In addition to spending four summers with the acting group at the Ramsdell, he was assistant stage manager, stage manager, director of a Children's

Theatre, and acted in 28 productions. Jones graduated from high school in 1949 and attended the University of Michigan with plans to study medicine; he found theatre's call more compelling. He graduated cum laude in 1955 with a B.A. degree in drama.

Jones was born in Arkabutla Township, Mississippi, in 1931 but moved to Manistee County where he was raised by his maternal grandparents. Jones, among the best known African American film and stage actors, is also part Irish and part Choctaw and Cherokee. He is famous for his deep, authoritative voice which was that of Darth Vader in *Star Wars*, a role for which he was originally uncredited.

As a child, Jones developed a stutter so severe that he refused to speak for fear of ridicule. He recalls the trauma of being ripped away from his mother and the only home he had ever known and riding the train from Mississippi to Manistee. This, coupled with beginning school and his stutter, made talking too difficult. He was rendered functionally and intentionally mute until high school. Then Donald Crouch, one of his teachers, recognized Jones' gift for writing poetry and helped him begin the battle towards speaking coherently without the stutter. Crouch convinced Jones that the words he was writing, the words that sounded so beautiful in his mind, would sound even more compelling if spoken aloud. The teacher believed public speaking would help Jones gain confidence, and he urged him to recite a poem each day in class. The voice Jones refused to use as a child has become one of the most famous and widely recognized voices in Hollywood.

Jones' first film role came in 1964 as a B-52 bomb room operator in *Dr. Strangelove, or How I Learned to Stop Worrying and Love the Bomb*. He was nominated for a Best Actor Award for his portrayal of Jack Johnson in the film version of *The Great White Hope*. While often cast as an African American, as in the mini-series *Roots* where he played author Alex Haley, his voice transcends ethnicity and is sought merely for its powerful sound. He spoke as Mufasa in the 1994 Disney animated feature *The Lion King* and the sequel, *The Lion King II: Simba's Pride.* Jones had roles in *Under a Killing Moon, Field of Dreams, Cry, the Beloved Country, Clear and Present Danger, Conan the Barbarian, Patriot Games, Coming to America,* and *The Hunt for Red October.*

Jones has also starred on Broadway in *On Golden Pond,* during which he was hospitalized for pneumonia, and *The Great White Hope.* He was the first established celebrity to appear on *Sesame Street.*

Even as an adult and world-renowned actor, Jones has to think carefully about what he is about to say to avoid stuttering. The slow, deliberateness of his speech is partially due to choosing the right word; the one that will not trip up his tongue.

Jones admits that his grandfather was not thrilled with the idea that his grandson wanted to be an actor, but his Grandma Maggie quickly came around. In Jones' words:

> "This is a woman whose bedtime stories were about lynching and hurricanes and floods and rapes and murders. Those were her bedtime stories! For me to go into drama, that kind of turned her on a little bit. I got a job over at the little opera house in Manistee, Michigan, the county seat. We had a summer theater there. She was always the first to be there, in the front row. Wanted to see me in these dramas. So, she opened the door, as far as the family was concerned, about allowing this to happen."

James Earl Jones describes himself as a plodder, someone who keeps heading toward his goal, one little step at a time. The only advice he offers anyone is the same as that offered by Carl Sandburg, "Take no advice, including this."

Harry W. Musselwhite moved from Grand Rapids to Manistee and became owner, editor, and publisher of the *Manistee Daily News-Advocate* from 1915 to 1928. In 1932 Musselwhite ran for U.S. Representative and served Michigan's 9th congressional district to the 73rd Congress for one term (March 1933 to January 1935) before he returned to the newspaper business.

<<>>

Toni Trucks, an actress of theater, film, and television, first tested her skill on the stage of the Ramsdell Theatre. She subsequently starred in numerous movies and TV series, including the part of Lisa Davis in *Seal Team.* Her parents, although divorced, both live in Manistee.

<<>>

Robert Pershing Wadlow, known as the Gentle Giant, was the tallest man who ever lived. He died in Manistee when he was only 22 years old. Wadlow's height, verified at his death, was 8 feet 11.1 inches. He weighed 439 pounds. By the time Wadlow was eight years old, he was taller than his father. For a while, he toured with Ringling Brothers but dreamed of law school and a normal career. Wadlow had minimal feeling in his legs and had to wear braces. On July 4, 1940, during a professional appearance at the Manistee National Forest Festival, one of his braces irritated his ankle. The resulting injury became infected. Due to an autoimmune disorder Wadlow suffered, neither a blood transfusion nor surgery could stave off the sepsis that raged through his huge body. He died less than ten days later.

● GHOST STORIES AND A MONSTER

The Dogman of northwestern Michigan. Dogman is a monster firmly entrenched in the lore of northern lumber camps and backwoods from the mid-1800s to today.

Dogman walks upright on hind legs and looks a bit like his monster kin, Wolfman.

The first reported Dogman sighting was in 1887 when lumberjacks in Wexford County spotted an animal they believed to be a dog. For lack of anything better to do, they began chasing it. To escape its pursuers, the tormented creature ran inside a hollow log. One of the lumberjacks grabbed a stick and poked inside the log. The beast let out an unearthly scream, crawled from its refuge, and stood upright. There, face-to-face and eye-to-eye with the men, stood a being with a man's body and a dog's head. The terrified men broke camp and never returned to the area. From that time forward, the creature made an appearance about every ten years.

In 1897 near Buckley, a farmer was found slumped over his plow, an apparent heart attack. The circumstances probably would not have been considered unusual except for the huge dog tracks that ringed the ground about the deceased's body.

Exactly a decade later, a demented widow reported weird dreams about dogs circling her house at night. These dogs walked like men and yelled like banshees. Ten years passed before the next incident. A sheriff is alleged to have happened upon a wagon with dog prints in the dust around it. No driver could be found but nearby, four horses lay dead with their eyes wide open. A veterinarian was called to the scene, but he found no medical reason for their deaths.

In 1937 a boat captain reported that several of his crew saw a pack of wild dogs roaming Bowers Harbor. That same year, or possibly the next, Robert Fortney picked up his shotgun and killed one of a pack of dogs that lunged at him as he stood on the banks of the Muskegon River. One dog did not run off in fright. Instead, it reared up on its hind legs and glared at Fortney with slanted, yellow eyes. Fortney was unsure what to call the animal that locked eyes with him. He had heard the stories about Dogman but did not want to feed those crazy tales. Still, he admitted, that was what it looked like—a man with a dog's head.

In 1957 a preacher found claw marks high on an old church door. If it was a dog, it was a mighty tall one, at least seven feet, he reckoned, to leave marks where they scarred the wood. Ten years later a van of hippies reported being awakened in the middle of the night by a half dog/half man scratching on the windows. People wondered what those free spirits had been smoking. Ten more years passed, and the next incident involved screams reported in the night near the Village of Bellaire when someone saw the creature. Again, another decade passed, and there was the report of an attempted break-in at a local cabin. The cuts on the door were believed to have been made by very sharp teeth or claws.

Two local fishermen became believers one evening at dusk when they were casting near Manistee. The sun was setting in its usual spectacular fashion when they saw an animal swimming toward their boat. One man immediately thought it was his old coon hound coming to join them, but when it got closer, he realized the beast had a dog's head and a man's body and was doing a human-style English crawl instead of a dog paddle. The two men, frightened nearly out of their wits, picked up their oars and clubbed Dogman until it finally retreated. The fishermen, not wanting to appear sissies, declined to talk further about their experience.

Dogman may be nothing more than a bunch of wild stories, but it stirs the imagination and frightens local folks around the upper part of Lake Michigan. To be safe, there are nights when you should not go out alone. And a note: all the years with reported sightings end in seven.

<<>>

Haunted Ramsdell. The theatre is well known for its ghosts who seem to enjoy the performances as much as the live audience does. There is a White Lady that people describe as a long-haired ghost who roams the theatre. She is believed to be Ramsdell's daughter. A worker in the basement of the theatre reported this young girl in a white dress standing in the doorway. He leaned closer to get a better look. She turned to him and said, "Follow me to your fortune," and disappeared before his eyes. The frightened worker gave a description that sounds very much like the White Lady described by others. It is hard to decipher her message. How was the startled worker supposed to follow her if she disappeared?

The ghost of Ramsdell himself makes occasional appearances, wearing a dapper, Victorian tuxedo.

The theatre may be haunted, but it is also a place worth the price of admission just to see the opulent interior.

16. LUDINGTON

Ludington enjoyed a 2020 population of 8,317. Ever since French Jesuit missionary and explorer Father Jacques Marquette first landed on the narrow peninsula dividing Lake Pere Marquette and Lake Michigan, Ludington's destiny has been tied to her water.

Father Marquette preached Easter Sunday, 1675, at a Native American village on the shore of the Illinois River. His health had deteriorated, and death was imminent. His last earthly wish was to return to his beloved mission at St. Ignace, but on May 18, he collapsed and died enroute. His remains were laid to rest in Ludington, or at least that is the story told there. A memorial and large iron cross mark the approximate location of his believed grave. Historians haven't weighed in with authoritative evidence of the actual burial site.

Frankfort claims Father Marquette died in their small village and, like Ludington, has erected a monument at the purported death site. A third story recounts that immediately preceding his death, Father Marquette planted a cross on a bluff overlooking Lake Michigan at the site that eventually became Cross Village. Regardless of where he died, there is agreement that his bones were eventually removed to St. Ignace where he wished them buried.

The area around Ludington was a wilderness in 1845 when Burr Casswell began setting traps and fishing at the mouth of the Pere Marquette River. Captivated by the beauty that surrounded him, Casswell moved his family to the area two years later and began a small community known as Pere Marquette Village.

In 1849 the Casswells built a two-story, wood-frame house on their farm. In 1855 the first floor of their home was converted into the county's first courthouse. In 1976 the Mason County Historical Society restored the building which now stands as part of White Pine Village. (See Museums for additional information.)

The town was later renamed for industrialist James Ludington who lived in the area and owned several logging operations there in the late nineteenth and early twentieth centuries. The city enjoyed an era of prosperity in the late 1800s due to both lumbering and the discovery of salt deposits nearby. By 1892, 162 million board feet of lumber and 52 million wood shingles had been produced by the Ludington sawmills. Logging was instrumental in turning Ludington into a major port for transportation of "green gold."

In 1897 the Pere Marquette Railroad constructed a fleet of ferries to transport rail cargo across Lake Michigan to Manitowoc, Wisconsin, where the cargo cars resumed their rail journey. The fleet later expanded to carry automobiles and passengers across the Lake. In the mid-1950s, Ludington became the largest car ferry port in the world.

Today, only one car ferry, the *S.S. Badger*, makes regular trips across the lake from Ludington to Manitowoc. It is one of only two lake-crossing car ferries on Lake Michigan; Muskegon has the other.

You may want to take the ferry to Manitowoc and spend the afternoon. (See Other Things to See or Do for additional information.) Or, you may enjoy 18 miles of hiking and biking trails through forests of hardwoods along Ludington State Park's seemingly endless stretch of Lake Michigan beach. Big Sable Point Lighthouse, one of the tallest lighthouses on the Great Lakes, maintains its vigil along that sandy shore. You should also check out the Pumped Storage Project. (See Other Things to See and Do for additional information.) It is a one-of-a-kind educational experience for the entire family.

• MUSEUMS

Port of Ludington Maritime Museum, 217 South Lakeshore Drive, provides a compelling history of the car ferries and other maritime stories. The museum is housed in the old Coast Guard Station; the building is on the National Register of Historic Places. The three-story building overlooks Lake Michigan's rugged shoreline and the North Pier Light. There is an interactive display that allows the visitor to simulate steering the *S.S. Badger*. Gift shop on the premises. The museum is operated by the Mason County Historical Society, which also administers nearby White Pine Village.

<<>>

Sandcastle Children's Museum, 129 East Ludington Avenue was closed as this travel guide was written. The guiding mission of the museum remained the safety, welfare, and unstructured play opportunities for children. That goal is not possible to achieve with COVID-

19 restrictions. However, Sandcastles reopened when it felt safe to do so, but you should call before planning a visit. New Covid variants could change the status. Inside this amazing museum, children have enough play stations spread out over three floors to keep younger children happy for a long time. The museum fosters children's curiosity and encourages hands-on discovery. Most of the stations are replicas of local businesses so kids play-experience an ice cream shop, grocery store, playdough table, dress up, and much more. Your main problem may be tearing them away when it's time to go.

<<>>

White Pine Village, 1687 South Lakeshore Drive. This historic village allows you to rediscover life in small-town Michigan as it was in the late 1800s. The entire family will enjoy this interesting and educational experience. The village features more than 25 buildings/sites of history on 23 acres. View artifacts of lumbering, music, farming, small rural villages, maritime, sports, and the development of business and industry. Buildings include a sawmill, a one-room school, and a courthouse among many others. The village has numerous special events.

● BEACHES, PARKS, AND TRAILS

Buttersville Park and Camping, 991 South Lakeshore Drive. Park Amenities include 44 campsites with electric hookups, and showers, picnic area, grills, restrooms, playground, beach, boating access, fishing, swimming, playground, pets allowed, and a sanitation station. A shelter can be reserved.

<<>>

Cartier Campground, 1254 North Lakeshore Drive, 164 sites, reservations accepted. Amenities: electric, water and sewer hookup, modern restrooms, showers, boating access, store, fishing, playground, and sanitation station. Pets allowed.

<<>>

Copeyon Park, South Washington Avenue. Open year-round. Amenities: picnic area, playground, and fishing.

<<>>

Kibby Creek Park, Pere Marquette Highway. Amenities: picnic area, rustic restrooms, artesian well.

<<>>

Ludington City Park, West Ludington Avenue. Amenities: picnic area, tables and grills, restrooms, swings, play area, and band shell that can be reserved.

<<>>

Ludington Municipal Marina, 400 West Filer Street, 150-slip marina, 62 transient slips. Amenities: fish cleaning station, laundry, restrooms, showers, fuel, ice and internet access. Reservations accepted.

<<>>

Ludington State Park, 8800 West M-116 at Lake Michigan, is 5,300 acres with 347 campsites (reservations accepted). Voted third best state park in the country. Amenities: electric hookup, modern toilets and showers, boat access, fishing, and concessions. Cabins available. Other amenities: picnic areas, grills, fishing, beaches, bathhouses, playground, canoe and boat rentals, swimming, great hiking trails, biking trails, restaurant, internet access, and general store. Pets allowed.

Ludington State Park is not only a fabulous recreational park, it is a park with a history. It was built at the spot where the once-busy village of Hamlin stood. Hamlin had sawmills, a school, several businesses, and a wooden dam. The dam broke in 1888 washing away pieces of Hamlin. In 1912 the dam burst a second time and swept away what remained of Hamlin. The dam was rebuilt, but at a new location that didn't bring as much danger.

In the mid-1930s, the Civilian Conservation Corps turned the prior location of Hamlin into the beautiful park that is now Ludington State Park.

<<>>

Mason County Campground, 5906 West Chauvez Road, 279 acres with 54 campsites. Reservations accepted. Amenities: water and electric hookups, modern restrooms and showers, playground, sanitation station. Pets allowed.

<<>>

Mason County Picnic Area, 5906 West Chauvez off Pere Marquette Highway, is part of the Mason County Campground. Amenities include shelter, picnic area, playground, disc golf course, and restrooms.

<<>>

Memorial Tree Park, North Washington Avenue at Ivanhoe. Amenities include shelter (reservations needed), picnic area, grills, playground, and ball field.

<<>>

Nordhouse Dunes, a National Wilderness Area within the Manistee National Forest offering 3,450 acres of a unique ecosystem that is the only designated wilderness in the Lower Peninsula. The trails are suited to the hiker who wants a moderate challenge. If you climb the dunes it will be more challenging. The trails are not accessible, and at times they can be crowded which probably isn't what you want in a wilderness area. However, the beachfront is lovely, and if you pick the right day, this is a perfect place. From Ludington take US 10 East to Stiles Road, turn north (left). At Townline Road turn right, then left on Quarterline Road. Turn west (left) on Nurnberg Road and follow it to the end.

<<>>

The Pere Marquette River is the first designated National Wild and Scenic River in Michigan which is ironic since it's a calm and peaceful river. If you visit in

September, you will see the salmon run. You can take a leisurely two-hour kayak trip, fish, or enjoy the scenery.

<<>>

Stearns Park Beach, Stearns Outer Drive. Amenities: picnic area, grills, playground, beach, skate park, mini-golf, restrooms, and summer concessions. Parking is available. This huge, busy park is named in honor of Justus Smith Stearns who was a local businessman, entrepreneur, and one of the most prominent lumbermen in the Midwest. Stearns Park Beach was originally part of Stearns' sawmill property. In 1910 the wealthy lumber baron donated the land on which the park stands to the city. Today, this beautiful park is a gathering place for locals and visitors alike.

<<>>

Summit Park, South Lakeshore Drive. Amenities: shelter (reservation only), picnic area, grills, playground, restrooms, ball field, tennis court, and beach.

<<>>

Suttons Landing, Iris Road off Pere Marquette Highway. Amenities: shelter, picnic area, restrooms, boat launch, and boardwalk along the river.

<<>>

Victory Township, Upper Hamlin Lake Victory Park Road. Amenities: picnic area, grills, and boat launch.

<<>>

Waterfront Park, 1122 South William Street between the City Municipal and Harbor View Marinas. Newly developed 5.3-acre city park with an amphitheater. Bronze sculptures take the visitor on an interesting trip through local history. Other amenities include a playground and picnic shelter. The waterfront walkway extends from downtown Ludington to the south end of William Street, north to Stearns Park. One of the nicest parks in Ludington.

Wilson Hill Park, Upper Hamlin Lake-Barnhart Road. Open dawn to dusk. Amenities: picnic area, grills, boat launch, and ball field.

<<>>

Cruises and fishing charters available in Ludington.

● OTHER STOPS TO CONSIDER

Amber Elk Ranch, 2688 West Conrad Road. Tour a working 130-acre elk ranch as you ride through beautiful pastures to watch these magnificent animals. The ranch started as the hobby of its owners and has grown into a successful business.

<<>>

Father Marquette Shrine, 852 South Lakeshore Drive. This monument honors the Jesuit priest who was one of the area's earliest founders and an integral part of Michigan's history. (See background to Ludington at the start of this section.) Small park with a boat launch and views of Lake Michigan and Pere Marquette Lake. Only a short distance from Buttersville Campground and beach area.

<<>>

Historic Murals. Located on downtown buildings. The murals offer an interesting way to become familiar with Ludington's history. They depict locally famous people and places and wildlife scenes.

<<>>

Ludington Pumped Storage Project, 3525 South Lakeshore Drive. Fifty years ago, the Ludington Pumped Storage Facility, the largest power plant of its kind in North America, was built for slightly less than $400 million. In 2020 they were in the final stages of an $800 million renovation of what has been described as a modern marvel of the world. It may look like a crystal-clear lake at the top of a large grassy hill, but when you check out the base you will discover huge turbines that generate reliable, safe, and economical electrical power for thousands of consumers. The pumped storage hydroelectric generating plant is essentially one giant battery. In the middle of the night, water is pumped up from Lake Michigan and held until the stored energy is needed. It then flows through the turbines, creating the largest power plant in the state. The plant produces power sufficient to service a city of 1.4 million people. It is an educational experience that will fascinate your whole family. You can view the plant's 824-acre reservoir from special observation decks.

<<>>

S.S. Badger, 701 Maritime Drive, a 410-foot car ferry (cars, motorcycles, and RVs) operating between Ludington and Manitowoc, Wisconsin. Spacious outside decks for walking or lounging. Restaurant and deli snack bar, children's playroom, video arcade, movies, entertainment, and a gift shop. Manitowoc has a population of approximately 35,000 and is a nice-sized city for a day or weekend visit. Consider spending time in Manitowoc wandering museums, shops, and restaurants along the water.

Courtesy of the *S.S. Badger*.

● LIGHTHOUSES

Big Sable Point Lighthouse, access in Ludington State Park, but a two-mile hike each way. The fully restored lighthouse is open for tours seasonally. You can climb to the top or visit the gift shop located in the original keeper's quarters.

At Grande Point au Sable, the Lighthouse Board recommended a beacon, and in 1867 Big Sable Point Lighthouse was constructed. That same year, sailors as far as 19 miles out on the lake saw the constant white light for the first time. Weather took a toll and by 1900, the tower had deteriorated and required repair. In 1949 Big Sable Point became the last Great Lakes light to be electrified. Automation eliminated the need for a keeper although the Coast Guard staffed the light until 1972.

In 1949 a seawall was built to minimize the harsh effect of the waves. But without occupants after 1972, deterioration increased. In 1987 the Big Sable Point Lighthouse Keepers Association formed to guarantee the preservation of this historic landmark. Restoration work began on the seawall, the original Fresnel lens was replaced, the building exterior and tower were painted, and floors were refinished.

The Big Sable Point Lighthouse is listed on both the state and national registers of historic places. More than 100-feet tall, it is one of the tallest lighthouses in Michigan.

<<>>

The Ludington Light is a 57-foot-tall, steel-plated lighthouse, which stands at the end of the breakwater on the Pere Marquette Harbor. Given its location where the Pere Marquette River meets Lake Michigan, it is often called the Ludington North Breakwater Light. The light's base is a prow-like structure, which is designed to break waves.

The station was established in 1871, was automated in 1972, and remains operational. The original Fresnel lens can be seen at Historic White Pine Village as part of their maritime exhibit.

William Gerard, the light's first keeper, lived in an old house during his tenure at the Lighthouse. (For a story of Gerard's heroic actions during the wreck of the *Souvenir* see Shipwrecks.)

● SHIPWRECKS

The **West Michigan Underwater Preserve.** (See also Montague Listing under Shipwrecks in this guide.)

<<>>

The Lake Michigan Triangle. Everyone is familiar with the southern Atlantic's Bermuda Triangle. Famous for its shipwrecks, downed planes, and unexplained disappearances, it's a staple of sea lore. However, the Lake Michigan Triangle rivals it.

Charles Berlitz, a supporter of Bermuda Triangle theories, believed Lake Michigan was subjected to forces similar to those in the Bermuda Triangle. Jay Gourley in his book, *The Great Lakes Triangle* said, "The Great Lakes account for more unexplained disappearances per unit area than the Bermuda Triangle."

The surface area of the triangle is created by connecting its three vertices: Ludington to Benton Harbor and then to Manitowoc, Wisconsin. It is a treacherous region where huge ships and even a commercial airline have vanished. (See Shipwrecks and the Crash of Flight 2051 under South Haven and also *Fatal Crossing* under Books and Movies with Connections to South Haven in this guide.)

<<>>

The ***Pere Marquette No. 18***. On September 9, 1910, the railroad car ferry *Pere Marquette No. 18* took 29 passengers and crew to the bottom of Lake Michigan. The remaining 33 passengers managed to escape.

What caused the *Pier Marquette* to sink remains a mystery. She was not victim to a vicious storm, and although the waves were high, it is not likely they caused her to go down. She was not overcrowded, and to all appearances, she was in excellent condition. We might know more if Captain Peter Kilty had survived. He and all of his officers went down with the ship.

The *Pere Marquette No. 18* was riding low in the water, and at some point, she was steering with difficulty. Seven feet of water was discovered in the stern, and water was pouring into the ship through portholes that may have been broken by the punishing waves. Twenty-nine rail cars were pushed overboard to lighten her load. The captain ordered his ship due west at full steam hoping to hit shoal water near Sheboygan in time to avert disaster.

During this drama, the captain also sent what may have been the first ship-to-shore radio distress signal in history. "*No. 18* is sinking in mid-lake, for God's sake, send help." That terse plea, sent at 5:20 a.m., saved the 33 survivors who would otherwise have perished.

The *Pere Marquette No. 17* responded to the distress signal and maneuvered around the side of the stricken steamer to be in position to take additional people aboard when the *Pere Marquette No. 18* sank without warning. The bow bucked high in the air, and the ship slid stern first into the great sea. As it sank there was an explosion that may have killed many of those still aboard. Fortunately, the *Pere Marquette 17* was able to assist some passengers floundering in the water.

After that first wireless message was received, seven additional messages were dispatched describing for the first time, the horror of a ship going down as it was happening. The message above and the first two that follow came from the *Pere Marquette 18*, the remainder from the *Pere Marquette 17,* as she responded to offer assistance:

"No. 18, sinking between Ludington and Milwaukee, for God's sake save us." (5:20 a.m., the same time as the original message.)

"Help, quick, Carferry 18 is sinking." (5:20 a.m.)

"Steamer 18 went down." (From *Pere Marquette 17* at 7:30 a.m.)

"Steamer 18 is gone. No 17 standing by. Will stay until all are saved." (7:35 a.m.)

"Frank Young, James Fray, and Cochrane were saved. All officers of No. 18 lost. Not one saved." (9:00 a.m.)

"We have picked up 30 of crew of 18." (11:00 a.m., and it was actually crew [no officers] and passengers.)

"33 lives saved altogether. We picked up five bodies. Captain Kilty, Purser Sczypank, Mrs. Turner, Cummings, and one unknown. Bodies on board *No. 17* to be taken to Ludington at 4:00 p.m." (1:00 p.m.)

In the aftermath of the tragedy, passengers who were saved, described the efforts of the *Pere Marquette 18* crew and accorded them the highest praise for their actions under harrowing conditions. According to survivor Seymore Cochrane of Chicago, he was reading a magazine in his berth when he heard shouts that the boat was sinking. He wrestled a door from its hinges and floated on it until he was picked up more than an hour later by *No. 17.* Later in an interview, Cochrane said, "There is no other way of reasoning than to say the crew sacrificed their lives to save the passengers. The boat was well-equipped with lifeboats, and if the members of the crew had not been cock full of manliness, they might have saved themselves and let the passengers perish. But, thank goodness, they were not that kind of men."

<<>>

The **Souvenir**, a schooner, ran aground on the clay banks south of Ludington on November 27, 1872. The unlucky ship had been damaged in prior wrecks, but that night tragedy blew in on the gale-force north winds spitting ice and snow and reducing visibility to nothing.

The next morning, the *Souvenir* could be spotted with one man on deck clinging to the wheel. No life crew was available and the sea was too violent to permit a rescue attempt. Horrified spectators on the shore signaled to the man to tie a line about his body and let the end float to shore where he could be pulled in. The man signaled back an unwillingness, whether from being too exhausted to make the effort or from a belief it would be suicide.

Lighthouse keeper William Girard arrived, climbed in a small boat, and bravely rowed to the distressed ship. He went alone because no one else had the courage to assist him. Girard reached the vessel and found the man still alive. The near-frozen fellow expired a few moments afterwards. The other seven crew members were already gone. Reports don't mention if they had washed overboard or died from exposure aboard ship.

• THE FAMOUS OR INFAMOUS WITH TIES TO LUDINGTON

Merrie Amsterburg, an American singer-songwriter, was born in Ludington. She plays several instruments, and her music is influenced by folk, rock, and pop. She has won two Boston Music Awards, a Boston Phoenix Award, and a Jam Magazine Award.

• BOOKS WITH TIES TO LUDINGTON

David K. Petersen, **Ludington Car Ferries**, tells the story of the car ferries that transported trains across Lake Michigan.

Art Chavez, **SS *City of Midland*** (Illustrated). The historic steamship *City of Midland,* one of the car ferries that transported railroad cars, automobiles, and passengers, sailed Lake Michigan waters for nearly half a century. She was the flagship for the Pere Marquette Railway's Lake Michigan ferry fleet. Her sleek profile, stylish passenger accommodations, and comfortable furnishings made her a passenger favorite.

17. PENTWATER

Pentwater's 2020 population was 837. A quaint turn-of-the-century town nestled on the shores of Lake Michigan, Pentwater has been nicknamed the Nantucket of the Midwest. Residents refer to it as "a little piece of heaven," and cherish its slower pace of life. The first land in the Pentwater area sold for $1to $1.25 per acre. The village has no traffic signals, but vehicles halt to let mother ducks lead ducklings across the street. Life is near-perfect along the sandy stretch of white sand beach that entices travelers to Pentwater. Charming shops, B&Bs, restaurants, antique stores, and a full plate of summer activities keep visitors busy once they arrive.

The city revels in its location on Lake Michigan and little Pentwater Lake, the former a mighty giant, and the latter two miles long with varying widths between ½ and ¾ of a mile. Lake Pentwater's annual ice harvest cooled local ice chests during hot, steamy summers before modern refrigeration was available.

There are three explanations offered for how Pentwater was named. The first suggests that Native Americans gave it a name meaning penned-up waters. The second is that it is a variation of paintwater from the dark color of Pentwater Lake. And, the third says it comes from the word pentagram meaning five points and refers to Pentwater's five bodies of water: Lake Michigan, the Channel, Pentwater Lake, the flats, and the Pentwater River. In the 1800s, land in the area was home to about 800 Native Americans, predominantly Pottawatomie, Ojibwe, and Odawa.

The town was originally named Middlesex by Charles Mears who built a sawmill there in 1856. His accomplishments earned him the city's respect; often he is referred to as its founder. He was only twenty-three years old when he arrived in the nearby White Lake Area in 1837. He made his fortune in virgin timber.

Mears' first mill was located on Silver Creek, and it quickly became a full-fledged lumber community. He built many lumber settlements before branching into other businesses. He owned thousands of acres stretching from White Lake to Big Point Sable. Before ending his storied career, he constructed 15 mills at five harbors. He was one of the largest lumber barons in Western Michigan. It is not surprising that he is honored as the founding father of Pentwater.

In truth, however, E.R. Cobb and Andrew Rector had already built a lumber mill and a boarding house on the south end of Hancock Street by 1853, three years before Mears arrived on the scene. Their mill and boarding house were separate from Mears' settlement at Middlesex. On March 16, 1867, Cobb's village was incorporated and officially named Pent Water, and Middlesex was eventually absorbed into Pent Water. For many years, the area west of Hancock continued to be called Middlesex. It may be more accurate to say that Rector and Cobb first founded Pentwater, and Mears was one of the area's most important early citizens.

Mears established a ferry service across the channel in 1858. He also built a 660-foot-long pier into Lake Michigan from the north bank of the channel, so even the largest boats could haul lumber to yards in Chicago and drop cargo in the village of Pentwater on return trips. Mears' efforts to provide a deeper and wider channel were assisted by the federal government in 1868 when it began a 20-year project to enhance the size of the channel.

In 1861 the first newspaper was printed in Pentwater. At the time the village boasted three stores, two steam sawmills, one printing press, several fisheries, two lawyers, one minister, and 300 village residents. It was the only village in all of Oceana County.

Smoke from the Chicago fire of 1871 could be seen all the way to Pentwater, and in 1889 Pentwater blazed in its own devastating fire. The conflagration started in a cigar store on the west side of Hancock Street. The surrounding wooden one-story stores burned.

A lighthouse and a lifesaving station were established in Pentwater to increase shipping safety. The Pentwater lights stand at the mouth of the Pentwater River, the southern boundary of Charles Mears State Park. (See Lighthouses for information about Mears Park and the lighthouse.)

The waters around Pentwater are believed to hold the skeletons of at least 40 ships. The 1940 Armistice Day storm is the most notorious to hit the area. It claimed 59 sailors that inky black, moonless night in November; winds of 80 miles an hour (with gusts reaching 110 miles), and 30-foot waves battered everything in their path. (See Shipwrecks in this section.)

The State Park located on the north side of the village bears Mears' name. His daughter, Carrie, deeded 600 feet of beach north of the channel to the state in 1920. That property marks the beginning of Mears Park.

This guide does not recommend places to stay, but one B&B is worth seeing for its architecture and historic significance. The turn-of-the-century Victorian **Hexagon House**, 760 Sixth Street, is situated on three beautifully manicured acres. It was built around 1870 as one of the first boarding houses for lumbermen. The builder and first owner was S.E. Russell who was an agent of Charles Mears. In the 1920s and 30s, Russell's two daughters inherited the property and turned it into a summer tourist camp. They also ran a homemade pie business and a boat rental business from the house. The surviving sister sold the property sometime in the 1950s, and after that, the house changed owners several times until it finally began its current life as a B&B.

Courtesy of the Hexagon House B&B.

• MUSEUMS AND GALLERIES

Art on the Town, 110 South Hancock, is a cooperative that features the art of 30 local artists in such media as paintings, sculptures, jewelry, blown glass, and ceramics.

<<>>

Pentwater Historical Society Museum, 85 Rutledge Street. This small museum, tucked away in a church basement off the main street, contains interesting local history about the Armistice Day Storm, local buildings, shipping, Charles Mears, and more. Worth a bit of time if you are in the area. Displays are well-organized, and the volunteers are helpful.

175

Art Galleries and Antique Shops. Pentwater is known for its art galleries and antique shops. You can spend hours shopping for past and present treasures. Pentwater also plays host to arts and crafts fairs during the summer months. You are almost guaranteed to find something special!

• BEACHES, PARKS, AND TRAILS

Charles Mears State Park, 400 West Lowell Street. Sandy swimming beach, playground, accessible walkway, picnic shelter, great fishing, and campground with 175 paved sites located on Lake Michigan. Beach has swings and a bathhouse. The park is adjacent to Pentwater's North Pierhead Light and has a one-mile interpretive trail for hiking. The Arcadia Dunes Nature and Recreation Area includes the Old Baldy Trail and St. Pierre Trail. Old Baldy is a dune with a spectacular view of Lake Michigan. The dune and trail start at the North end of the state park, just across from the bathrooms/shower house and playground. The trail consists primarily of a stepped boardwalk that ascends rapidly up the wooded dune. After a couple of steep ascents, hikers are rewarded with a lookout point offering an excellent view of the state park, beach, piers, and Lake Michigan. Continue up to another short, less steep walk and you reach the northwest corner of the park and the top of Old Baldy.

Visitors to Charles Mears Park can enjoy a playground, picnic shelter, and excellent fishing. There is a section of the beach that allows pets.

<<>>

Chester Street Park, 129 Chester Street. A narrow park on the south side of the Pentwater Chanel. Long boardwalk, benches, and the place for a relaxing walk.

<<>>

Halcyon Nature Center, 780 Sixth Street. Offers 2½ acres of native trees, a pond with two small islands, and nature trails with labeled flowers, rocks, and trees.

<<>>

Pentwater Municipal Marina, 519 South Hancock Street. This public marina provides 44 slips divided into 17 seasonal slips, 22 transient slips, and five spots for charter vessels. It accommodates boats up to 45 feet in length. Amenities include pump-out service, fish cleaning station, restrooms, shower building, picnic area with grills, gazebo, paved walkways, benches, and pet walking area.

• OTHER STOPS TO CONSIDER

Jomagrha Winery, 7365 South Pere Marquette Highway. Located one mile from Lake Michigan and four miles north of Pentwater, this winery has a limited production of its French-hybrid plantings and other wines from the harvests of local vineyards. Several wineries along the Lake Michigan coast, including Jomagrha, are part of a wine trail. (For additional information see listing under Other Stops to Consider in Holland.)

<<>>

Farmers Market, Mondays and Thursdays during the summer at 10:00 a.m. on the Village Green.

• LIGHTHOUSES

The North and South Pierhead Lights serve as beacons to guide pleasure boats into Pentwater's harbor during the busy summer season. Directions: US 31 into Pentwater. Turn west on Lowell Street at the north end of town, and drive ½ mile to Charles Mears State Park. From there you can walk the beach to the pierhead lights.

Established in 1890 and 1873 respectively, the lights have undergone numerous changes throughout the years. In 1937 the Army Corps of Engineers replaced the original timber piers with concrete and reinforced the tower with a steel skeleton.

The current South Pierhead Light stands 25 feet tall and the North Pierhead Light is 17 feet tall. Together they are one of the few remaining pier range light systems located on the Great Lakes.

• SHIPWRECKS

The **West Michigan Underwater Preserve**. (See also Shipwrecks under Montague listing in this guide.)

<<>>

The **Novadoc** went down on November 11, 1940, when a gale strength storm raged in what became known as the Great Armistice Day Storm. The storm's strength sank five vessels and claimed 66 victims.

A 20-mile span of Lake Michigan between Little Point Sable at Silver Lake and Big Point Sable north of Ludington has earned a reputation as the Graveyard of Ships. It claimed its first recorded ship, the *Neptune*, in 1848. The five ships that went down on Armistice Day 1940 brought the graveyard's total to nearly 70 vessels.

The first two boats to go down in the 1940 storm were small commercial fishing tugs from South Haven. The **Indian** departed harbor about 7:30 a.m. to pull in its daily catch. It never returned. The **Richard H**, an aging steam tug, was last seen trying to make shore in the early afternoon.

The remaining vessels, the **Novadoc, Anna Minch,** and the **Davock**, would take more than a few strong gusts to destroy. The *Novadoc* was a 250-foot-canaller, a ship small enough to fit through the Welland Canal. The doc at the end of its name stood for Dominion of Canada, and the ship had departed Montreal on a route to Chicago to pick up a load of sulfite coke intended for Quebec.

In Lake Michigan, Captain Steip had tried to set the *Novadoc* a course along the eastern shore to take advantage of the shelter it provided from the wind. The fickle wind shifted to the southwest and increased in strength and speed. The ship ended up perilously close to the center of the lake, and the waves became too high to allow the tossed vessel to reach any harbor on the east side of the lake. The crew had no choice but to ride out the storm.

Near Pentwater at Little Sable Point, Lightkeeper William Krewell watched the masthead lights of the floundering ship as she rolled in the mountainous, foamy waves. The men aboard the ship later described seeing the lighthouse in the distance, but only when they were precariously perched at the top of each new wave.

The *Novadoc* ran aground on a shoal at 7:00 p.m. The crash severed the ship and buried each half in sand. All electric lines were cut. In this broken condition, the storm continued to pummel her. The crew spent the night huddled in the captain's cabin. Just before daybreak, the door to the cabin gave way and rushing water forced the men into the captain's inner office. There they prayed that the wall separating the office from the rest of the quarters would hold. With daylight, the weary crew found they had no lifeboats remaining to carry them to shore.

The stranded men sent up rockets to let potential rescuers on the shore know they were alive. In return, the crowd built a fire to show the crew they had not been forgotten. Help would get there as soon as it was safe to send a boat out. The storm abated somewhat as darkness fell the second night. The cold men aboard the *Novadoc* found a container and cut up pieces of kindling from chairs and other furniture to start a fire to warm their frozen limbs.

The next morning, Captain Steip made his way to the far end of the boat and discovered two of the cooks had washed overboard. Later that morning, the surviving crew was rescued by the **Three Brothers**, a little fishing boat willing to brave the still-churning sea to save the marooned men.

As the *Three Brothers* readied to launch, their crew was warned the proposed rescue attempt verged on insanity—it could not be done—their boat was too small and the waves too high. *The Three Brothers* pushed off in spite of the dire predictions. They reached the *Novadoc* where the grateful crew embraced them as heroes. Once safely ashore, Captain Steip is said to have reached in his pocket and produced a roll of bills, handing it to Clyde Cross, captain of the *Three Brothers*, in gratitude for saving his life. Cross, in an "Aw shucks" way, is alleged to have responded, "Hell no, captain. Glad to be of service." Cross later said he saw that there was a job that needed doing, and he did it. The press hailed him as an All-American hero.

The Coast Guard was not as generous in its praise. It denounced Cross as a glory seeker who had ignored the unwritten law of the sea by refusing to come to their aid when they had asked for his help in launching the Coast Guard lifeboat. Whatever anyone's position on the wisdom of *The Three Brothers* going to the aid of the *Novadoc* when it did, the cold, wet, and frightened survivors were grateful.

In an unfortunate footnote, the little fishing tug, *The Three Brothers,* became a victim of Lake Michigan a few years later. Fortunately, no lives were lost and during her sailing days, she could brag that she rode out the Great Storm of 1940 and saved seventeen men.

The *William B. Davock* and the *Anna C. Minch* were also lost in the Armistice Day Storm. There were no survivors on either, and therefore the story of their last minutes or hours remains a mystery. They went down not too far from where the *Novadoc* was stranded. The *Minch*, a 380-foot-steel propeller, sits in 20 to 40 feet of water about eight miles off Pentwater. Because she broke in two, it is believed she collided with the *Davock*. The 310-foot-steel-hull propeller, *Davock*, rests in about 150 feet of water, also eight miles from Pentwater.

• THE FAMOUS OR INFAMOUS WITH TIES TO PENTWATER

Charles Mears is revered as a founder of Pentwater. He was a businessman and developer.

<<>>

Adolph Walter Rich, born in Hungary, immigrated to the United States and spent part of his life in Pentwater. He was a manufacturer, merchant, and philanthropist who is best known for founding the Jewish agricultural colony at Arpin, Wisconsin.

18. SILVER LAKE

The Silver Lake area is Michigan's Sand Playground. It is not an incorporated city, has no post office, and the addresses of its restaurants and shops are Mears, Shelby, or Hart. Still, this geared-for-fun recreational destination offers so much action, it deserves mention in this guide.

The famous dunes of the area tower between the shores of Lake Michigan and Silver Lake. Silver Lake Park has 500 acres of drivable dunes. You can test your skill with your own 4-wheel drive vehicle or rent a jeep, dune buggy, or quad from one of the nearby rental businesses. If you prefer, you can take a dune tour and leave the driving to someone else. Sand-surfing (also called sandboarding) is yet another option. The Silver Lake area has much to offer, but its sand activities top the list. You'll find equipment for whatever you choose to do.

The Silver Lake Dunes are a beautiful and interesting backdrop for a perfect hike. The Hart-Montague Trail lets you go a distance of 22 miles hiking, biking, or cross-country skiing in season. A refreshing swim and a picnic are the perfect conclusion to an invigorating hike or ride.

Golfing enthusiasts will find courses to challenge any skill level. Miniature golf entertains the entire family. There are go-karts, paddle boats, and bumper boats waiting with your name on them.

Ready for a dune ride. Courtesy of Jon Royce.

• MUSEUM

Oceana County Historical Park and Museum, two blocks west of downtown Mears, is a complex of structures and buildings throughout Hart and Mears. The Swift Lathers Museum is the main building of the park's seven structures. Other buildings of interest include the Robinson Museum, the Transportation Museum, the Boynton Cottage Museum, and the Swedish Mission Covenant Church. The Old Town Hall, located one block east of the main museum, is part of the complex. Together, the museums represent the local history of the nineteenth and twentieth centuries.

• Beaches, Parks, and Trails

Hart-Montague Bicycle Trail. Offers 22½ miles of walking, skating, biking, snowmobiling, or cross-country skiing depending upon the season. (See Montague in this guide for additional information.)

<<>>

Silver Lake State Park, 9679 West State Park Road. A 3,000-acre park with 500 acres of drivable dunes and staging area and 25 acres of camping with more than 200 campsites. Boat launch and swimming beach, bathhouse, picnic tables, shelters, grills, and firepits. Great place to explore, hike, and fish. Hunting (grouse, white-tailed deer, rabbit, and squirrel) allowed in designated areas in season. The park has four miles of Lake Michigan shoreline, mature forests, and is the only park in Michigan that allows off-road and all-terrain vehicles on designated routes. The park also has frontage on Silver Lake.

• Lighthouse

Little Sable Point Light, 287 North Lighthouse Drive, Mears, is one of the tallest lighthouses in the state at over 100 feet and 130 steps to climb the tower. Often crowded, there is a small sandy beach and swimming area. A paved walkway with benches leads to the lighthouse.

The lighthouse was designed by Colonel Orlando M. Poe. Following the loss of the Schooner *Pride* in 1866, public outcries for a light at this locale were heeded.

Congress approved funding in 1871, but construction didn't begin until 1874 due to lack of roads to the site. Originally designated the Petite Point Au Sable Lighthouse, the name was changed to the current Little Sable Point Light which is its designation on the National Park Service list of lighthouses.

In 1954 the lighthouse keeper's dwelling was razed because it was no longer needed. Electricity reached the lighthouse, and it was automated.

The lighthouse is open for the public to climb the tower.

19. MONTAGUE
20. WHITEHALL

Sometimes two cities are such close neighbors that they require discussion as two parts of a whole. Montague and Whitehall, on opposite sides of the White River, are two such cities. The history of one was the same as, or at least impacted by, the history of the other. The White River is nearly 24 miles in length and passes through White Lake before emptying into Lake Michigan to which it is connected by a dredged canal. In 2020 Montague on the north side of the river had a 2020 population of 2,401, and Whitehall had a 2020 population of 2,709.

In 1675 Father Marquette stopped in the area and learned that the Native Americans called the stream *Wabish-Sippe*, meaning the river with white clay in the water, which gave rise to the names of White River and White Lake.

Residents of Montague and Whitehall received a special bonus from the giant glaciers that carved the Great Lakes nearly 20,000 years ago. The forces of that moving behemoth of ice left the deep channel approximately seven miles long and one mile wide that provides the water connection from the White River to Lake Michigan.

Early Native Americans chose to live in this area because the water routes enhanced their ability to travel. Later the connecting waters provided the same advantage to fur traders, lumbermen, settlers, and eventually the tourists.

The lumber era of the 1800s brought a boom to the cities of Whitehall and Montague on opposite sides of the White River. Montague's first permanent settler, Nathanial Sargent, arrived in 1855 and built a home. In 1883 the village was officially incorporated. Noah Ferry, another of the town founders, named it in honor of his father, William Montague Ferry, who had founded the cities of Grand Haven and Ferrysburg in neighboring Ottawa County. Ferry brought a post office to Montague, and the street where it stands is named in his honor. The Ferry Reformed Church on Old Channel Trail is also named for Noah Ferry.

The same year Sargent built his home in Montague, William Barnart bought property in Whitehall from the United States government in a land grant signed by President James Buchanan. Barnhart had been lumbering since 1844 and planned to set up business in Whitehall.

Around 1859 Charles Mears, another noted lumber baron of the era, platted the village of Whitehall and named it Mears after himself. In 1862 the village was renamed Whitehall, and five years later it was incorporated. Mears remains the name of a small village a few miles north near Silver Lake.

In 1857 George Rogers built the first steam-powered lumber mill in Montague. His life ended tragically a short time later when he fell overboard and drowned while crossing White Lake in the steamer *Oceana*.

During the heyday of lumber, the two cities were nearly as large as they are today. Their growth was advanced because great steamships could dock and pick up lumber for Chicago. It is estimated that 85 percent of the timber used to rebuild Chicago after the horrific fire of 1871 started its journey in White Lake. In the late 1800s, there were 19 steam-powered lumber mills around White Lake.

Noah Ferry joined the Union forces when the Civil War broke out, and he became captain of a company of 102 men known as the White River Guard. In early 1863, he was promoted to Major, but that same year he was killed in battle against Robert E. Lee's forces at Gettysburg.

A gruesome train derailment near White Lake devastated the community on April 9, 1894. The accident was one of the worst tragedies of the logging era. Seven men died of fatal burns when a locomotive rounded a curve and plowed directly into a tree that had fallen across the track.

By the close of the century, the forests had been decimated, and 1903 marked the last log drive of any consequence. With the close of the lumber era, the residents needed another source of support for their struggling economy and turned their attention to resorts and tourism. Chicagoans longed to escape the hot, gritty summer of the big city and refresh their bodies and spirits in the cooling waters and relaxed atmosphere of quaint little towns near Lake Michigan. By 1890 the White Lake area was recognized as a premier tourist destination.

Train transportation helped tourism flourish; a ticket from Chicago to White Lake in the summer of 1917 cost $4 for a round trip. During the roaring 20s, automobiles became the preferred means of transportation replacing steamers and trains for the journey. In a single day, the entire family, along with as much luggage as they cared to pack, could arrive in White Lake from destinations as far away as Indiana and Illinois. Spending the summer, or at least a portion of it, in a fashionable resort on White Lake or nearby Lake Michigan was a testament to their newfound wealth.

Today, tourists are captivated by the magnificence of the forests, dunes, and beaches. Picturesque White Lake is admired for its esthetics and recreational opportunities more than its practical use in shipping. The white pine is valued for its natural beauty, not its commercial value.

Whether your sport is kayaking, tubing, rafting, canoeing, fishing, or waterskiing, this major hub of water activity is a perfect place to play. Townspeople welcome visitors to their many annual events including: music festivals, fishing contests, and arts and crafts fairs.

• Museum and Galleries

C&O Railroad Caboose Museum, 124 West Hanson Street, Whitehall, behind the White Lake Chamber of Commerce. The caboose is well-preserved and maintained. Grab a brochure, watch the short film, and enjoy the railroad history of Whitehall and Montague. A short, but pleasant stop in your busy day.

<<>>

Dr. Meinhard's Apothecary Shop Museum, 124 West Hanson Street, Whitehall, behind the White Lake Chamber of Commerce. This historic building is where Dr. Meinhard practiced medicine and operated his apothecary in the early 1900s. His business was originally located in front of his house on 811 South Mears Avenue. In 2011 the building was moved to its present location and became a museum, depicting what it may have looked like when operated as an active practice. Artifacts are from the same period. A medicinal herb garden is outside between the building and the

Caboose Museum. (See above listing for Caboose Museum.) Parking lot shared by Visitor's Center, Caboose Museum, and Dr. Meinhard Museum.

<<>>

Montague City Museum, Church and Meade Streets (8717 Meade), Montague, helps you experience the lumbering era through the displayed artifacts. You can also see the pageant dress worn by Montague's Miss America, Nancy Ann Fleming. The building housing the Montague Museum was the former United Methodist Church, constructed in 1872. It features vivid stained-glass windows, red-carpeted aisles, and a stereo system that provides pleasant browsing music. Limited summer hours.

<<>>

Terrestrial Forming Pottery Studio, 5385 Lamos at Michillinda Road, Whitehall. Known locally as Peter the Potter's Place, Peter Johnson creates sculptured pottery that is both functional (lead-free and dishwasher safe) and art. For decades, Johnson has worked on his old-English-designed treadle-kick wheel. Peter mixes his own clay and glazes and fires his self-built kilns about every two months. He favors earth tone glazes reminiscent of the woodland Native Americans whom he studies. The barn-like studio is tucked into the woods near Lake Michigan. He may be willing to give you a tour.

● ANOTHER STOP TO CONSIDER

The **World's Largest Weathervane** rises a majestic height of 48 feet on the north shore of White Lake. It weighs 4,300 pounds. Perched atop the weathervane is a replica of the ***Ellenwood***, a lumbering schooner whose home port was White Lake. On October 1, 1901, the *Ellenwood* ran aground during a nasty, northerly storm. She was about eight miles north of Milwaukee and far from her home port. The crew abandoned her and headed for safety in the ship's yawl. The beleaguered schooner was bashed and battered by the mighty waves until she tore apart and sank. The next spring, a portion of her wooden nameplate washed ashore at White Lake. The *Ellenwood* rests in a watery grave of her home port.

A 22½-mile rail trail opened in 1988 and beckons bicyclers, inline skaters, and hikers. It is a paved recreation trail built on the former C&O Railroad right of way. The trail is handicap accessible. (See Other Things to See or Do.)

• BEACHES, PARKS, AND TRAILS

Goodrich Park, located next to the White Lake Municipal Marina. Amenities include a large playground, barbeque grills, picnic tables, a covered picnic area, large trees for shade, and beautiful views of White Lake.

<<>>

Hart-Montague Bicycle Trail State Park, Business 31 and Water Street, Montague. Michigan's first linear state park, this 22.5-mile paved recreation trail is used by hikers, walkers, runners, bicyclists (bicycles can be rented at many hotels and other businesses in the area), rollerbladers, skateboarders, and in the winter, snowmobilers and cross-country skiers. You can ride horses beside the trail, but not on the asphalt.

The trail was originally a railroad track established in the late 1800s. To entice the railroad to the area, residents raised $30,000 and included the land for the right of way. They also provided the labor to grade the rail bed; a task that required picks, shovels, and teams of horses. Ownership of the railroad changed several times over the years, but it was part of the C&O line in 1982 when it was abandoned. The railroad donated the land to create this trail.

Enjoy the entire trail nonstop, or stroll along pausing at shops, or grabbing a snack at one of many close-by restaurants. The trail is handicap accessible and weaves through White Hall, Montague, and nearby communities.

<<>>

Historic Walking Tour, maps at the Welcome Center (C&O Railroad Depot), 124 West Hanson Street, Whitehall. The tour takes you past 16 historic homes of community founders. The homes and yards are privately owned and not open to the public, but a leisurely walk past them is the perfect way to experience the feel of these two little cities. You will also meander past lovely churches with inspiring architecture.

<<>>

Manistee National Forest and White Lake's natural marshland provide habitats and homes to more than 100 Mute and Tundra swans. Outdoor enthusiasts can hike the area and delight in nature. (See Manistee in this guide for additional information on Manistee National Forest.) The forest is not a contiguous area and touches many places along Michigan's west coast.

<<>>

Medbury Park, on the White Lake Channel to Lake Michigan. Dog-friendly park where you can sit and watch boat activity. Easy walk to White River lighthouse.

<<>>

Meinert County Park and Pines Campground, 8355 Meinert Park Road, Montague. This small county park on Lake Michigan's shore has 67 modern campsites with open and shaded options. Other amenities: campsites that offer water, electrical, and sewer hookups. The park has a sandy beach, flush toilets, showers, dumping station, ice, and firewood available. Ranger service and security.

<<>>

Montague Marina, 4770 Goodrich Street. Docking and 66 seasonal and transient slips. Clubhouse with galley, ice, showers, washrooms, picnic area, parking, and charters. Seasonal.

<<>>

Municipal Boat Launch, Launch Ramp Road, Montague. Fish cleaning station and restrooms available. Montague City Hall sells day-use passes.

<<>>

White Lake Municipal Marina, 100 North Lake Street, Whitehall. Docking, 50 slips, diesel fuel, gas, parking, pump-out, ice, bathhouse with showers, and large playground. Located at Goodrich Park. Seasonal.

<<>>

Whitehill and Montague have several charter companies, private marinas, camping spots, and horseback riding.

● OTHER STOPS TO CONSIDER

Farmers Market, Water and Church Street, Montague. Seasonal local produce. Open Wednesday and Saturday 8:00 a.m. to noon.

<<>>

Country Dairy, between New Era and Shelby, adjacent to the Hart-Montague Bike Path, 10875 Ochs Road. Tours (fee charged and must be scheduled in advance) of milk-bottling process and a working farm. You can watch not only white and chocolate milk being processed, but vanilla and strawberry as well. The tour of this working dairy farm and milk processing facility includes the cheese-making process and the Show Barn where the cows are fed and milked. You may even spot a new calf or two. Gift store on the premises.

<<>>

The Electric Forest, seven miles north of Montague. This guide doesn't include many festivals or special events because of their short duration and penchant for changing dates and even being discontinued. However, the Electric Forest may be worth checking out if you are going to be in Montague in early summer. Tens of thousands of fans travel from all parts of the country and the world to gather at the JJ Resort for the music and camping adventure. The Electric Forest brings together a passionate group of music fans who enjoy community spirit and great music set against the natural beauty of the area.

<<>>

White Lake Music Shell, Launch Ramp Road, Montague. Free concerts Tuesdays at 7:30 p.m. from June to August. Located on the shores of White Lake, the concerts vary to include jazz, folk, country, swing, and international groups.

• LIGHTHOUSE

The White River Lighthouse, 6199 Murray Road, Whitehall. The historic lighthouse was built in 1875 and currently houses a maritime museum. You can climb the old spiral stairs for a spectacular view of Lake Michigan and White Lake.

By the mid-1800s, the need for a lighthouse was clear. It took several years to improve the harbor to make building a lighthouse feasible. The octagonal lighthouse tower, set in the northwest corner of a gabled-roof 1½ story dwelling, is 38 feet tall and made of limestone. The reward for climbing the old tower's spiral stairs, besides history, is the view. The lighthouse was automated in 1945. It was deactivated in 1960.

In 1919, 87-year-old keeper William Robinson was told that he had to retire and let William Bush, his grandson, who had been serving as his assistant, take charge of the light. Robinson couldn't bear leaving. The lighthouse had been his home for more than 40 years. The dedicated keeper fell into a depression. The day he

192

was scheduled to move out, he died a peaceful death in the lighthouse he had always loved.

The White River Light Station Museum currently houses nineteenth and early twentieth-century photographs related to the lighthouse and other artifacts of the area.

● SHIPWRECKS

The **Contest**, a schooner that was beached in 1882 in the White Lake Channel, remained buried under a Lake Michigan dune for 44 years. On December 14, 2018, torrential waves and wind blew away a large chunk of the dune and revealed the shipwreck's remains. People walked to the bluff to get a glimpse of this relic of the past. They knew the sand would again bury the skeleton, and the window for observation could be short.

<<>>

The **West Michigan Underwater Preserve**'s, official address is 5200 Anderson Road, Montague. This is Michigan's newest underwater preserve and is dubbed Lucky 13. It is the 13th preserve, began with 13 major shipwrecks, and became official on September 13, 2012. The WMUP covers over 345 square miles from just north of Big Sable Point near Ludington to just south of Grand Haven. From North to South, the preserve includes the wrecks of *G.F. Forester, Comanche, Minch, Novadoc, Davock, Pizzazz, Daisy Day, Brightie, Interlochen, State of Michigan, Salvor, Helen, Henry Cort, Hamilton Reef, Crane, and Ironsides.*

● THE FAMOUS OR INFAMOUS WITH TIES TO WHITEHALL

Nancy Anne Fleming, born in Muskegon on May 20, 1942, considered herself a native of Montague. On September 10, 1960, she was crowned Miss America

1961. She had competed in the Miss Michigan pageant as Miss White Lake.

<<>>

Adella M. Parker was born in Whitehall on February 1, 1870. She moved with her parents to Seattle and attended law school at the University of Washington from which she graduated in 1903. She was the sole woman in her law school class. She became a suffragist, politician, lawyer, and educator.

<<>>

Ruth Thompson was born in Whitehall on September 15, 1887. She became a lawyer and the first female State Representative of Michigan, the first female U.S. Representative from Michigan, and the first female on the U.S. House Judiciary Committee. She gained national recognition as an advocate for children's rights.

• GHOST STORY

Ghosts of the White River Lighthouse. The ghost of Captain William Robinson still roams about the place he called home. (See Lighthouse in this section.) He and his wife Sara lived in the lighthouse for more than four decades. William died in the lighthouse the day he was supposed to move out. He was 87 years old, and retirement was not his choice. He and Sara had 13 children together, and her spirit wasn't about to be separated from that of her husband so she also wanders about the premises helping him keep an eye on everything. Unexplained noises emanate from the lighthouse, mostly in the dark of night. Various artifacts are moved about as though someone is simply carrying on their routine.

As you climb the lighthouse steps, if you feel a chill or the touch of something against your shoulder, say "Hi" to Captain Robinson. He's glad you are visiting his lighthouse.

White River Light Station. Courtesy of Steve Schneider.

21. MUSKEGON

Muskegon is the largest city along the West Michigan coast. Its 2020 population was 36,903.

In spite of its miles of sugar-sand beaches, Muskegon seems less touristy than her sister beach towns. The reason is at least partially due to Muskegon's industrial persona which in the mid-1900s was associated with foundries, a history summed up as pelts, pines, and piston rings. Such a glib characterization shortchanges Muskegon and travelers to this area as well.

It would be a shame to ignore Muskegon's rich history, wonderful parks (the beach at Pere Marquette Park has been on *USA Today*'s list of cleanest beaches in the U.S.), museums, and cultural events.

It is believed that the first people to the Muskegon area were nomadic hunters who came seven to eight thousand years ago following the retreat of the glaciers.

Woodland cultures, such as the Hopewellian, came after the hunters, and they dominated the area about 2,000 years ago.

Europeans began recording the history of the area when it was primarily occupied by Odawa and Pottawatomie tribes. The name Muskegon is derived from the Odawa term *Masquigon* meaning marshy river or swamp. The Masquigon (or Muskegon River) River is identified on French maps of the late seventeenth century confirming that by then the French had reached the west coast of Michigan.

While it is uncertain exactly when the first Frenchman visited the Muskegon area, we do know that Father Jacques Marquette traveled northward through this area on his last trip to St. Ignace in March 1675. A party of French soldiers under the command of René-Robert Cavelier, Sieur de La Salle's lieutenant, Henry de Tonti, passed through in 1679.

History documents French fur-trading activity during the next century, but the exact locations of the earliest posts cannot be pinpointed. By the early 1800s, trading sites had been created around Muskegon Lake where traders were drawn by a large number of beavers in the river networks. Credit for the first documented trading post goes to Magdelaine La Framboise in 1810. Her husband, Joseph, had made trips to the area since 1783. In 1812 Jean Baptiste Recollet established a post near what is now North Muskegon.

It was not until the mid-1800s that Muskegon seemed to catch on. The riches related to the timber garnered the attention of speculators coming from the east. They brought with them enough money to erect lumber mills. The typical lumberman was in good health and young. Generally, he was between 20 and 30 years old, came from New England, New York, or Pennsylvania, and had done well enough in his prior endeavors to finance his lumber venture.

The lumber boom came before the area was ready for it. There were no adequate means of transportation to foster its growth. Stagecoach was slow, and the railroad was not yet a presence. However, by the mid-1800s Muskegon's port rivaled that of Chicago.

By 1869 railroad fever hit and various lines made Muskegon a stop on their route. Inside the city, however, even 15 years after the railroad, horses and mules pulled streetcars along 3½ miles of track. It was 1890 before they were replaced by electric cars.

Muskegon became known as the Lumber Queen of the World. After the fire of 1871, the city of Chicago rebuilt with Muskegon timber. During the lumbering era, the city boasted more millionaires than any other town in America.

Around the turn of the twentieth century as the lumber industry died, a community catering to entertainers sprang up along the massive dune called Pigeon Hill in a section of the city known as Bluffton. In 1903 the Keatons (Buster and his parents) and other vaudevillians summered in the area.

Today, you can follow the history of Muskegon through a guided walking tour or by visiting fascinating museums including the Muskegon County Museum, the Hackley House, and the Hume House built by lumber barons of the era. Charles Hackley's name is virtually synonymous with Muskegon; his legacy lives on through family donations and gifts to the city. You can take a self-guided walk and explore the best and most interesting sites of Muskegon's past.

Whatever else you do, you will want to visit Muskegon's beaches and parks. They are among the best along the west coast.

Art Cats Gallery, 1845 Lakeshore Drive in the eclectic Lakeside District of Muskegon on the shore of Muskegon Lake. The owner of this gallery creates whimsical pieces, and many other artists display their works of jewelry, pottery, mosaics, glass, original paintings, prints, and sculpture here.

<<>>

The Great Lakes Naval Memorial and Museum, 1346 Bluff Street. Tour the *USS Silversides* and the *USCGC McLane*, two World War II Ships. The *USS Silversides* served with the Pacific Fleet along Japan's coast, the East China Sea, and through key enemy shipping routes. Her mission was to stop raw materials and supplies from going to Japan. The *USCGC McLane* was authorized by President Calvin Coolidge's administration to enforce prohibition. The museum has an overnight encampment program that is a great way for a scout troop or other group to enjoy an unusual learning experience.

<<>>

The **James Jackson Museum of African American History**, 7 East Center Street, Muskegon Heights. The museum's focus is local Muskegon County African American history but includes state and national history. There is an Obama Corner.

<<>>

The **Lakeshore Museum Center**, 430 West Clay Street. This is the main museum building and a repository of Muskegon's past. It has nine dioramas tracing early history and depicting scenes from 1937 forward. The Coming to the Lakes exhibit displays 10,000 years of history including a 21-foot mastodon. Children will delight in the "Mastodon on the Loose" scavenger hunt.

If you ever questioned what Michigan was like 400 million years ago, this is the place to find answers. In its infancy, Michigan was covered in saltwater and huge prehistoric fish swam along coral reefs.

Another gallery examines a dune, grassland, wetland, forest, and urban habitat. A hands-on science center allows visitors to create a tornado.

The Lakeshore Museum Center was formerly called the Muskegon County Museum. Muskegon county residents expressed a collective interest in creating a museum for the preservation of historical records and artifacts as early as the late nineteenth century when a reunion of area settlers discussed the importance of preserving local history. From that point forward, efforts were directed at creating a museum, adding to it, and refining it until it became a multi-site complex of five historic structures. In 2019 the Lakeshore Museum Center was voted the Trip Advisor's #1 Tourist Attraction in Muskegon.

The Fire Barn Museum, Hackley and Hume Historic Site, Heritage Museum, and Scolnik House of the Depression Era, are parts of the complex and in close proximity to each other.

▪ **The Fire Barn Museum**, 510 West Clay Street between Fifth and Sixth Streets. The C.H. Hackley Hose Company No. 2 was formed in December 1875. Charles Hackley sponsored twelve volunteer firemen in the first of what would be many gifts he made to the city. Initially, the firefighters used hand-drawn carts which they later traded for horse-drawn carts as they rushed to respond to neighborhood fires. The museum is a living memorial to the brave men and women who have served as Muskegon firefighters over the years. In 1976 the Muskegon Heritage Society and the City of Muskegon joined forces to build a re-creation of the C. H. Hackley Hose Company No. 2 building as a bicentennial project featuring a collection of antique fire fighting apparatus.

· **The Heritage Museum**, 561 West Western Avenue. On June 2, 2020, the Muskegon Heritage Museum officially merged with the Lakeshore Museum Center. The Heritage Museum houses a large collection of exhibits, artifacts, and photos showcasing the economic, industrial, and social history of the greater Muskegon area. Exhibits include a working steam engine with a line shaft that runs 11 machine tools, a working Brunswick pinsetter, a spring winding machine, and over 80 other displays representing local businesses. The Museum has nearly 10,000 square feet of display space on three floors.

· **The Hackley & Hume Historic Site**, 484 West Webster Avenue (Northeast corner of Sixth Street and Webster Avenue) is the site of the magnificent homes built by two of Muskegon's most famous lumber barons, partners Charles H. Hackley and Thomas Hume. In 1887 Hackley purchased the lots on which these homes stand and construction took place over the next two years. You will experience how these two families lived, the history of the lumbering era, and the beauty and charm of these Queen Anne Victorians with their exquisite late nineteenth-century craftsmanship, woodworking, and painstaking restorations.

Historic Hackley and Hume Homes. Courtesy Pixabay Free Images.

▪ **The Scolnik Museum**, 504 West Clay Avenue. Set inside one of the houses in a historic neighborhood, this museum shows what life was like during the Great Depression. Originally a single-family house, it had been adapted by its owner to rent out the upstairs, so the original spiral staircase and other features no longer exist. The house is furnished in the period including magazines and music and games. The kitchen illustrates how meals were prepared, the washboard in the laundry takes you back to a time before modern conveniences.

<<>>

Muskegon Museum of Art, 296 West Webster Avenue. Permanent collection of fine American and European paintings, sculptures, prints, and drawings. Also changing exhibits and special programs to entice the museumgoer. Guided tours available by appointment.

<<>>

The SS *Milwaukee Clipper*, 2098 Lakeshore Drive. She was called the Queen of the Great Lakes, and you can take a guided tour through four of her six decks. The steamship was a former passenger steamer and Lake Michigan car ferry. She is the oldest remaining passenger ship on the Great Lakes and is listed as a Historical National Landmark.

<<>>

The *USS LST 393*, Mart Dock on the waterfront, just off Shoreline Drive. The tour takes from 30 to 45 minutes, and you can explore the technology and living conditions of WWII sailors. You can walk where heroes walked and learn of the *LST 393*'s impressive wartime record in this veterans museum with exhibits that honor those who served America and fought for their country's freedom.

<<>>

The Frauenthal Theater, 425 West Western Avenue. If you are looking for theater or concerts while you are in Muskegon, the city offers the lovely Frauenthal Theater where you can check the current schedule and perhaps attend a performance.

● BEACHES, PARKS, AND TRAILS

The Hart-Montague Trail. This 25½-mile trail offers scenic overlooks, picnicking, and restrooms. Mile markers help you chart your progress. (See listing under Montague.)

<<>>

Hartshorn Public Marina, 920 West Western Avenue. Steps from downtown, this is Muskegon Lake's only public marina. It offers 54 transient slips and shore power, but no pump-out or gas.

<<>>

Heritage Landing, 1050 7th Street, has become the site of many community festivals and events. In a former life, it was an industrial scrap yard but has been transformed into a gathering place near downtown. You'll enjoy the views of Muskegon Lake's sunsets. The family-friendly park has a play area for kids and is also the dock for Great Lake cruise ships.

<<>>

Kruse City Park, Sherman at Beach Street. Enjoy the dunes and overlooks from the walkways. Also provides restrooms, playground, picnic tables and shelter, nature trails, and basketball courts. The dog beach may be closed due to erosion.

<<>>

Margaret Drake Elliot City Park, 1651 Beach Street just north of Pere Marquette Park at the Muskegon Channel. The park is five acres and within walking distance to Lake Michigan beach.

<<>>

The Monet Garden of Muskegon, 470 West Clay Avenue, is a pocket park created on a vacant lot transforming it into a small slice of beauty. It is open to the public and maintained by the Master Garden Club. The garden was inspired by the famous Monet Garden in France. Benches are provided so you can relax, and the area is illuminated after dark.

<<>>

Muskegon State Park, 3560 Memorial Drive, US 31 to the M-120 Exit in North Muskegon, then follow signs to the park. Provides a great expanse of beautiful Lake Michigan sandy beach (two miles along Lake Michigan and one mile on Muskegon Lake) that is as gorgeous as any in the state, and forested dunes stretch to meet the shoreline. The park contains three campgrounds. Amenities include electricity, shower/toilet, and picnic tables. There are also two mini-cabins. Day visitors love the beach for swimming and soaking up the sunshine. Enjoy hiking 12 miles of marked trails. There is a lighted boat launch at Snug Harbor where trailered boats of all sizes can be launched. In the winter, visitors, including novice adventurers, will find plenty to do at the popular Muskegon Winter Sports Complex. An Olympian-designed luge track, sledding hill, an ice-skating trail through the woods, cross-country ski trails, ice skating, and ice fishing.

<<>>

Musketawa Trail. The Rails to Trails Conservancy has led the way in converting the state's abandoned railroad corridors to trails. The Musketawa Trail is a four-season, 26-mile paved recreational trail that runs from Muskegon to Marne, past farmlands and wetlands, over creeks, and through villages. It is perfect for bikers, snowmobilers, horseback riders, inline skaters, cross-country skiers, hikers, wheelchair travelers, and nature lovers who want to enjoy meandering any part of the trail. Along the way, you will find the longest of 13 railroad trestles (216 feet long) over Crockery Creek. At Ravenna you can take note of the 100-year-old rebuilt railroad water tower, railroad signs and signals, and metal arts bike rack. A railroad caboose has been added as a historical centerpiece of the trail. You will eventually reach East Muskegon with connections westward to the Laketon Trail and on to the beautiful, nine-mile Muskegon Lakeshore Trail.

<<>>

Pere Marquette Park, 1601 Beach Street at Lakeshore Drive. This city park offers a wide 2½ mile expanse of Lake Michigan frontage, playground, picnic tables, volleyball courts, a restaurant, and access to lighthouses and the Muskegon Channel. Handicap accessible. Site of the *USS Silversides*.

<<>>

Pioneer Park, 1563 North Scenic Drive, has 235 modern campsites with water and electric hookups at every site. The campground can accommodate tents and RVs. No reservations are taken so first come, first served. Modern toilets and showers. Access to Lake Michigan. For the day-use visitor, there is a beach, swimming, play area, softball diamonds, volleyball area, and tennis and basketball courts.

<<>>

P. J. Hoffmaster State Park, 6585 Lake Harbor Road. This 1,130-acre park offers forested dunes along three miles of Lake Michigan Shore. The sandy beach is spectacular. The campground is located in a wooded valley and has 293 sites with electric and modern shower/toilet buildings available. The day-use area has picnic sites, a picnic shelter, a swimming beach, ten miles of trails to beckon the hiker or birdwatcher, a dune climb stairway, and an observation deck. Winter brings cross-country skiers to the marked three-mile trail for intermediate skiers. Pets must be on a leash and are not allowed on the beach. The Gillette Sand Dune Visitor

Center houses an exhibit hall depicting the ecological zones of the unique dune environment. There are nine multimedia presentations on the dunes and seasonal nature subjects in the 77-seat auditorium.

<<>>

Muskegon has several marinas with transient slips, cruises, and ferry service to Wisconsin if you want to enjoy a side trip.

• OTHER STOPS TO CONSIDER

Farmers Market, 242 West Western Drive. The place to buy fresh Michigan produce, flowers, pastries, honey, flowers, and more. Open May through November, Tuesdays, Thursdays, and Saturdays from 8:00 a.m. to 2:00 p.m. They also have a flea market on Wednesday from 8:00 a.m. until 2:00 p.m. from May through October. The market claims it is more than a market, it's an experience.

<<>>

Hackley Public Library, 316 West Webster, a gift from lumber baron Charles Hackley to the City of Muskegon Public Schools, the library opened in 1890. The building is an architectural adventure, and the librarians are used to visitors wandering in to look at the stained glass, marble staircase, and woodwork. If you need to use a computer, you can even give yourself an excuse—though one isn't needed. The library is in the same neighborhood as the Lakeshore Museum Center.

<<>>

Ice Fishing. When Michigan's 11,000 inland lakes freeze over (usually by late December), you can try your luck ice-fishing for perch, walleye, pike, bluegill, and other delicious freshwater fish. You will need an ice auger to drill a hole, a seat of some sort (sitting on the ice is neither practical nor comfortable), a pole, a bit of luck, and a fishing license (available at most area sporting goods stores).

<<>>

Michigan Adventure, 4750 Whitehall Road, eight miles north of Muskegon. Sixty ways to enliven your stay. It is Michigan's largest water park and you can fly, whirl, propel, cruise, topple, twist, tumble, turn, and slide through all sorts of water adventures from tame to tumultuous and everything in between. One thing is certain, you will get wet. On a hot Michigan summer day, that is perfect.

<<>>

Muskegon Winter Sports Complex, 462 Scenic Drive, located at Muskegon State Park. (See Parks in this section).

<<>>

Walking Tours. Muskegon is the perfect city for a lovely, walking tour. Learn, exercise, and relax. Life is good when you stroll among Muskegon's historic sites during a 90-minute walking tour. Explore Muskegon's rich history including the story of the Hackleys, Spaniolas, and the McCracken building, as well as learn about current and past occupants of businesses you'll pass. For information contact the Muskegon Lakeshore Museum.

• LIGHTHOUSES

The Muskegon South Pierhead Lighthouse, 1453 Beach Street on the pier behind the Coast Guard Building, Muskegon Heights, stands 53 feet tall and marks the entrance to the channel that connects Lake Michigan with Muskegon Lake. This site is accessible by the pedestrian walkway between the National Oceanic and Atmospheric Administration and the United States Coast Guard Station. The South Pierhead Light has two spiral staircases and a shipman's ladder. You can view

206

the South Pierhead Lighthouse from the beach or by boat and tours are available during the summer months.

Muskegon's first lighthouse and nearby keeper's quarters were built in 1851. The dwelling was a red brick structure topped with a wooden light tower at the center. Not much is known about this lighthouse since no photos have survived, but its existence underscores the concern for improving shipping safety.

In 1870 a new lighthouse was constructed on the same parcel of land as the original light. The new lighthouse included a keeper's dwelling that was painted white. The short, square wooden tower on the front side of the structure rose above the house's gable roof.

The channel was difficult to keep navigable and maintain because of silting. Larger ships were built, and they required wider and deeper water entryways to harbors. The original piers were extended farther and farther into Lake Michigan so Muskegon could continue to be a prosperous port. Changes, replacement, reconstruction, and preservation took place over the years, and by 2008 both the South Pierhead Light and the South Breakwater Light were deemed excess property. Notice went out seeking a new caretaker and offering the lights at no cost to a qualified entity. In 2010 the Michigan Lighthouse Conservancy gained possession of both the South Pierhead Light that was first lit in 1903 and the South Breakwater Light that was built in 1930. The South Pierhead Light was added to the National Register of Historic Places in 2005. You will get additional fascinating history when you tour the lighthouse.

<<>>

The Muskegon South Breakwater Lighthouse is located about a half mile from shore. The walk out on the pier makes a pleasant one-mile round trip during which you can savor the views. The rectangular base of the tower is a 10-foot entrance area. Above that entrance level, sits a

63-foot-tall pyramidal tower that was built in 1931. The tower and base are both painted red.

South Breakwater Lighthouse. Courtesy of Pixabay Free Images.

The tower's interior is sparse. Since it wasn't manned, but intended only to hold equipment, the space didn't provide creature comforts. The floor and landings are unpainted concrete. The breakwater light has no rails on the concrete pad and can become slippery when wet.

● SHIPWRECKS

The **Henry Cort** was a busy ship during her career. Originally named the *Pillsbury,* she was sold in 1896, renamed the *Henry Cort,* and repurposed to haul bulk iron ore for the Pittsburg Steamship Company, a subsidiary of the U.S. Steel Corporation. She served faithfully, but not without blips along the way. In 1917 she sank in 20 feet of water after a collision with the steamer *Midvale* while breaking ice in Lake Erie. The crew walked across the ice and boarded the *Midvale.* There were no injuries. After several months submerged, the *Cort* was raised in 1918, underwent major repairs, and returned to service. In 1927 she was sold to Lake Ports Shipping and Navigation Company of Detroit. In 1933 she was again confounded by ice and settled to the bottom of the Detroit River near Ecorse.

The *Henry Cort* ended her career near Muskegon on November 30, 1934, when she hit the breakwater during 45-mile-an-hour winds. The U.S. Coast Guard rushed to the *Cort*'s aid. Hundreds of spectators watched from shore while the Coast Guard shot a line from the pier to the *Henry Cort*. All 25 crewmen climbed hand over hand, or used an improvised breeches buoy and were brought to the relative safety of the pier. There they huddled together before making a dangerous march over the slippery breakwater rocks, dodging waves taller than they were to reach safety. One of the Coast Guard's crew died in the rescue attempt after being washed overboard from the surfboat. His body was never recovered. The *Cort* broke in two and was declared a total loss. Today, she sits outside of the north breakwater in about 30-feet of water.

<<>>

Unidentified ship near Muskegon. On November 30, 2019, a storm surge uncovered a wreck off the Lake Michigan coast near Muskegon. It is not unusual for ships to go down and remain buried for decades, only to be uncovered during a major storm that whips around the sand covering them.

Divers from the Western Michigan Underwater Preserve worked with a state marine archaeologist to identify the vessel. They determined the boat was about 86-feet long, 21-feet wide, and was a nineteenth century flat-bottomed scow. The divers believed the scow was transporting a steam crane between Muskegon and Grand Haven when it sank. A crane in the area had been a dive site for many years. The scow had likely been buried for decades.

<<>>

209

The **West Michigan Underwater Preserve**. (See Shipwrecks under Montague listing in this guide.)

• THE FAMOUS OR INFAMOUS WITH TIES TO MUSKEGON

Virginia Bell was born on July 30, 1927, in Muskegon, Michigan. She served in the Women's Army Corp in Japan during World War II. After her service, she joined the All-American Girls Professional Baseball League and was a pitcher and outfielder.

<<>>

Joseph R. Beyrle was born on August 25, 1923, in Muskegon. His son, **John Ross Beyrle**, was born on February 11, 1954, in Muskegon. Father and son shared a birthplace and ties to Russia. The father is believed to be the only American soldier to serve in both the U.S. Army and the Soviet Red Army in WWII. He was captured by the Germans and became a prisoner of war. After several escape attempts, he successfully joined a Soviet tank battalion, was wounded, and eventually sent back to the United States. He died in 2004. His son, John Ross, became an American diplomat and served as Ambassador of the United States to the Russian Federation from July 3, 2008, until January 10, 2012.

<<>>

Nancy Fleming was born in Muskegon and raised in Montague. She was crowned Miss America in 1961. After her reign, she worked in the entertainment industry as a program host and interviewer for ABC-TV, Cable Health Network, and PBS. In 1978 Fleming married radio and television personality, Jim Lange, who remained best known for the *Dating Game*. The couple lived just north of San Francisco in Marin County. Jim Lange died in 2014. (See Montague listing in this guide for additional information.)

<<>>

Joseph Frank Keaton. Back at the turn of the twentieth century, about 1902, at a time in Muskegon history when lumber was giving way to industry and tourism, a community of entertainers sprang up in the shadow of a massive dune known as Pigeon Hill in the Bluffton section of the city. Bluffton was located between Lake Michigan and Muskegon Lake, and it became home to Joseph Keaton, his wife Myra Cutler, and their son, Joseph Frank Keaton, who was better known as Buster. Buster was the sixth in the family line to be named Joseph Keaton.

These entertainers performed at a summer showhouse built by the elder Keaton and his friends at Lake Michigan Park. The Keaton family fell in love with the community while performing there. From 1907 forward, they returned each summer and referred to Muskegon as their adopted home; the city in turn, adopted them as its most famous citizens.

Buster was born October 4, 1895, and by age three he was part of his parents' act, *The Three Keatons*. The act resulted in accusations of child abuse against Buster's parents because the plot involved young Buster goading his father, who then threw him against the scenery, into the orchestra pit, and sometimes even into the audience. Buster always denied any abuse, saying he was trained to take trick falls safely. His parents also ran afoul of the law with child labor violations.

Later Buster gained fame as a silent film comic actor and a filmmaker. His comedy included a deadpan expression that earned him a second nickname of The Great Stone Face. His most popular films were *The General, Sherlock Jr., The Navigator, It's a Mad Mad Mad Mad World,* and *Our Hospitality.*

After vaudeville and silent films, Buster turned to talking movies. He wrote, produced, acted, and directed films. MGM bought out Keaton's filmmaking unit in 1928, and Keaton found his subsequent work too regimented and restrictive. He had successful TV series, *The Buster Keaton Show* (1950) and *Life with Buster Keaton* (1951). Keaton cancelled his own show because he could not keep up with the demand of producing a new show each week.

At age fifty-five, Keaton appeared on the Ed Wynn Variety Show and recreated one of his vaudeville stunts that required him to prop one foot on a table, swing his other foot next to it and hold that impossible position in midair for a moment before he crashed to the floor. When asked by TV host Garry Moore how he did those falls, he opened his jacket and revealed the bruises. Buster died on February 1, 1966.

<<>>

David Cornell Leestma, astronaut and retired Captain in the United States Navy, was born May 6, 1949, in Muskegon. He graduated first in his class from the U.S. Naval Academy in 1971. NASA selected him to become an astronaut in 1980, and he became the first member of NASA Astronaut Group 9 to go into space.

<<>>

Harry Morgan, born Harry Bratsberg, enjoyed a TV and film career that lasted six decades. His major roles included Pete Porter in both *December Bride* and *Pete and Gladys*, Officer Bill Gannon on *Dragnet*, Amos Coogan on *Hec Ramsey*, and Colonel Sherman T. Potter in *M*A*S*H*. Morgan's credits include more than 100 films. He was raised in Muskegon. In 1933 he graduated from Muskegon High School where he was a statewide debating champion.

<<>>

Earl Edwin Morrall was born May 17, 1934, in Muskegon. He quarterbacked in the National Football League for 21 seasons. He is most remembered for helping the Miami Dolphins win Super Bowl VII. Morrall began his football career at Muskegon High School where he led the team to a state football championship in 1951. He attended college at Michigan State University and played under head coaches Biggie Munn and Duffy Daugherty.

<<>>

Donald Arvid Nelson was born on May 15, 1940, in Muskegon. He first learned basketball shooting in the chicken yard where a spokeless bicycle wheel was nailed to the shed as the hoop. From that humble beginning, he went on to become a professional basketball player and head coach. He had the most regular season wins of any coach in NBA history with 1,335 victories to his credit. He coached the Milwaukee Bucks, the New York Knicks, the Dallas Mavericks, and the Golden State Warriors after completing an All-American career at the University of Iowa.

<<>>

James Newell Osterberg Jr. better known as **Iggy Pop**, was born on April 21, 1947, in Muskegon. Pop was a musician, singer, songwriter, record producer, and actor. He was known as the Godfather of Punk for his primitive raw style of rock and roll.

<<>>

Vonda Kay Van Dyke was born on May 19, 1943, in Muskegon. In 1964 she was crowned the 1965 Miss America. She was the only Miss America who was also Miss Congeniality.

<<>>

Richard Lee Versalle, an operatic tenor, was born on December 3, 1932, in Muskegon. He served in the U.S. Navy, then went into business while studying singing. He made his operatic stage debut when he was 45 years old. He sang Augustin Moser in *Die Meistersinger von Nürnberg* at Chicago Lyric Opera.

Jonathan Walker was known as the man with the branded hand. Walker is Michigan's most famous abolitionist. As a young man, Walker was a fifth-generation sea captain from Massachusetts. Early in his life, he swore to work toward ending slavery, a practice he described as an abomination. His goal was not unpopular in Massachusetts, but decidedly less acceptable when he moved his family to Florida in the 1840s to gain work on the railroad. In Florida his neighbors quickly pegged him as a slave sympathizer.

In 1844 Walker attempted to assist the escape of seven runaway slaves to the British West Indies in an open boat. Along the way, Walker became violently ill and unable to captain the ship. The crew of slaves knew nothing about sailing, and it is likely all aboard would have drowned if they had not been rescued by a sloop that took them to Key West.

The rescue was not all good news, however, because Walker was sent to Pensacola where he was put in prison and chained to the floor. He was tried, convicted, fined, and put on a pillory. His ill-fated mission also earned him the brand "SS" on his hand. The Double S, ordered by the United States government, stood for Slave Stealer.

At least one blacksmith refused to make the branding iron, saying brands were for animals. But another less principled smithy made the tool, and a United States Marshall inflicted the burning iron to Walker's hand. Those nearby heard the sizzling flesh. After being branded, Walker was returned to jail where he served eleven months before northern abolitionists paid his fine and secured his freedom.

1848 Engraving of Jonathan Walker. Public Domain.

In 1850 after his release, Walker moved to Michigan and lived near Muskegon until his death on May 1, 1878. He was seventy-eight years old. Poet and fellow abolitionist, John Greenleaf Whittier, paid tribute to Walker in his poem, "The Branded Hand." The poem became a rallying cry for those advocating the end of slavery. A monument to Walker's memory was erected on his grave and dedicated on August 1, 1878.

• BOOKS WITH TIES TO MUSKEGON

Norma Lewis and Christine Nyholm, **Muskegon (Images of America)**. Liberally illustrated, this is a history of the city that claims it built Chicago.

<<>>

Alvin F. Oickle, **The Man with the Branded Hand: The Life of Jonathan Walker, Abolitionist** (2011). Captured in 1844 while attempting to smuggle slaves to freedom, Walker was tried, convicted, and the only man ever branded in a courtroom by a United States marshal. (See the Famous or Infamous with Ties to Muskegon.)

• GHOST STORIES

Ghosts of the Frauenthal Theater. Visitors, performers, and staff at the theater have reported being followed around by a small apparition in black clothing. Visitors to the theater insist there is no way they would feel safe in the theater alone at night—that a heavy presence seemed to be nearby.

22. GRAND HAVEN
INCLUDING FERRYSBURG AND WEST OLIVE

Grand Haven boasted a 2020 population of 11,354. *Coastal Living* named Grand Haven "The Happiest Town in America." Count for yourself the many reasons.

Historically, fur trading gave birth to Grand Haven or Gabagouache as it was then known. In the language of the Odawa, *Gabagouache* described the widening of the river and the slowing of the current as the flow reached Lake Michigan. In the early 1600s, the area was a major trade route for the Odawa as they took advantage of Michigan's largest river, the Grand, snaking its way into the interior of the state. For nearly two centuries, Gabagouache was economically dependent on pelts.

By the late 1700s, John Jacob Astor's American Fur Company operated twenty trading posts in Western Michigan, and Gabagouache was Astor's principal post with its existence confirmed back to at least 1809.

From 1809 to 1821, Astor's posts were managed by Madame Magdelaine La Framboise who was half-French and half-Odawa. When she retired to Mackinac Island, her job was turned over to Rix Robinson who is often credited with laying the foundation for settling Western Michigan. In later years, Robinson served as a Michigan State Senator.

In 1822 William Ferry, a Presbyterian minister, became the first permanent resident of the area, and appropriate to his profession, he built the first area church. Neighboring Ferrysburg is named in his honor.

In the early 1800s, white pine was crowned king, replacing the fur industry. Sawmills required a transportation system to get lumber to markets, and Grand Haven's strategic water vantage point met the need.

By 1834 Ferry and Robinson began developing the town. They formed the Grand Haven Company and platted and sold lots. Gabagouache became Grand Haven in 1835, taking its name from the fact that it provided a large safe haven for ships at the mouth of the Grand River. By 1837 the town had more than 200 residents.

By 1870 the population burgeoned to 6,000, and lumbering still supported the economy. Several sawmills, a shingle mill, and a sash and door factory were established in Grand Haven. In that year, the Grand Trunk Western Railroad constructed a depot along the waterfront. Today the depot is a fascinating museum.

The late 1800s gave a clue of what was to come. Grand Haven edged toward becoming a popular health resort, famous for its Magnetic Mineral Spring. Grand Haven did not suffer as much with the demise of the lumber industry as did her sister cities. She transformed into an active port renowned for sport fishing as well as a tourist hotspot. The Grand Haven Lighthouses were first built in 1839 on the south pier, marking the channel into the river. There are currently two lighthouses, each painted red. The outer light was built in 1875, and the inner light was built in 1905. They are connected by a lighted catwalk that runs along the pier to the shore. (See Lighthouses in this section for additional details.)

Grand Haven is home to the U. S. Coast Guard Station which coordinates all Lake Michigan Coast Guard activity. The Coast Guard came to Grand Haven in 1932, and its presence has been significant ever since.

It is an easy task for travelers to plan a busy itinerary that takes in local sites and activities. The problem will be budgeting time to hit everything you want to see or do. The choices are varied. You can explore the river bayous by canoe or kayak. You can walk Grand Haven's scenic 2½ mile boardwalk, or you can rent a bicycle and peddle your way around miles of beautiful countryside. And those are just for starters.

Expect to fall in love with Grand Haven and the smaller Ferrysburg. When they lay claim to your heart, you will find yourself filled with the desire to make repeat visits.

Gallery Uptown, 201 Washington Avenue. This gallery claims it is the oldest artist-operated gallery in the state. Award-winning local artists exhibit their work here, and each month, a themed show features new works by gallery members and invited guests. You will find paintings, drawings, mixed-media, reproductions, wearable art, jewelry, pottery, wood, glass, and limited edition works by local artists.

<<>>

Carlyn and Company Gallery, 205 Washington Avenue. Handcrafted work from many artists. Carlyn Gallery opened in 1989, specializing in fine arts and crafts. After nearly two decades, the gallery added sustainable products. The building was returned to its original style through a recycling restoration and reopened as Carlyn and Company. Throughout the years, Carlyn and Company has been a home for approximately 80 local artists to sell their handmade goods to the public. You will find handcrafted jewelry, accessories, and art for the home.

<<>>

Tri-Cities Historical Museum, 1 North Harbor Drive, downtown Grand Haven on the lakeshore. Follow the history of Grand Haven from the Native Americans to the pioneers, including the lumberjacks and the French voyageurs. The lifestyle of each era is revealed through exhibits showcasing period rooms, medicine, agriculture, lumbering methods, maritime history, and tourism. The museum is a portal to the history of Northwest Ottawa County. Located in two separate buildings, each with historic ties to the area, the museum has continued to grow since it was started back in 1959. In 1972 the museum only occupied the former Grand Trunk Railroad Depot which was built in 1870.

While at that location, take time to check out the train outside near the museum. The Steam Engine #1223 of the Pere Marquette Railroad with the locomotive tender, a boxcar, two cabooses, and a concrete coaling tower are on display. Storyboards accompany each railroad car. This remains the lakeside location where there is a new Maritime Gallery with wonderful ship models.

The Depot/Lake location simply outgrew its space, and in July 2004, the doors to a second site opened: **The Akeley Building Museum**, constructed in 1871, located at 200 Washington. Both locations display artifacts from the life and times of the people, places, and events that shaped this area. If you want to expand on the short history included at the beginning of this Grand Haven section, you only have to stop at these museum locations. Temporary exhibits change from time to time. Don't forget to check the museum gift shop. It has great collectibles, toys, books, and gifts.

● BEACHES, PARKS, AND TRAILS

Escanaba Park. Within Lighthouse Connector Park along Harbor Drive. This paved walkway from downtown to the beach and lighthouse lets you watch the boats travel on the channel, or you may choose to sit on the grass and people watch.

<<>>

Grand Haven Skate Park, located in Mulligan's Hollow next to Imagination Station off Harbor Drive. Ramps include both a large and small halfpipe, 16-foot by 16-foot flat-top pyramid, grind-rails, and G-ramps. There is a full-sized bowl, hubba box, two five-stair rails, and one seven-stair rail. The cement park has 13,000 square feet of space for bikes, blades, and boards. The bonus is the view of Lake Michigan.

<<>>

219

Grand Haven State Park, 1001 South Harbor Drive. Located a half mile from downtown, this beautiful 48-acre park features the wide sandy shore of Lake Michigan along the west side of the park and the Grand River along the north side. Playground, paved seasonal camping sites, and views of Lake Michigan and the Grand Haven pier. An easy walk to downtown.

<<>>

Lakeshore Trail, 14035 Lakeshore Road. In-line skating, skateboarding, bicycling, or walking. Benches along the way. The Lakeshore Trail is Ottawa County's showpiece, a 20-mile paved pedestrian path running parallel to Lakeshore Drive. It follows rolling dunes and provides many recreational opportunities along the way. With famous state parks at either end, the trail meanders through three Ottawa County beach parks and natural areas: Rosy Mound Natural Area, Kirk Park, and Tunnel Park.

<<>>

Hemlock Crossing & Pine Bend Park, 8115 West Olive Road, West Olive. 239 acres of woods and wetlands along the Pigeon River. More than six miles of trails for hiking and cross-country skiing meander through bottomland and upland forest, old pine stands, and along the river. Scenic overlooks add to your experience. You can rent a kayak or canoe. In the winter you can rent snowshoes. Facilities include two small picnic shelters, a kayak/canoe launch, and the Nature Education Center. During warm weather modern restrooms are available. In the winter, there are pit toilets.

<<>>

Imagination Station, Mulligan's Hollow (Mulligan Drive off Sherman). The old Imagination Station has been replaced by a new playground created and designed by area children and constructed by the community.

<<>>

Kirk Park, 9781 North Lakeshore Drive North (15 miles north of Holland State Park in West Olive). Known for its forested beauty and sandy beaches, this park has a swimming beach, picnic tables, grills, playground, scenic Lake Michigan views, hiking, ungroomed cross country ski trails, horseshoe pit, modern restrooms (seasonal), and parking lot. Best of all, 2,000 feet of sandy beach and scenic dune overlooks. Off-leash dog area.

<<>>

Kitchel-Lindquist-Hartner Dunes Preserve, 20001 Berwyck Street, offers four trails to explore and different types of vegetation and wildlife. Mostly undeveloped. One trail runs along the location of the early city of Grand Haven.

<<>>

Linear Park, Jackson to Third Street (left on Harbor Island). Great walking and jogging park with views of the channel and boat activity. Linear Park contains a paved non-motorized path 250 feet in length along the Grand River South Channel. Facilities include a trailhead with a paved parking lot, fishing decks, and a small picnic shelter. Located adjacent to the Grand Haven Board of Light and Power, it provides an environmental buffer between the coal yard and the Grand River. Additional amenities include a picnic shelter, benches, fishing decks, and a connection to the Grand Haven Waterfront Trail.

<<>>

Pigeon Creek Park, 12524 Stanton Street, West Olive. Trails wind through more than 400 acres of rolling, forested land surrounding Pigeon Creek. It is a great place for cross-country skiing with a warming lodge and ski rentals. For joggers, there is a 4-K lighted trail. Also, equestrian trail, picnic tables, and grills.

<<>>

Rosy Mound County Park, 13925 Lakeshore Drive, on the Lake Michigan shoreline just south of Grand Haven. This is a natural area that encompasses an example of the Great Lakes dune system with its beach, foredunes, and dunes. Boardwalk and an out-and-back hiking trail. The stairway over the dunes will lead you to views that make the effort worth it. The park is open year-round, and the views remain as awesome with a blanket of white shrouding them.

Grand Haven Beach. Courtesy of Bob Royce.

<<>>

Grand Haven Municipal Marina. 101 North Harbor Drive. Amenities include 57 transient slips, electricity, water, ice, restrooms, and showers.

<<>>

Grand Haven also offers wineries, chocolate makers, fishing charters, tours, and a variety of sport equipment rentals.

● OTHER STOPS TO CONSIDER

Bicycle Rides. There are over 100 miles of bike paths throughout Northwest Ottawa County. Popular paths and trails run along Lake Michigan's shoreline on

Lakeshore Drive between Grand Haven and Holland, circling Spring Lake, and along the Grand River to Eastmanville. Maps are available at the Chamber of Commerce.

<<>>

Farmers Market, 300 North Harbor Drive, downtown under the bright blue canopy near Chinook Pier. Saturdays and Wednesdays, 8:00 a.m. to 1:00 p.m., seasonal. Garden fresh produce, flowers, herbs, honey, and more.

<<>>

Lynne Sherwood Waterfront Stadium, on the Waterfront Boardwalk, hosts many summer activities including the Musical Fountain, big band dances, worship services, Anchorage Cup Sail Races, Powerboat Runs, Trawlerfest, and Coast Guard Festival activities.

<<>>

World's Largest Musical Fountain, at Washington and Harbor. A synchronized display of water and lights on the harbor. Every summer evening at dusk you can enjoy these dancing waters. Special performances on Fridays and Saturdays during Tulip Time and in September. It is one of the *musts* when visiting Grand Haven.

<<>>

Ride the Harbor Trolley, catch it at the Chinook Pier. Offers transportation services between the Tri-Cities of Spring Lake, Grand Haven, and Ferrysburg. Harbor Transit started in 1975 and has grown from a small Dial-A-Ride service into a public transit authority that remains dedicated to exceptional, convenient community transportation. You will get a narrated tour of the area. Operates seven days a week from Memorial Day weekend to Labor Day. Restrictions applied during COVID-19.

<<>>

Stroll the Waterfront Boardwalk, 2½ miles of the Grand Haven Harbor starting with the shops at Chinook Pier.

You pass restaurants, marinas, charter fishing boats, and parks and end at the lighthouses on the pier. The Boardwalk intersects with downtown shops and restaurants. Great place to jog or maybe meander along holding hands with someone special. No matter how you do it, the views will be worth every minute you spend.

Coast Guard Memorial with Coast Guard Building in Background.
Courtesy of Bob Royce.

• LIGHTHOUSES

Grand Haven South Pierhead Inner Light and the Grand Haven South Pierhead Entrance Light, 1001 South Harbor Drive. The two lights share a common history. Established in 1839 on the south pier where the Grand River enters Lake Michigan, both are painted red and connected by a lighted catwalk that makes them accessible to each other, to the shore, and the Grand Haven Boardwalk.

The inner light is cylindrical, and the fog house outer light stands on a huge concrete foundation. These are among the most photographed lighthouses on the Great

Lakes. The pier boardwalk is the place for strolls, perfect sunsets, and photo opportunities.

The lighthouses were offered for sale in 2009 under the National Historic Lighthouse Preservation Act. The City of Grand Haven now owns the pier and lights, but they are maintained by the Army Corps of Engineers.

Grand Haven Pier Lights. Courtesy of Bob Royce.

● SHIPWRECKS

The ***Milwaukee***'s captain, Robert McKay, recklessly ignored the second chance that luck graciously dealt him. The price tag for his ingratitude was his life. Fifty-two additional crew members went down with him. The man responsible for the foolhardy decisions of that dreadful night was alternately called a madman or dubbed "Heavy Weather McKay." On October 22, 1929, he guided his 383-foot, railroad car ferry *Milwaukee* into the safety of the harbor for which she was named.

Rarely had a seasick crew been more relieved to step foot on solid ground than the men who had their queasy stomachs turned upside-down and knotted inside-out by a bullying storm. Bruising north winds had tried to take them under with every wave that washed over the deck on their way to port. But the crew emerged victorious.

Once they tied up in the harbor, the nauseated men, like the troopers they were, began pulling boxcars ashore. When the task was finished, twenty-five additional cars bound for the Grand Trunk Western's rail station at Grand Haven stood waiting to be loaded onto the ferry for the return trip. The men again set directly to the task. Time was money and car ferries never squandered either. However, as the crew reloaded the *Milwaukee,* they must have considered the worsening weather, and hoped McKay would postpone the return trip long enough to let the storm abate. They knew better than to bet their paychecks on it. The Grand Trunk Western Railroad did not like to see their ships idle, storm or no storm, and this storm would be remembered as one of the worst to ever hit Lake Michigan.

With the final eastbound railcar loaded and in position, Captain McKay, to no one's real surprise, announced his decision to depart immediately. Barely out of the harbor, the ferry was rocking and rolling. The captain of the lightship three miles from Milwaukee watched the ship bouncing east until the rain and spray enveloped her and then erased her from sight.

A second Grand Trunk Ferry departed Milwaukee four hours after Captain McKay. It reached the dock in Grand Haven on the morning of October 23, having staggered into harbor after a fifteen-hour battle with the killer storm. It had taken nine hours longer than usual to cross. The crew of the second ferry was surprised to learn McKay's *Milwaukee* had not arrived before them. Everyone hoped she had been forced to abandon her normal course and sought shelter or turned north hoping for an easier trip.

The morning of October 24, Michigan and Wisconsin Coast Guard stations were alerted that the *Milwaukee* was long overdue. Debris was spotted floating in the water near Racine, Wisconsin, but it could not be definitively identified as wreckage from the missing *Milwaukee*.

On the morning of October 25, two bodies floated off Kenosha, Wisconsin, both wearing lifejackets from the *Milwaukee*. Bodies continued to roll in. The next day, a lifeboat was found, but the four crewmen inside were dead of hypothermia. A second lifeboat was found later in the day, but its canvas cover was still lashed in place, and no one was aboard. It was obvious the *Milwaukee* was lost.

Grand Haven was home to thirty of the ferry's crew and the little community was devastated. Earlier that fall, on September 11, the *Andaste* had gone down in a storm while making its Grand Haven to Chicago run with a load of gravel. Thirteen of the twenty-five crewmembers who disappeared with the *Andaste* were also from Grand Haven.

Several days after the first bodies were found, a surfman at the South Haven station discovered the *Milwaukee*'s message case floating along the shore. Inside was a note signed by the ship's purser: "*S.S. Milwaukee*, October 22, '29, 8:30 p.m. This ship is taking water fast. We have turned around and headed for Milwaukee. Pumps are working, but sea gate is bent in and can't keep the water out. Flicker is flooded. Seas are tremendous. Things look bad. Crew roll is about the same as on the last pay day."

The note explained much of the mystery concerning the sinking of the *Milwaukee*. If the sea gate was damaged, there was nothing to stop water from flooding onto the main deck. The sea gate is a heavy steel gate that is dropped into place to close off the end of the main deck after the cargo of rail cars has been loaded. Without a functional sea gate, water would eventually fill the entire ship. Later investigation concluded that the sea gate may have broken when Captain McKay attempted to turn the ship around, perhaps causing one of the rail cars to come loose and crash into the gate. The flicker referenced the crews' quarters that were located below the main deck near the stern of the ship. The purser mentioned the crew roll so the ship's owners would know who had been aboard.

Later, a second note, sealed in a bottle, washed ashore. "This is the worst storm I have ever seen. Can't stay up much longer. Hole in the side of the boat." It was signed McKay. The note may have been a macabre joke. No one would ever know if there was a hole in the side of the *Milwaukee*, but it seems that if true, the purser's entry would have mentioned it. It was suspected that the note was fake.

<<>>

The **Ironsides** was a very sturdy vessel built in 1864 to haul iron ore on Lake Superior during the Civil War. She had twin engines, and her 231-foot length was braced by dual *hogging* arches on her sides. The demand for ore declined after the Civil War, and she was converted to use as a freight and passenger vessel. On September 15, 1873, she was carrying a general freight cargo when she foundered off Grand Haven in about 120 feet of water. Today, divers visit the ship's final resting place. This can be a challenging dive because of depth, limited visibility, and accumulated fishing tackle. The wreck has begun to settle and collapse into the sand. Still, the engines and some of the hull provide an interesting dive for qualified divers.

<<>>

The **West Michigan Underwater Preserve**. (See Shipwrecks under Montague in this guide.)

Howard L. Bailey was born on July 31, 1957, in Grand Haven, Michigan. He played college ball at Grand Valley State University and three seasons of major league baseball, pitching for Detroit Tigers.

<<>>

Cornelius "Neal" Ball was born on April 22, 1881, in Grand Haven. He played major league baseball for the New York Highlanders, Cleveland Naps, and Boston Red Sox. He was mainly a shortstop but also played second base, third base, and outfield. He is most remembered for his July 19, 1909, unassisted triple play.

<<>>

Garrett Clark Borns was born on January 7, 1992, in Grand Haven. He attended Grand Haven schools. He became an American singer, songwriter, and classical pianist. He modified his name for the stage to BØRNS. While still in high school, he performed with a cover band known as "Brown Chicken Brown Trout" which performed at the Grand Haven Waterfront Film Festival in 2010.

<<>>

Daniel Brian Bylsma was born on September 18, 1970, in Grand Haven. He played professional ice hockey and coached for the Detroit Red Wings.

<<>>

Madame Magdelaine (Marcotte) La Framboise, a descendent of celebrated Odawa Chief, Returning Cloud, was born in Northern Lower Michigan about 1780. La Framboise and her husband, Joseph, managed John Jacob Astor's fur interests on the west side of Michigan, and after Joseph was murdered in 1809, Magdelaine continued to operate the business until she retired to

Mackinac Island in 1821. (For more information about Magdelaine La Framboise, see listing under Mackinac Island in Book Two, *Exploring Michigan's Upper Peninsula Coasts*, and the historical novel, *Ardent Spirit*, by J.K. Royce.)

• BOOKS AND MOVIES WITH TIES TO GRAND HAVEN

Wallace K. Ewing, and Elizabeth Dobbie for the Tri-Cities Museum, **Grand Haven (Then and Now)**, Illustrated. As fur trading in Michigan came to an end, pioneers migrated to Grand Haven for lumber. By the time the last acre of trees was harvested, Grand Haven had shifted from dependence on lumber to manufacturing and tourism. The images illustrating this book show the foundations upon which the community was built and changes wrought through the years.

<<>>

Wallace Ewing and David Seibold, **Grand Haven Area: 1860-1960**, another of Ewing's attempts to share Grand Haven history.

<<>>

J. K. Royce, **Ardent Spirit**. This is a fictionalized biography of the life of Magdelaine La Framboise, the Odawa-French fur trader. (See The Famous or Infamous with Ties to Grand Haven.) La Framboise was inducted into the Michigan Women's Hall of Fame for her contributions to business. Royce creates a novel as historically accurate as possible from the records available. The resultant story offers a peek into the history of Mackinac Island, the Lake Michigan shoreline, the fur trade, and the life of one remarkable woman.

Brother Jim Boynton, who served summers at Ste. Anne's Church on Mackinac Island when the author researched there, read the novel and tracked down Royce to share his opinion, "You did an excellent job and really captured how I imagine Magdelaine's life to be . . . her thoughts and interactions."

• GHOST STORIES

Haunting of the Kirby House. The popular Grand Haven restaurant sits on property originally believed owned by Reverend William Ferry who built a church on Mackinac Island, and who also is well known in Grand Haven and Ferrysburg. Accounts say Ferry's dwelling was the first permanent home built in Grand Haven. In 1866 the Ferry residence burned to the ground. The Kirby Hotel was constructed on the site seven years later. From then on, the property has been reinvented as several hotels and restaurants. Currently, a well-known eatery in the area, the Kirby House's employees report many other-worldly experiences—apparitions, voices, things moving about. They attribute the strange happenings to a ghost they lovingly call Emily.

A second story involves another employee seeing a young child playing on the second floor when the building was closed.

A third unnerving tale comes from the time when the upstairs was undergoing renovation. Construction workers claim they saw the shadowy silhouette of a tall thin man wearing a long coat and a wide-brimmed hat. When the specter looked directly at them, the workers were horrified to see the spirit's beaming red eyes.

<<>>

The Blue Man. Sightings are reported of an apparition described as a blue man at the top of Ferry Hill in the Lake Forest Cemetery. This is the special, old section of the cemetery where the city's founding fathers, including William Ferry, are buried. Winding stairs provide access to the plots of some of the most prominent families of

Grand Haven's and Ferrysburg's past. The Blue Man is speculated to be William Montague Ferry who was born in 1796. William became a Presbyterian minister and moved with his wife to Mackinac Island where they were missionaries before moving to Grand Haven in 1834 where he planned to pursue his future and fortune in the heavily wooded Grand Haven area. The cities of Ferrysburg, Montague, and Whitehall were either named for him or members of his family, or have streets, buildings, or other references to him. Ferry died on December 30, 1867, leaving an estate worth more than $100,000, a huge sum of money in those days. The inscription on his tombstone reads, "First toil, then rest; First grace, then glory." But there is a chance he is not resting well. Maybe on some clear night, with the moon illuminating the way, a hazy blue figure will appear and clarify the mystery that surrounds William Montague Ferry.

23. HOLLAND

Holland had a 2020 population of 33,137. In September 1846, a group of 60 Dutch immigrants cast their fate to the steerage section of the sailing brig *Southerner* and headed for New York, their first port of call in America. Their leader, Reverend Albertus C. Van Raalte, who was bringing his wife and five children to a strange new place, prayed he was taking them to religious freedom and a land of opportunity.

The Van Raaltes made their way from New York to Detroit. Albertus then went on alone to search for the perfect place to settle his loved ones and start his Dutch Colony in the new world. He was convinced he had found it at the mouth of the Black River which flowed into Black Lake and into beautiful Lake Michigan.

Within six months, the colony had grown to nearly 800, all of whom initially agreed with Van Raalte that he had made the perfect choice for their settlement. The first summer changed the minds of many of the immigrants when the undrained swamps of the area produced illness, death, and despair. Housing and food were in short supply. Some believed Van Raalte had brought them to this strange new country to die. Van Raalte ministered to his colony providing them with daily doses of quinine and other medicinal concoctions. Somehow most survived.

Changing the fortune of the little group and aiding in their survival was the beautiful, warm fall and mild winter of 1847. By spring the immigrants were able to begin building—and build they did. By 1852 in addition to their cabins, they had a tannery, a tailor, two hotels, eight stores including a jewelry store, a blacksmith shop, and machine shops.

The New Hollanders next turned their attention to two projects that demonstrate their foresightedness. They needed a channel to connect them to Lake Michigan so they could transport goods. They sought government assistance for the project, but when it was not forthcoming, they dug it by hand.

The next project they tackled was manually constructing the River Avenue Bridge. Their strong Dutch work ethic and ingenuity became the cornerstone of the city's success.

The first Holland Harbor Lighthouse was built in 1872. It is nicknamed Big Red. (See Lighthouse in this section.)

In 1932 the First State Bank of Holland was robbed by Depression-era gangsters. It is believed Edward Wilhelm Bentz orchestrated the heist, but he was never arrested. (See The Famous or Infamous with Ties to Holland.)

Today the greater Holland area is a thriving, award-winning community, home to hundreds of businesses, 1,500 acres of park, Lake Macatawa, and many local attractions and events to tempt travelers. You'll find much more than windmills and wooden shoes.

Holland's galleries offer something for every art lover's or collector's taste. There are autumn and winter gallery walks. Holland has heated sidewalks to make winter shopping easier. Because of the deep religious influence in Holland, you will find more restaurants and businesses closed on Sundays than in other coastal towns.

Repairing Holland's heated streets. Courtesy of Bob Royce.

• MUSEUMS

Cappon House. Courtesy of Pixabay Free Images.

Cappon House, 228 West 9th Street at Washington Avenue, **and Settlers House**, at 190 West 9th Street. Cappon House was the nineteenth-century Victorian home of immigrant Isaac Cappon who became Holland's first mayor. Cappon built this

Italianate home for his family of sixteen children. The dwelling is filled with authentic period furniture, exquisite woodwork and fixtures, and a gallery of family photographs.

The Settlers House, built by Thomas Morrissey, a ship's captain and a carpenter of Irish Canadian descent, was built in 1867. The tiny one-room cottage eventually became home not only to Morrissey and his wife, but to five children. The dwelling is furnished with local objects from the area's settlement period of 1845-1880 and items from the Holland Museum's collection. It is a good representation of how a working-class family lived.

A Visitor Center in the Cappon barn is the starting point for touring both the Cappon and nearby Settlers houses.

<<>>

Carolyn Stitch Studio, 29 West 8th Street, is one of many downtown galleries you can check out. This one has whimsical art, cards, and gifts.

<<>>

Holland Museum, 31 West 10th Street at River Avenue adjacent to Centennial Park. Holland's history and heritage, from founding by Dutch immigrants through today's vibrant city, lives again through 400,000 artifacts, special exhibits, and permanent galleries that include Dutch art. The Cappon House and Settlers House are part of the museum. (See Cappon and Settlers House under Museums.) The Spark!Labs exhibit permits children and families to create, collaborate, test, experiment, problem solve, and explore the invention process. Admission to Spark!Lab is included with your ticket price. The number of visitors was limited during COVID-19.

<<>>

Kruizenga Art Museum, 271 Columbia Avenue. Hope College art museum that focuses on education but also strives to appeal to the broader public with exhibits that challenge innovation and thinking.

<<>>

Lake Effect Gallery, 16 West 8th Street. Gallery and studio displaying the art of about 22 local artists with a selection of local scenes. Wearable art, sculpture, glass, metal, and jewelry. The Gallery features an ever-changing collection of West Michigan Lake Shore artists' work, both original and custom prints. Lake Effect Gallery is a place to peruse affordable, friendly art for the home and work environment.

<<>>

Holland Civic Theatre, 50 West 9th Street. A small, intimate venue that presents community theater. Easily confused with the Holland Civic Center Place which is a much larger and more varied venue. (See Holland Civic Center Place below.)

<<>>

Holland Civic Center Place, Symphony Orchestra, 150 East 8th Street. Hosts sporting events, films, concerts, and other events. (Don't confuse with the listing above.)

• BEACHES, PARKS, AND TRAILS

Centennial Park, River Avenue between 10th and 12th Streets. Small but lovely Victorian City Park with fountains, flowers, mature trees, benches, and a gazebo. Historical markers: one recounts the founding of Holland. Summer concerts are held in this park.

<<>>

DeGraaf Nature Center, 600 Graffschap Road. Open year-round. Has weekly events and provides you with an opportunity to enjoy woodlands, shrubs, marshes, and trails. There is an interpretive center. Nice place for hiking and cross-country skiing.

<<>>

Holland State Park, 2215 Ottawa Beach Road. Beautiful sandy beach and a popular place to view the local lighthouse, Big Red. (See Lighthouse for related story and see photo by Gary Martin on front cover.) Two large campgrounds, picnic areas, a playground, beach house, boat launch, and concession stands. One of Lake Michigan's most popular parks.

<<>>

Kollen Park, 240 Kollen Park Boulevard, west end of 10th Street at Van Raalte Avenue, close to downtown on the shores of Lake Macatawa. Beautiful shade trees and benches along Heinz Waterfront Walkway create a pleasant place to watch the summer activity. Playground, restrooms, grills, and picnic tables.

<<>>

Lake Macatawa Beach and Park, East of Holland State Park on Lake Macatawa. Swimming and hiking, 211 camping sites, and a boat launch available to campers.

<<>>

Laketown Beach, 6710 142nd Avenue. A smallish and rustic, but imminently swimmable beach. Limited parking. May be less crowded than the state parks. A dune stairway provides access to the water. It is quite a hike, but if you aren't opposed to exercise, you may find this is a hidden gem.

<<>>

Matt Urban Park, 270 East 32nd Street. A 23-acre sports complex where soccer and baseball are played. Includes four lighted ball diamonds, a lighted soccer field, two lighted basketball courts, picnic grounds, two playgrounds, and public restrooms.

<<>>

Mount Pisgah, 2238 3rd Avenue, off Ottawa Beach Road. Climb the towering dune east of the Holland State Park. It rises 157 feet above Lake Michigan and is accessible by a boardwalk and stair system. Your reward for this strenuous climb is unforgettable views of Lake Macatawa, Big Red, and of course, the great lake. Benches let you pace yourself. Parking is limited.

<<>>

Oak Grove Campground and Resort, 2011 Ottawa Beach Road. Family resort located within walking distance of Lake Macatawa and Lake Michigan beaches. Close to fishing, boating, golfing, and miles of paved bike trails. Beachside bike rentals where you can rent tandems, 21-speeds, single-speeds, kid's bikes, baby seats, and burley carts. Extras: heated swimming pool, whirlpool, game room, basketball, playground, and high-speed internet. Seasonal.

<<>>

Sanctuary Woods Preserve, 4750 66th Street at the west end of 32nd Street. Hiking through wooded dunes and trails. You can take your dog. Has dune stairs and lovely views of both Lake Michigan and Lake Macatawa.

<<>>

Smallenburg Park, Fairbanks Avenue at 14th Street. Playground, picnic facilities, and skateboarding. Offers ice-skating in the winter.

<<>>

Tunnel Park, 66 North Lakeshore Drive, two miles north of Holland State Park. A 22-acre park along the shoreline of Lake Michigan. The park earned its name because it creates a unique tunnel through the dunes. There is a dune stairway to Lake Michigan. This is a park you'll enjoy for swimming, sunbathing, children's playground, and picnicking.

<<>>

Van Raalte Farm Park, 24th Street, one mile east of US 31 (16th Street). City park with picnicking and hiking during the warm months and cross-country skiing and sledding down the lighted hill during the winter.

Benjamin Van Raalte, son of Holland's founder, built the home that still stands in the center of this park.

<<>>

Windmill Island Gardens, 1 Lincoln Avenue. Flowers. Flowers. And more flowers. A profusion of color and beauty awaits you. The canals and landscaping take you on a mental excursion to Amsterdam. An authentic Dutch windmill, the only one operating in the United States, grinds locally-grown wheat into flour that you can purchase in the gift shop. From the 250-year-old windmill's fourth floor deck, you can survey 36 acres of canals, dikes, and manicured gardens. There are costumed guides, a street organ, a hand-painted Dutch carousel, a playground, picnic areas, horses in the pasture, and a gift shop.

<<>>

Window on the Waterfront, 50 Columbia Avenue (at 6th Street). Charming 30-acre park with a paved trail that winds along the Macatawa River, perfect for walking or biking. Wildlife can be spotted from several observation points. A favorite place to bird-watch. Park amenities include walking and biking paths, viewing decks, boardwalks, athletic field, over 100,000 tulip bulbs in beds, and in the winter, an ice-skating rink.

<<>>

Winstrom Park, 1774 Perry Street at 160th Avenue. Frisbee golf, tennis courts, basketball court, playground, soccer fields, baseball diamonds, pet-friendly.

<<>>

You can also find paddleboat rides on Lake Macatawa, dinner cruises, and kayak and canoe rentals.

● OTHER STOPS TO CONSIDER

First National Bank of Michigan, corner of 1 West 8th Street and Central Avenue. This isn't a tourist site, but if you are walking 8th Street, enjoying the shops and

239

restaurants or you are in need of banking services, you might consider the building's most unforgettable day.

The dignified-looking structure has housed banking operations for more than a century. It opened as First State Bank in August 1916, changed names and ownership several times over the years, and became First National Bank of Holland in 2018.

But it is a day nearly a century ago that provided the most remembered and written-about morning in the bank's history. The stock market had crashed on October 29, 1929, and in its rubble, bank robbery became big business. Machine Gun Kelly, John Dillinger, Pretty Boy Floyd, and Baby Face Nelson captured the nation's collective imagination and became household topics of conversation.

On Thursday, September 29, 1932, a few minutes after Holland's First State Bank opened, armed robbers with guns drawn, burst through the doors. According to employees, five men entered, and two more stood watch outside. The crooks scooped up approximately $70,000—$26,000 in bonds and the remainder in currency—before fleeing through the back door. Police Chief Peter Lievense arrived before the robbers escaped. A gun battle ensued. Bullet holes riddled the Warm Friend Building at 5 West 8th Street. A plaque recounts the shootout that scars its west wall.

No evidence suggests any of the bandits were hit that day. They may have worn bulletproof vests. Chief Lievense took a bullet in the side. Butcher Peter De Jongh from Kuiper's Market in the Warm Friend Building was shot in the chest. Both men survived.

Warm Friend Plaque and bullet holes.
Courtesy of Bob Royce.

In spite of the harrowing heist, the bank reopened for business by noon that same day. No one was officially charged with the robbery, but law enforcement believed Edward Wilhelm Bentz was the perpetrator and brains behind the caper. J. Edgar Hoover called him, "the shrewdest, most resourceful, intelligent, and dangerous bank robber in existence."

During his career as a Depression-era outlaw, Bentz shunned the spotlight. even though he pulled heists with assistance from Harvey Bailey, Albert Bates, and the better-knowns, Kelley and Nelson. Bentz put his intelligence and the savvy he learned from an early life of petty crime to work for him. He spent hours in libraries where he studied the financial institutions he planned to hit. He knew the bank's assets and how much he could hope to get. He planned his escape routes in detail. He had the moxie or audacity to case the place by introducing himself as a possible investor or as a businessman thinking of opening an account. He was sometimes given a personal tour of the building layout.

Prison Mugshot of Eddie Bentz. Courtesy of Wikimedia Commons.

Bentz semi-retired after the Holland job. By his own admission, he'd pulled more than a hundred robberies. But he made the catastrophic mistake of listening to his friend Baby Face Nelson who was readying to get into the business and pull his first job. Nelson wanted Bentz to help plan and participate in a Grand Haven heist on the People's Savings Bank on August 18, 1933. The plan went seriously wrong. The getaway driver panicked and fled, stranding his partners. Still, all but Eddie Doyle escaped. For the first time in many years, Eddie Bentz was a wanted man.

Bank robberies had become so prevalent that in 1934 they were designated federal crimes, and federal investigators had jurisdiction to track down and arrest fugitives. Bentz was hunted and taken into custody by federal agents on March 13, 1936. It is reported that at his sentencing, he asked the judge to send him to Alcatraz because that's where all of his friends were. His request was granted. He was paroled from the Rock in 1948, but had charges pending in other states and served additional time in Massachusetts and Wisconsin. In 1967 he returned to his hometown of Tacoma, Washington, and died there of a heart attack in 1979. He was 85 years old.

<<>>

Historic Felt Mansion, 6597 138th Avenue. Beautiful grounds, rich history. Tours are available and free to seniors on Mondays. Built by Dorr Felt over the period between 1925 and 1928. Like many of us today, Felt was drawn to the beauty of Lake Michigan's coastline. Visitors can wander the grounds, see the Carriage House, the interior of the Mansion, and explore other farm buildings. (See the Ghost of Felt Mansion under Ghost Stories.)

<<>>

Holland Farmers Market, 150 West 8th Street, downtown Holland. More than 65 vendors provide every variety of fruit and vegetable grown in Michigan, plus flowers, honey, spices, cheese, and meats. Generally, the hours have been 8:00 a.m. to 2:00 p.m. Wednesdays and Saturdays. Seasonal, check to confirm.

<<>>

Nelis Dutch Village, 12350 James Street. Not a Disneyesque theme park, but rides, petting zoo, playscape, and other activities younger children will like. You may even be able to teach the little ones a bit of Dutch history. Restaurants, shops, a bit touristy, but you may find this a worthwhile stop.

<<>>

Outdoor Discovery Center, 4214 56th Street. Outdoor educational preserve that teaches through demonstration and interpretive exhibits. A 130-acre environment with approximately five miles of trails. Visitor Center and restrooms.

<<>>

Walking Tour of Holland's Statues, varied locations throughout the city.

- *Ben Franklin,* A wise-looking Ben sits on a park bench on River Street reading the Declaration of Independence. Mark Lundeen created the work.

Ben Franklin Statue. Courtesy of Bob Royce.

- *Contemplation,* a life-size bronze sculpture of the artist's sister sitting on a bench with a book. Artist: Billie Houtman Clark. 10th and College.
- *Grandpa's Workbench,* in the courtyard of Evergreen Commons, portrays a grandfather building stilts with his grandchildren. Sculptor: Gary Alsum. Located at the foot of River Avenue.
- *The Immigrants Statue,* at Lake Macatawa, captures immigrants arriving on the shores of Lake Macatawa. The statue was a gift of the Dutch Province of Drenthe, presented to Holland in 1997 to commemorate Holland's Sesquicentennial. The artist was Bert Kievit.

243

• *Joy of Music* is a group of five including three musicians and two singing children. It is located in Alpenrose Park. The sculptor was George Lundeen.

Joy of Music. Courtesy of Bob Royce.

• *Padnos Sculptures*, created from scrap metal with assistance from Stuart Padnos at Louis Padnos Iron and Metal Company. Padnos' sculpture of a Dutchman wearing wooden shoes and holding tulips is located at 7th and Lincoln. His other sculptures are located on Pine Avenue between 3rd Street and 7th Street.

• *Perro Del Sol V*, colorful steel work created by Hope College professor, Billy Mayer. River Avenue at 12th.

• *The Pledge of Allegiance*, a group of children honoring the flag. Artist: Glenda Goodacre. 8th and College.

• *The Protector* depicts a police officer dressed in a Holland Police Department uniform. He is holding the hand of a small girl. The statue was donated to the city and paid for through personal and corporate donations. Artist: Neil Brodin. 8th and Pine.

• *Queretaro Fountain.* Donated by Holland's sister city Queretaro, Mexico, in 1999 as a symbol of the friendship between the two cities. Located at 11th street near Kollen Park.

• *Secret Garden*, a life-size sculpture of two young girls sitting on a bench reading a book. Artist: Mark Lundeen. 10th and Central.

• *Statues of Hope College*, several statues on Hope Campus between College and Columbia from 9th to 13th Streets.

▪ *The Valentine*, located on the grounds of Freedom Village. Romantic statue portraying an older couple sharing a valentine. George Lundeen created the statue.

▪ *Water Lily*, a young girl sits on a stump holding a water lily from which water flows into the pool below. Artist: Rosalind Cook. 6th and Central.

▪ *Van Raalte Statue* was created by artist Mark Lundeen for the city's sesquicentennial in 1997. The statue of Reverend Albertus C. Van Raalte faces Hope College and Pillar Church, both founded by Van Raalte. 10th Street at Centennial Park.

<<>>

Lake Michigan Shore Wine Trail. West Michigan has quickly become a juggernaut in the wine world. The cool temperate climate and sandy clay soil suit the vineyards. Wineries flourish and there are at least 25 from which you are treated to an innovative collection of wines.

The countryside, from the Indiana border north to Holland and from the lakeshore east to the vineyards beyond Paw Paw, grows nearly 12,000 acres of grapes.

The wineries hold special events. You can sample wine before purchasing, taste local cuisine, and learn about pairing food and wine. Enjoy the adventure. Cheers!

<<>>

More to Do. The above suggestions of things to do are only a short list of what's available in Holland. You will find go-carts, miniature and regular golf, indoor ice-skating, wineries, breweries, shopping, history, and much more.

● LIGHTHOUSE

Holland Harbor Lighthouse (Big Red), 2215 Ottawa Beach Road. The lighthouse provides one of Michigan's most popular photo-op sites. Great views from the North Pier boardwalk, Holland State Park, and Mount Pisgah. Big Red is at the entrance to the channel connecting Lake

Michigan with Lake Macatawa. It is on the south side of the channel. Two modern lights mark the ends of the breakwaters that extend into Lake Michigan.

The United States Lighthouse Board was slow to respond to Holland's request for a channel from Lake Macatawa to Lake Michigan and a lighthouse for the safety of ships docking there. The frustrated citizens dug the channel themselves and after decades of unanswered requests, the lighthouse board finally recommended construction of the first light at Holland Harbor, and the request was approved by the U.S. Congress. In 1886 the harbor's first lifesaving station was established. The lighthouse was automated in 1932.

In 1970 the Coast Guard recommended abandonment of Big Red, but local citizens came to the rescue creating Holland's Harbor Lighthouse Historical Commission to preserve and restore the beloved landmark.

Public access to Big Red is limited because you must cross private property to reach it. (See photo of Big Red by Gary Martin on front cover.) Regarding this photo, Martin says,

> "That's my all-time favorite. There is one week in the spring and one in the fall when the sun rises and shines directly down the channel leading in to Lake Makatawa and reflects off the side of Big Red onto the sand. You have to have wet sand and just enough wave action to keep the sand wet to capture the reflected light as reflected in this photo. It took five years of going up to Big Red for the conditions to finally come together to capture the image that you see. There were a bunch of close but no cigar tries. and it was great when persistence finally paid off!"

• SHIPWRECKS

The **Andaste** disappeared beneath the roiled waters of Lake Michigan on September 9, 1929. Twenty-five men went to their deaths with her. The *Andaste* was not the most elegant ship to sail the lakes. She was a semi-whaleback, slope-sided, 266-foot-long steamship built in 1892 with a cargo capacity of 3,000 tons. She was made for function, not beauty.

The *Andaste* was captained by Albert L. Anderson of Sturgeon Bay, and on the day of her demise, she was docked in Ferrysburg taking on a load of gravel. She cast off and passed the Grand Haven piers at 9:03 a.m. headed for Chicago where she was scheduled to arrive the next morning. Her voyage was routine; it was a trip she had made four times a week for years.

By 10:00 a.m. winds kicked up and quickly morphed into a full-blown gale. The *Andaste* did not arrive the next morning as scheduled, but her tardiness was not given much thought since the old ship had been late before. By Wednesday a full day late, simple delay no longer explained her tardiness. By Thursday it was assumed the *Andaste* was lost. She had no radio. There was no way to determine what had happened until the ship's debris told the story.

Wreckage drifted ashore at beaches from Grand Haven to Holland. At Castle Park, just south of Holland, the first body was recovered. Mr. H. H. Stibbs was scanning the water in front of his cottage and saw debris. His son, J. H. Stibbs, a competitive swimmer, swam out to recover what he could. He returned, towing a life ring with a dead sailor.

Other bodies washed ashore at Jenison Park in Grand Haven. Of the initial 14 victims to float to shore, 11 were wearing lifejackets. Continued search efforts during the next two weeks recovered the remaining bodies, as well as considerable flotsam: cabin doors, several hatch covers, and part of a stairway. Much of the wreckage was tangled in fishing nets. The youngest victim was 14-year-old Earl Zietlow, a sailor on his first and last voyage.

The best evidence suggests the *Andaste* went down 25 or 30 miles out on the lake. A cottage owner, between Grand Haven and Holland, testified at an inquest that he was awakened by a violent storm at 1:00 a.m. the night the *Andaste* went missing. Looking out his window, he saw the lights of a ship not too far from shore, and the lights remained visible until about 4:00 a.m. And then, nothing.

<<>>

The Southwest Michigan Underwater Preserve is a five-mile-wide strip of water offshore from Allegan, Berrien, and Van Buren Counties. Preserve boundaries run from just north of Holland to Bridgman. The towns of Holland, South Haven, Douglas, Saugatuck, Benton Harbor, St. Joseph, and New Buffalo are part of the preserve. On November 13, 1999, the preserve was dedicated as the tenth preserve along Michigan waters. There are numerous shipwrecks in the preserve area as well as geological formations including clay banks and underwater rock piles.

• THE FAMOUS OR INFAMOUS WITH TIES TO HOLLAND

Harry Bannister, an American actor of stage, film, and television, was born in Holland, Michigan, on September 29, 1889. Married to actress Ann Harding, the two appeared together in two films, *Her Private Affair* and *The Girl of the Golden West*.

<<>>

L. Frank Baum authored many children's stories, the most famous of which remains the *Wizard of Oz*. The Baum family maintained a second home they called The Sign of the Goose in Macatawa.

<<>>

Edward Wilhelm Bentz, a Depression-era bank robber, is believed to have pulled the heist on the First State Bank on 8ᵗʰ Street in 1932. (See story under Other Stops to Consider.)

<<>>

Kirk Cousins attended Holland Christian High School where he starred in football, baseball, and basketball for the Maroons athletic teams. He went on to quarterback at Michigan State University and then played professional football for the Minnesota Vikings.

<<>>

Elisabeth "Betsy" Dee Prince DeVos was born on January 8, 1958, in Holland. She married Amway founder and CEO Dick Devos. In 2017 Betsy was appointed by President Donald Trump as his Secretary of Education. She served in that capacity until her resignation in 2021 just before the end of Trump's term.

<<>>

Cornelis Pieter "Pete" Hoekstra was born in the Netherlands. His family moved to the United States when Pete was three. He attended Holland Christian High School and then received a BA degree in political science from Hope College in 1975. With a long political career as a Conservative Republican and a member of the U.S. House of Representatives, he most recently served as House Chair of the Intelligence Committee under President Donald Trump.

<<>>

Rhoda Janzen is a professor of English and Creative Writing at Hope College. Born into a Mennonite family, she authored *Mennonite in a Little Black Dress*. It is autobiographical and describes the crisis in her life.

<<>>

Morley "Josey" Jennings was born on January 23, 1890, in Holland. He played baseball, football, and basketball, and ran track at Mississippi State University.

After his career as a distinguished athlete, he became a coach at Baylor and athletic director at Texas Tech.

<<>>

Paul de Kruif, a scientist and writer, assisted Sinclair Lewis with his Pulitzer Prize-winning novel *Arrowsmith*. For his efforts, he received 25% of the royalties. It is believed that the characters in the novel may have been based upon people Dr. de Kruif knew, possibly even with himself as the model for Martin Arrowsmith. De Kruif retired to Holland and died there in 1971.

<<>>

Rob Malda, founder of Slashdot, was born May 10, 1976, in Holland. He attended Holland Christian High School and Hope College. He was named in the *MIT Technology Review* as one of the top 100 innovators under 35 years old in the world.

<<>>

Lisa McMann, born February 27, 1968, in Holland, is a writer of short stories, children's books, and young adult fiction.

<<>>

James Andrew Michael, musician (alternative rock, hard rock, alternative metal, and heavy metal), was born in Holland on September 26, 1967. He writes and produces music and is the lead singer for Sixx:A.M.

<<>>

A. J. Muste, a political activist and pacifist, attended Hope College in Holland.

<<>>

David Myers, a psychologist and author of many psychology textbooks, attended Hope College in Holland.

<<>>

Milton John Nieuwsma is an American writer and journalist who is best known for his work about the Holocaust. He moved to Holland in 1997 and continued his writing career from there.

250

<<>>

Nathan Oostendorp was born in Holland and co-founded the tech website Slashdot. He also founded the online community Everything2. Oostendorp attended the University of Michigan where he earned a master's degree in Information Economics and while there published several academic papers about online communities.

<<>>

Erik Dean Prince was born in Holland on June 6, 1969. He is a brother of Betsy DeVos, attended Holland Christian High School, was a former navy seal, is the founder of Blackwater and a staunch Republican who has been a major financial contributor to the party.

<<>>

Ronald Maurice "Skip" Schipper coached college football at Central College in Pella, Iowa, and later became college athletics administrator there. He spent his later years in Holland where he died in 2006. He was a member of the College Football Hall of Fame.

<<>>

Willie Snead played part of his high school football career at Holland Christian High School where his father was the head coach. Later, a standout at Ball State, he went on to play professional football with the Cleveland Browns, Carolina Panthers, New Orleans Saints, and Baltimore Ravens.

<<>>

Sufjan Stevens attended Hope College in Holland. He became a singer-songwriter and instrumentalist mastering several instruments. He recorded an album, *Michigan*, a collection of folk songs and instrumentals with ballads about Michigan including Detroit, Flint, Holland, the Upper Peninsula, Tahquamenon Falls, and the Sleeping Bear Dunes National Lakeshore. Along with his scenic descriptions are his feelings about faith, love, and the regeneration of Michigan.

Matt Louis Urban, a lieutenant colonel in the United States Army, was one of the most decorated soldiers of WWII. He died on March 5, 1995, in Holland.

<<>>

Mary Jeanne van Appledorn, a composer of contemporary classical music and piano, was born in Holland on October 2, 1927.

<<>>

Andrew William Van Hekken was born July 31, 1979, in Holland where he attended both elementary and high school. The top pick of the Seattle Mariners in the third round of the 1998 major league baseball draft, he was later traded to the Detroit Tigers where he pitched a complete game shutout in his first major league appearance.

<<>>

Luke Witkowski was born on April 14, 1990, in Holland. He was selected as the 160th overall pick by the Tampa Bay Lightning, eventually played a short stint with the Detroit Red Wings, and then returned to Tampa as a free agent.

<<>>

Valerie van Heest is an author, explorer, and museum designer. She serves on the board of the Michigan Shipwreck Research Association. She led investigations of over a dozen shipwrecks and testified in the Lady Elgin case. (See Lake Michigan at the beginning this guide.) She relocated to Holland and joined the committee to establish the Southwest Michigan Underwater Preserve. In 2000 the state of Michigan approved Southwest Michigan Underwater Preserve as the tenth underwater preserve.

• BOOKS AND MOVIES WITH TIES TO HOLLAND

Walter Vande and Randall Vande, **Holland: The Tulip Town**. On April 26, 1927, a Holland High School biology teacher, suggested that the city present a Tulip Day every spring. Two years later, on May 18, 1929, after scores of visitors viewed more than 100,000 tulips along Holland's curbs, Tulip Time became an annual festival that grew into a celebration with dancing, floats, bands, wooden shoes, food, and fun. This is the history of tulips and their relationship to Holland.

• GHOST STORIES

The Castle Ghost. German-born Michael Schwartz left his homeland because of Prussian militarism. Mr. Schwartz made an early fortune in real estate in Chicago which permitted him the luxury of retiring at a young age. Desiring to leave the problems of the city behind him, he settled in Castle Park, a small community a few miles south of Holland where he hoped to build his dream manor, a replica of an estate he recalled in his native Germany. He wanted to insulate his wife and six daughters from the incivilities of Chicago and the crude ways of this brash young country.

Building the brick and stone mansion was the easy part. More difficult was keeping his beguiling daughters away from the attentions of local boys, especially when two years later the family moved from Castle Park to Holland. One of the Schwartz daughters met a local Dutch boy from their new neighborhood and made plans to marry him. Her father was outraged and forbade the union.

The lovers, not to be thwarted, made covert plans to sneak away in the middle of the night and elope. With the plans complete and the buggy ready, they made their escape, but not without waking Herr Schwartz who grabbed a gun and was in quick pursuit by horseback. His horse made better speed than the buggy, and Schwartz reached the young couple before the vows were exchanged. He locked his errant daughter in his home's tower where she pined away, heartbroken, until the time of her death. On moonlit nights she can be seen in the tower window, facing Holland and searching for the lover she lost.

24. SAUGATUCK
25. DOUGLAS
INCLUDING FENNVILLE AND SINGAPORE

The City of Saugatuck had a 2020 population of 1,031 and Douglas a 2020 population of 1,370. Sometimes sister cities seem to be part of one whole. Often, they are on the opposite sides of a bridge—cities that grew, prospered, and still seem to flow almost as single unit. Saugatuck and Douglas on opposite sides of the Kalamazoo River and connected by the Chain Ferry, are two such cities. You may visit them together.

Once called the Paris of the Midwest and now considered the Art Coast of Michigan, the area around Saugatuck and Douglas evolved from humble fur trading and lumbering origins. The region sprang to life in 1825 when a fur trading post was established there.

Douglas calls itself The Village of Friendly. It began as two cities, divided by what is now Center Street. Jonathan Wade platted Dudleyville on the south side of Centre Street in 1866. William Dutcher platted the north side in 1861. The two merged in 1870 as the Village of Douglas which became the City of the Village of Douglas in 2004 when residents voted to incorporate as a city.

Douglas is well-regarded for its quality galleries. Artists, captivated and inspired by the water and dunes, have moved there and opened studios. Art on Center refers to six fine art galleries located on Center Street in downtown Douglas.

Singapore, founded in approximately 1830, now a ghost town, was instrumental in the development of the area. Singapore's city father, Oshea Wilder, settled on the river near the Lake Michigan shore. He had dreams that his outpost would rival Chicago as a lake port and metropolis. In 1846 two Great Lakes sailors purchased the heavily-wooded south bank of the Kalamazoo

Singapore Marker.
Courtesy of Bob Royce.

River near Douglas as a town site. They cleared the land and waited for settlers to come. They waited patiently, but not much happened until 1851 when the owner of a recently burned lumber mill in Singapore moved his operation to their location at what is now Douglas.

Life was not easy during the first 20 years for the small towns of Saugatuck, Douglas, and Singapore. Residents spent their energy trying to merely survive. Prosperity was a dream for the future. Lumbering brought economic success to the area, and the Douglas Hotel was built in 1870, the same year the small city was incorporated.

The next year the Chicago Fire—one of the most significant events in early Michigan history—occurred. This unfortunate disaster created an almost inexhaustible need for lumber to aid in rebuilding. Every mill in Michigan, including those along the Kalamazoo River, responded to the strong market demand. The remaining mill in Singapore cut everything in sight. This deforestation included removing trees from the coastal dunes. The wanton devastation signaled the death knell for Singapore, which during its existence referred to Saugatuck as the Flats.

Within four years, the dunes, no longer grounded by the tree roots, buried the small village of Singapore. Before the fire, Singapore boasted two hotels, several general stores, and a renowned wildcat bank.[4] Many buildings were moved to other locations when the sand started creeping in their doors, but the story persists that one resident refused to move, even as the sand enveloped his home. Eventually, he had to enter and leave the dwelling by a second-floor window; but still he refused to budge—until the sand reached his roof.

Two factors that greatly influenced other Lake Michigan coastal towns left Saugatuck and Douglas unaffected. Both escaped the damage of the great fires of 1871 and 1881 that scorched so many of their sister cities, and neither had a railway station.

In 1877 the last sawmill closed and the giant Douglas mill converted its production to baskets. This proved to be a stroke of genius, as the now cleared land was planted in fruit trees and fruit growers needed baskets to hold and ship the harvested fruit.

The new fruit business kept boat travel bustling along the Chicago route from Saugatuck and Douglas. When the fruit was unloaded in the Windy City, the boats returned with tourists anxious to escape the sweat and swelter, grit and grime of the city and relax on the beautiful shores of Lake Michigan.

---

[4] A wildcat bank is an institution established in remote and inaccessible locations chartered by state law without federal oversight.

One local story reported that when an out-of-state party offered to buy some land from an area farmer, William McVea, he ran to his newly installed telephone and placed a call to a surveyor insisting that the surveyor come first thing in the morning, "These damn fools want to pay $500 for a pile of sand in my cow pasture." Many not-so-foolish investors wish they now had that pile of sand.

Today, during the summer season, Illinois license plates along elegant Lake Shore Drive are as prevalent as those from Michigan. Early on, Saugatuck became a magnate for short-term visitors, and many hotels and amusements were created for them. Douglas had relatively few day-trippers, but catered to conservative resort residents who stayed for the entire season. Even today Saugatuck is the more bustling, tourist-driven of the two; Douglas is a bit more relaxed and laid back with fewer travelers clamoring for entrance to each shop and restaurant.

This is the B&B capital of Michigan. More bed and breakfasts are located in Saugatuck, Douglas, and Fennville than in any other part of the state. From award-winning beaches to scenic waterways and grassy dunes, from thriving art scenes to a culinary mecca that's become world-renowned, this is a unique place with recreation and relaxation for everyone.

A word about galleries. The main street of Saugatuck, plus many small side streets, feature brightly painted artsy facades luring you to check out their interiors. By all means you should do so. However, these establishments come and go, their days and hours change, even their phone numbers and websites aren't always current. Rather than provide inaccurate information, this guide includes only a handful of art galleries—and those showcase the art of numerous artisans not a solo artist's shop—that have been in business for many, many years. If a gallery isn't listed, it is no reflection on the quality of their art. Explore away. Dozens of galleries compete for your attention. You will find your favorite (and current) places. While you are shopping, you'll also find these small towns are flush with sophisticated boutiques.

• MUSEUMS AND GALLERIES

Amazwi Contemporary Art, 249 Culver Street, Saugatuck. *Amazwi* is the Zulu word for voices. Amazwi opened in 2004 with a desire to make the contemporary voices of Africa heard throughout North America. They accomplished this through sales of African art and artifacts. This business is hard to classify. Part museum, part art gallery, part shop, it is above all interesting. The incredible art isn't a collection of random paintings but includes baskets, metal art, hand-crafted jewelry, handwoven bowls, all made by the hands of people in Africa.

<<>>

Discovery Art Center, 347 Water Street, Saugatuck. A nationally recognized cooperative gallery featuring the work of area artists including oil paintings, traditional watercolors, jewelry, hand-painted china, photography, brass and crystal sculpture, and wearable art.

<<>>

Saugatuck-Douglas Historical Museum, 735 Park Street, Saugatuck. The museum opened in 1992 in the historic Saugatuck Pump House which was the village's first water pumping station. The building sits along the west shore of the Kalamazoo River at the foot of Mount Baldhead Park and is only a short walk from the iconic Chain Ferry that crosses the river between Douglas and Saugatuck. The structure was built in 1904 in a modest prairie-craftsman style.

In 1910 the building was enlarged to also serve as Saugatuck's first electric generating station. As need increased, the water and electric objectives were moved to a larger facility, and by 1970 the pump house had fallen into serious disrepair. Volunteers stepped in to restore and save the building from demolition. The Pump House is now designated a Michigan Historical Site and is listed on the National Register of Historic Places. Volunteers will share more about the building's interesting history.

Inside the museum, History Center volunteers create fascinating exhibits and historical displays that make this one of the most visited small-town museums along the Lake Michigan shore. Saugatuck's history goes beyond shipwrecks. It includes dancing, summer fun, artists, and gangsters that all permeate the background of Saugatuck and Douglas.

The museum boasts 1,500 square feet of riverfront garden with six learning stations. Each station provides a storyboard with historical and ecological information about the view you will enjoy from that outlook. Access to the gardens is either from stairs through the entry pavilion or by a gradually inclined paved switchback walkway which allows for universal access.

The museum is the perfect way to introduce yourself to Saugatuck and Douglas.

<<>>

Water Street Gallery, 98 Center Street, Douglas. The venue for contemporary sculptures, ceramics, painting, and photography. The gallery's vision is to inspire artists and customers in creating and enjoying innovative original works of art presented in a vibrant and welcoming gallery.

<<>>

Mason Street Warehouse and **Saugatuck Center for the Arts**, 400 Culver Street, Saugatuck is a place to find local theater. Professional quality productions, comfortable seating, a treasure for locals and visitors alike. The Center for the Arts also features exhibitions, concerts, and a beautiful flower and sculpture garden.

Downtown Saugatuck.
Courtesy of Pixabay Free Images.

Even restrooms in Saugatuck take on a Monet-like façade.
Courtesy of Bob Royce.

● BEACHES, PARKS, AND TRAILS

Coghlin Park, 64 Griffith Street, Saugatuck. A green grassy park where you can pause for a few minutes and watch the boats go by. Might be a nice place to wait for the shoppers in your family, if you'd rather rest your feet than search for treasures.

<<>>

Douglas Beach Park, 3099 Lakeshore Drive, Douglas. An underrated beach where you may not have to fight the crowds. Quaint picnic area, bathhouse, and stairs to the beach.

<<>>

Kalamazoo River. Rent a canoe, and launch it from a shallow place along the river. Maybe find a nice spot to jump overboard and swim if the weather is too hot. A relaxing place to drift and watch the wildlife.

<<>>

Mount Baldhead, 769 Park Street. Mount Baldhead includes a one-mile loop trail for hiking, walking, and trail running. Climb 302 steps to Mount Baldhead and descend onto the gray coastal sands. It is guaranteed to leave all but the fittest huffing and puffing. Mercifully, there are benches along the way, and there are no rules against resting. The view from the top is nothing short of spectacular as you look down on the forested dune. Slather on plenty of sunscreen; the sun can be fierce.

<<>>

Oval Beach Recreation Area, Perryman at Oval Beach Drive, near Park Street. *Conde Nast Traveler* rated it one of the 15 best shorelines in the world. The accolades don't stop there. *National Geographic* included it in the Traveler's Top Freshwater Beaches in the USA and MTV's Top 5 Beaches in the USA. Oval beach is not only eye candy with its dune backdrop, it has a feeling of seclusion. Picnic tables, a concession stand, and a beach house are available.

<<>>

Saugatuck Dunes State Park, 6575 138th Avenue, Saugatuck, take BR-31 to 65th Street north to 138th

Avenue, west to the park entrance. This 1,000-acre area of rugged dunes on Lake Michigan was acquired in 1971 from the Augustinian Order that once used the buildings on the property as a seminary. Today the land is a day-use park (no camping permitted). The park's major features are its 2½-mile shoreline of swimming beach and 300-acre natural area which contains a coastal dune system with three endangered plant species, numerous bird species, and 13 miles of sandy hiking trails. Pets are permitted on the trails. This is a relatively undeveloped park. It offers picnic tables, grills, and a picnic shelter. A favorite of bird watchers and hikers.

<<>>

Saugatuck Harbor of Refuge. Open 24 hours but no amenities.

<<>>

Saugatuck Harbor Natural Area, north of Oval Beach. Stretching along the rolling dunes, this sandy trail snakes through a 173-acre protected natural area with remnants of the historic Fishtown pier, wetlands, the Kalamazoo River channel, and a beautiful strip of Lake Michigan. Migrating birds fly overhead, and shy deer peek out from hiding places.

<<>>

Sergeant Marina, 31 Butler Street, Saugatuck, a block from downtown. Seasonal and transient slips available. Can accommodate up to 50-foot boats. Gas, diesel, and electricity available. Other amenities include bagged ice, in-slip pump out, clubhouse, WiFi, bathrooms, and showers.

<<>>

Wicks Park. Place to spread a blanket, or put up a chair and relax, maybe catch a local concert, boat watch, people watch, grab and enjoy take-out from nearby, or enjoy the shade on a hot summer day.

● OTHER STOPS TO CONSIDER

Saugatuck and Douglas provide many opportunities for kayaking, canoeing, cruises, equipment rental, wine tasting, golfing, food tours, bicycling, fishing charters, antiquing, shopping, dune rides, and galleries, galleries, galleries. These are small towns so you won't have to spend a lot of time searching—it's all there to greet you.

<<>>

All Saints Episcopal Church, 252 Grand Street, Saugatuck. This is a small historic church built in 1871 in Carpenter Gothic Style.[5] Worth a drive by.

<<>>

Crane's Orchards, 6054 124th Avenue, Fennville. The history of Crane's orchards can be traced as far back as the late 1800s when H. H. Hutchins cleared and planted the property along a beautiful inland lake that he named Hutchins Lake. Today the fruit orchards produce nearly all of the fruit that Crane's Pie Pantry Restaurant uses for their delicious and renowned pies. You can pick apples, peaches, and sweet cherries while enjoying scenery that will stay in your memory forever. The farm has a corn maze, hayrides in the fall, and other activities to add fun to your vacation.

<<>>

Saugatuck Chain Ferry, 719 Water Street. Diane, the Saugatuck Chain Ferry, is the only remaining hand-cranked chain ferry in the United States. She glides across the Kalamazoo River by a chain connected to both sides. She leaves each dock at 10 to 15-minute intervals, based on demand. A pleasant way to reach the beaches.

---

[5] **Carpenter Gothic**, sometimes called **Rural Gothic**, is a North American architectural style designation for an application of Gothic Revival architectural detailing and picturesque massing applied to wooden structures built by house carpenters.

The Saugatuck Chain Ferry has operated since 1857 although the present ferry was built in the 1960s and is owned by the City of Saugatuck.

Saugatuck Chain Ferry.
Courtesy of Pixabay Free Images.

The ferry's original purpose was to transport horses across the river. Today, it remains a way to cross the river, but for many, it's a fun experience to ride from one side to the other side and return on the next trip.

<<>>

Saugatuck Guided Walking Tours, Tourist Center, Saugatuck. Guided tours any way you want them. There are guided tours that last about an hour, or the Chamber of Commerce has a map you can pick up and take your own walking tour. A smartphone app even lets you set your pace and learn the history as you walk.

• LIGHTHOUSE

Kalamazoo (Replica) Lighthouse. Located on the south shore of Kalamazoo Lake in Douglas. On March 3, 1837, Congress appropriated $5,000 for a lighthouse at the mouth of the Kalamazoo River. Land was secured, and two years later the lighthouse was built. Erosion was a problem at the original location, so in 1859 a new lighthouse was constructed on a dune a distance from the river. This new lighthouse had a two-story dwelling with a square tower sitting atop its pitched roof. On April 3, 1956, a tornado, which was part of forty-seven tornadoes spawned over a two-day period, touched down on the beach near Saugatuck, and ravaged the 1859 lighthouse.

A replica was constructed, but it stands on Lake Kalamazoo. (See related Ghost Story in this section.)

● SHIPWRECKS

Mystery Ship. In March 2011, a 60-foot-long, single-masted sloop was found at the bottom of Lake Michigan. It was believed by the founding divers that the mystery ship may have lain at the bottom of Lake Michigan for as many as 180 years. The ship, in surprisingly good shape, stood upright in about 250 feet of water between Saugatuck and South Haven.

Researchers hopeful of discovering the ship's identity have been thwarted in their efforts.

● THE FAMOUS AND THE INFAMOUS WITH TIES TO SAUGATUCK OR DOUGLAS

Michael Gallagher was born in 1958. He was an investigative journalist for Gannett News Service. He started his career with the *Kalamazoo Gazette* in the 1980s. As a reporter for the *Lansing State Journal*, he wrote a series about drug smuggling in Michigan prisons. The FBI investigated his story and accused him of falsifying a source. The newspaper stood by him. He developed a reputation for doggedness in pursuit of stories. His investigative series for the *Cincinnati Enquirer* into misdeeds of Chiquita Brands International, a Cincinnati-based company, landed him in hot water again. He accused the company of mistreating its workers, polluting the environment, bringing cocaine into the United States on its ships, bribery, and other criminal acts. Chiquita notified police that its voicemails had been hacked and broken into dozens of times a day. Gallagher pleaded guilty to two felony counts of tapping into Chiquita's voicemail. He was sentenced to a 2½ prison sentence that was reduced to five years of probation. Gannett settled with Chiquita and ran a huge front-page apology for three consecutive days. Gallagher was fired. Chiquita never formally denied the claims. Gallagher moved to Saugatuck, and became editor of the *Observer*. He asked for and was granted expungement of his criminal record.

<<>>

Ralph Anson Kohl was born on August 21, 1923. He played football for the University of Michigan during their undefeated 1947-48 season. A knee injury sabotaged his professional career, but he became a coach and scout. He and his wife lived in Saugatuck for many years. He died in June 1997 at Holland County Hospital in Saugatuck.

<<>>

Rachel Reenstra was born February 16, 1970, in Saugatuck and graduated from Hope College with a degree in Theatre. She is a writer, actress, and comedian with roles in TV and movies. She is also an animal conservationist and three-time Emmy-nominated host for the ABC weekend series, *The Wildlife Docs*.

<<>>

Francis Brown Stockbridge was born on April 9, 1826. In 1851 he moved to Saugatuck and operated a sawmill. In 1869 he was voted in as a member of the Michigan State House of Representatives and in 1871 a member of the Michigan State Senate. He was elected as a Republican to the United States Senate in 1887 and was reelected in 1893. He served from March 4, 1887, until his death on April 30, 1894. While visiting a nephew in Chicago, he was struck by a cable car. Although the injuries he sustained didn't immediately kill him, it was argued by his colleagues that stress from the incident contributed to his demise. Stockbridge was the last person to serve in both the Michigan State Legislature and in the United States Senate until Debbie Stabenow was elected in 2000.

<<>>

Franklin Burr Tillstrom was born on October 13, 1917. He was a puppeteer and the creator of *Kukla, Fran, and Ollie.* He maintained a longtime summer home in Saugatuck, and the Saugatuck Douglas Art Club dedicated a memorial to Tillstrom in 1988. In 2013 he was inducted into the Chicago Gay and Lesbian Hall of Fame.

<<>>

Howard Eliot Wolpe was a seven-term U.S. Representative from Michigan and Presidential Special Envoy to the African Great Lakes Region during the Clinton administration. Prior to entering Congress, Wolpe served in the Michigan House of Representatives and as a member of the Kalamazoo City Commission. Wolpe made his home in Saugatuck and died there on October 25, 2011.

- BOOKS AND MOVIES WITH TIES TO SAUGATUCK

Reverend G. Corwin Stoppel has authored six mysteries set in Saugatuck. ***The Great Saugatuck Murder Mystery*** (Minister at the Episcopal Church is murdered), ***Murder of the Saugatuck Church Basement Kitchen Ladies*** (A woman is found dead on the floor of the church kitchen), ***Murder on the Saugatuck Chain Ferry*** (A very quirky murder set in the 1920s with dancing girls and mobsters), ***Murder at Nine Fingers Charlie's Art Emporium*** (A woman critical of the new gallery's opening is found dead there), ***Death by Pallet Knife*** (At the conclusion of an Ox-Bow open house, a body is discovered with a palette knife in the victim's heart), and ***The Murder of the Saugatuck Yarn Hoarder*** (Murder of the village gossip).

The **Road to Perdition**, a 2002 crime thriller starring Tom Hanks, Paul Newman, and Jude Law was set in 1930s Chicago. Filming took place in several western Michigan cities, including Saugatuck and West Olive.

• GHOST STORIES

The Ghost of Felt Mansion. Dorr Felt began construction of his luxurious summer home in 1925, six years after he purchased the property. The house was his gift of love to his wife Agnes. The story ended tragically when Agnes died of a stroke in her room shortly after the mansion's completion in 1928. Dorr Felt remarried, but his second wife hated the house where she felt Agnes' eyes watching her. The ghost of the first Mrs. Felt was not happy that Dorr had remarried.

The Felt family continued to own the mansion for an additional two decades before the daughters sold the estate to the St. Augustine Seminary and School. Buildings were added by the seminary in the 1960s, but declining enrollment forced closure in the 1970s.

The State of Michigan began using the seminary school as the minimum-security Dunes Correctional Facility, and the Felt Mansion was converted to a State Police post, along with offices and storage space for the prison. When the prison closed, the township purchased the land and buildings from the state with the agreement that the mansion and grounds would remain for public use only. This limitation made selling the property to a private buyer or enterprise impossible.

Inside the house, doors still open and close in Agnes' room, and voices can be heard. Visitors take pictures that reveal wispy white streaks, orbs, and mists. The ballroom is felt to be the most haunted area of the home. It is believed that Dorr's ghost has joined Agnes in wandering the mansion. Perhaps he always missed his first wife.

Near the mansion and behind the railroad tracks is the last remaining building from the Dunes Correctional Facility. It was used as the Trustee Building and housed eighty inmates. This building was reputedly an Asylum for the criminally insane, but that rumor is based on false information. That is not to say that the silhouettes of figures walking the grounds, and the screams heard, may not be ghosts who have some agonizing connection to the correctional facility or other ancient history of the grounds.

<<>>

The Ghost of George Sheridan. Lighthouse keeper Sheridan had a long history as a keeper of lights on Lake Michigan before he committed suicide and returned as a ghost to haunt the area of his last assignment. During his tenure, he served at the Chicago Harbor, Calumet, Michigan City, and finally Kalamazoo light at the mouth of the Kalamazoo River where it opens to Lake Michigan. Lighthouses provided Sheridan with many years of happy employment.

Sheridan's father was also a lighthouse keeper, and perhaps it is in the father's tragic history that we find the seeds from which sprang the son's melancholy. Aaron, George's father, was the head lighthouse keeper on South Manitou Island.

On March 15, 1878, Aaron Sheridan, his wife Julia, ten-month-old son Robert, and Chris Ankerson were returning from the mainland when their sailboat capsized about a mile from the lighthouse. All aboard except Ankerson drowned. Aaron Sheridan had six sons at the time of the tragedy, five were at home with the family babysitter when the accident occurred. The babysitter said the surviving sons—all between the ages of three and twelve—wandered the beach searching for the bodies of their parents and baby brother. George, along with his remaining siblings, was taken to live with a relative. George eventually followed in his father's career path.

George kept a watchful eye on the water surrounding his stations and was credited during his tenure with rescuing four men and three women from near tragedy.

When the Kalamazoo Lighthouse was discontinued in 1914, George was offered the position of assistant depot keeper at St. Joseph. The job came with a condition. Before assuming his duties, George had to seek treatment for his melancholia. He was admitted to Evanston Sanatorium. After treatment George returned to the Saugatuck-Douglas area but shortly afterward needed additional medical care and returned for more psychiatric treatment. While at Evanston, George visited his uncle at the Grosse Point Lighthouse. Keepers' jobs ran in the family, and George's uncle was a keeper at Grosse Point Lighthouse. While staying with his uncle, George failed to return from a walk. His body was found dangling from a rafter in the station's boathouse. His ghost returned to his last post and remains in the area of the replica of his now-defunct Kalamazoo Lighthouse.

26. SOUTH HAVEN

It is a marvelous planet on which we ride. It is a great privilege to live thereon, to partake in the journey, and to experience its goodness.

Liberty Hyde Bailey

The 2020 population of South Haven was 4,327. In 1787 Odawa, Miami, and Pottawattamie Native American tribes began using the area around South Haven as a place for trading. They called it *Ni-Ko-Nong*, which translated means beautiful sunsets. They banked their birch bark canoes in the sands along the lake.

In 1833 the United States government granted J.R. Monroe a land patent for 65 acres along the shoreline of Lake Michigan. Monroe married Fanny Rawson, and the newlyweds traveled by lumber wagon through the wilderness to the log cabin J.R. had built for his bride.

The Monroes were disappointed that the village they planned to help create around their home in South Haven never materialized. They abandoned their dream and their home and moved to Lawrence, Michigan. Their timing had been premature by a couple of decades. In the 1850s, the first permanent settlers arrived, and in 1869 South Haven was officially founded.

The establishment of the city coincided with the building of a sawmill which in turn caused construction of a hotel, a school, additional homes, and stores to provide needed goods and services to the new settlers.

Lumbering was the impetus creating the city; it was also its economic sustenance for four decades. After the lumbering era ended, the areas cleared of timber were used by fruit farmers to spark an industry that continues to flourish. The first annual Peach Festival was held in 1930, and today's Blueberry Festival continues to draw visitors eager to share the fun.

Both passenger and freight ships stopped at South Haven during its early days, and the South Haven Pier and Lighthouse guided ships to the safety of the harbor during violent Lake Michigan storms.

By the early 1900s, South Haven became known as the Catskills of the Midwest, and a swell of second homes grew into large resorts.

Today, South Haven offers visitors sugar-sand swimming beaches and unlimited boating and marine activity. It encompasses 120 square miles of beautiful countryside including woodlands, ravines, fields, and the famous dunes. It is the western stop on the Kal-Haven Trail, loved by both bicyclers and snowmobilers. A visitor can experience a winery tour and tasting, pick fruits and veggies for evening dinner, or simply enjoy the fruits of someone else's labor and purchase fresh produce at one of the many farm markets dotting the landscape.

South Haven is a dog-friendly city, and your best friend is welcome in all stores downtown except pharmacies, restaurants, or other food establishments where their presence is restricted by health regulations.

South Haven Lighthouse and Pier.
Courtesy of Bob Royce.

● MUSEUMS AND GALLERIES

Blue Star Pottery, 337 Blue Star Highway, is the studio of artist Mark Williams who founded and has owned Blue Star Pottery since 1973. Williams specializes in handmade stoneware and creates designs that are uniquely his.

<<>>

Liberty Hyde Bailey Museum, 903 South Bailey Avenue (Off Blue Star Highway and Aylworth Avenue). The Bailey Museum is a National Historic Site marking the birthplace of world-famous botanist and horticulturist Liberty Hyde Bailey who was known as America's Father of Modern Horticulture. At Michigan State University,

Bailey designed the nation's first horticultural laboratory. The museum houses articles used by the Bailey clan and other pioneer families of South Haven. It also displays spinning wheels, an operational cylinder phonograph, pianos, South Haven high school yearbooks, and copies of Bailey's books.

<<>>

Michigan Maritime Museum, 260 Dyckman Avenue. Hands-on and interactive exhibits about the people who sailed the Great Lakes. There are five buildings in the complex. One exhibit includes a gallery collection entitled Sailing through Time. Two U. S. Coast Guard buildings display period rescue equipment and three wooden rescue craft. The Boat Shed hosts workshops on shipbuilding and sailing. Visitors are invited to ask questions, watch the work being conducted, and offer a hand if they like. You can climb aboard the historic replica sloop, the *Friends Good Will.* The original *Friends Good Will* was built in Detroit in 1810 as a merchant vessel. The sloop was chartered by the federal government to take military supplies to Fort Dearborn at what is now Chicago. She was returning with furs and skins when lured into the Harbor of Mackinaw Island by the British who confiscated the ship and her cargo. She was renamed *Little Belt* and pressed into service fighting for the Royal Navy until 1813. A ninety-minute sailing experience you are not likely to forget awaits you. You can also take a sunset sail.

Another celebrity of the museum's fleet is *Coast Guard Motor Lifeboat 36460* which was built in 1941 and served for 35 years. A self-bailing and self-righting workhorse, she handled icy conditions and waves up to 60 feet high. A special feature was her watertight survivors' cabin. In 2012 Disney Productions started work on a new film, *The Finest Hours,* the true story of the Pendleton rescue. Disney asked to use *36460* in the movie. After Hollywood and her moment of fame, *36460* returned to the MMM and remains one of the stars of its fleet.

<<>>

South Haven Center for the Arts, 600 Phoenix Street, strives to enrich the community and provide opportunities to explore, discover, and experience the arts. The center presents exhibitions and special events. This is a good place to catch summer productions and view the art and exhibits before and after the performance.

• BEACHES, PARKS, AND TRAILS

Cable Street Tot Lot, 421 Cable Street. Younger children will love the playground. Benches, picnic tables, restrooms, and free parking.

<<>>

Dyckman Park, 536 Phoenix Street, Downtown. This beautifully landscaped park has picnic tables, benches, and restrooms. In the summer, the farmers market borders the park, and in the winter, an ice rink is groomed at that spot.

<<>>

Elkenburg Park, 309 Elkenburg Street. Southside neighborhood park with a picnic shelter, picnic tables, grills, playground, basketball courts, and public restrooms.

<<>>

Ellen Avery Park, south end of North Shore Drive. A park where you can enjoy boat watching and views. Picnic tables and benches.

<<>>

Hartman Park, 347 Prospect Street near Hartman School. Lots of grassy area for throwing a frisbee. Picnic tables, grills, and free parking.

<<>>

Heritage Water Trail. The 20-mile Bangor to South Haven Heritage Water Trail is a navigable waterway including the Black River, other rivers, lakes, and canals. It offers put-in and take-out points for canoes and kayaks, rest stops, maps, and information on paddling conditions. The educational/interpretive program enriches your experience. Nearby museums are identified. The goal is to promote environmental awareness and help people appreciate nature and history while relaxing and having a good time. This is one of nine designated water trails in Michigan. You can rent canoes and kayaks locally.

<<>>

Kal-Haven Trail State Park. Accessed at Wells and Bailey Streets in South Haven, the Kal-Haven Trail is a narrow strip that runs 34 miles from 10th Street near Kalamazoo to South Haven providing a route for the hardier cyclist to enjoy beautiful woods and farmland, a covered bridge, a camelback bridge, the Bloomingdale Depot, and a host of plants, flowers, birds, and wildlife. The trail is a favorite spot for hikers and snowmobilers.

<<>>

Monroe Park and Kids Corner, 563 Monroe Boulevard. Lake Michigan is the focal point of this park that provides stairs to a public beach across the street. Other amenities include a wooden playground structure, picnic tables and shelter, grills, and public restrooms.

<<>>

North Beach, North Shore Drive. Compare it to any river, lake, or ocean beach anywhere, and North Beach holds its own. Small wonder it is one of the most popular beaches on Lake Michigan. Among the amenities are a Lake Michigan lighthouse, a pier at the entrance of the Black River for boat watching, kayaking, canoeing, or fishing, perfect sand for beach volleyball or building sand castles, swimming, varying depth sand bars, restrooms, a playground, lots of space and opportunity to people-watch, and proximity to restaurants and concession stands. If there is any downside, North Beach is crowded on hot summer days.

<<>>

Optimist Tot Lot Park, 191 Bailey Street. Park suited to small children. Grills, picnic tables, playground equipment, public restrooms, baseball diamond, and a basketball court sized for tots. Free parking.

<<>>

Packard Park, 231 North Shore Drive. Amenities include a deck overlooking Lake Michigan, a large shaded grassy area, picnic tables, grills, and public restrooms.

<<>>

Public Boat Launch at Black River Park, Dunkley Avenue. Boat launch facilities with automated gate entry. Picnic tables, fish cleaning station, and public restrooms.

<<>>

Stanley Johnston Park, 202 Dyckman Avenue. Historic park with grills, picnic tables and shelter, gazebo, restrooms, play equipment, and lots of shady areas.

<<>>

Riverfront Park, Water Street, adjacent to Southside Marina. Beautiful views for boat watching. Picnic area, grills, walking path, and public restrooms.

<<>>

South Beach, 60 Water Street, located just south of North Beach. Usually less crowded than North Beach, but has a nice sandy beach, Lake Michigan views, swimming, close to shopping, playground equipment, and restrooms.

<<>>

South Haven Marina, 345 Water Street, provides 104 transient slips. There are four municipal marinas in South Haven with a total of 229 boating slips available for either seasonal or transient boaters. The marinas are Northside Marina, Southside Marina, Museum Marina, and Black River Park Marina. The slips are from 30 feet to 60 feet with broadside dockage. Amenities: restrooms, showers, water/electric, and pump-out.

<<>>

Van Buren State Park, 23960 Ruggles Road, Exit 13 off I-196. Located three miles south of South Haven on 400 acres of land along the Lake Michigan shoreline. The park has high dune formations and one mile of sandy beach. A place to lounge on the beach, walk through woodland trails, and enjoy a picnic lunch. Day use amenities include a picnic area, parking lot (550 cars), restrooms, changing areas, concession stand, hiking trail, and an undeveloped 70-acre dune area. Entrance fee. Campground available with 220 modern campsites with electricity, a picnic table, and a fire ring.

<<>>

Waterfront Skate Park, located next to South Beach and the Black River. Lets the older kids grab their skateboard or in-line skates for a day of fun.

South Haven Beach. Courtesy of Bob Royce.

• OTHER STOPS TO CONSIDER

The South Haven Ice Rink, 546 Phoenix, Downtown, offers family fun within walking distance to stores and restaurants. Enjoy a winter night, skating under the seasonal lighting. A large pavilion covers the rink so weather is rarely an issue. Skate rental available.

<<>>

South Haven is a vibrant community that offers almost any recreational activity a small town could provide: paintball, golfing, mini-golf, bowling, bumper boats, horse-drawn carriage rides, jet skiing, canoeing, kayaking, bicycling, sailing, cruising, charters, shopping, antiquing, galleries, and dining at all levels. You can rent equipment for your adventure.

Downtown South Haven. Courtesy of Joe Jurkiewicz.

• LIGHTHOUSE

The **South Haven South Pierhead Light** stands at the entrance to the Black River on Lake Michigan. Made of cast iron and 35 feet tall, it has offered guidance to ships since 1903 when it replaced the original 1872 tower. The light is still operational. The catwalk is an elevated walkway, constructed so that during high waves the lighthouse keeper could have safer access by entering the tower through a second-level entrance door. Only three other lighthouses besides South Haven still have an elevated walkway: St. Joseph, Grand Haven, and Manistee. In the 1920s, daredevils dove off the top of the lighthouse.

The 2½ story keeper's house was a wood, hip-roofed home located onshore at 91 Michigan Avenue. The dwelling was transferred to the city for preservation in 2000, and the Michigan Maritime Museum has renovated it as the Marialyce Canonie Great Lakes Research Library.

Responsibility for the South Haven Lighthouse was transferred from the Coast Guard to the Historical Association of South Haven in 2012. The Historical Association raised the money for a complete restoration.

Courtesy of the Appleyard Collection at the Michigan Maritime Museum. Note diver making a jump.

• SHIPWRECKS AND A PLANE CRASH

The **Chicora**. The *Chicora* went down on January 21, 1895. If other shipwrecks sustained more casualties, if other ships suffered more economic loss, if other ships more poignantly captured the public's imagination, probably none was drenched in more irony than the wreck of the *Chicora*.

Mid-January may not seem like the optimal time to be crossing Lake Michigan, but the steamship *Chicora* was an especially stout ship designed for winter passenger and cargo runs. She was tough enough to cut through an ice-packed lake, and she rode violent waves that would have destroyed lesser craft. The wooden-hulled *Chicora* traveled at 17 miles per hour. She had been tied up for winter at St. Joseph when her owners were asked to deliver a shipment of late winter flour from Milwaukee to St. Joseph. On Sunday, January 20, 1895, Captain Edward C. Stine readied his ship and struck out for the Wisconsin harbor. Aboard was a crew of 23, including Captain Stine's 23-year-old son who was pressed into service by his father to replace the second mate who was too ill to make the trip. Only one passenger was aboard, and he was said to be a friend of one of the ship's officers.

It was an unusually pleasant January day, and the *Chicora* reached Milwaukee without incident. The next morning, January 21, she readied for the return trip. The *Chicora* left port at 5:00 a.m., just minutes before a messenger arrived with a telegram from the ship's owner ordering the captain to hold off sailing. The barometer was falling fast in St. Joseph. One story reported that Captain Stine was ill and hurrying to get back to his doctor in St. Joseph.

Midway across Lake Michigan, the *Chicora* encountered winds that had shifted to the southwest bringing with them a dreadful January fury. Those anxiously awaiting the *Chicora*'s return to St. Joseph tried to stave off panic when she did not arrive as scheduled. It made sense that the storm hampered her progress, and she might be a bit tardy. As hours passed, and with fear gnawing at their guts, those waiting reported her overdue. Telegrams were sent up and down the Lake Michigan coast alerting all harbors to keep watch for the lost ship.

There were reports from South Haven that a ship was spotted limping toward shore. Its stern was dipping. Another report from the same area described a distressed ship blowing its horn and seeking assistance. When the storm abated, and it was safe to venture onto the water again, a group of men from Saugatuck began a search. What they found was disheartening and bode ill for the chances of the *Chicora*. Less than a mile from shore, a line of wreckage embedded in ice stretched from Saugatuck to South Haven.

A month later, a tug reported sighting a hulk floating on open water with men still clinging to it, apparently still alive. The *Chicora*'s second mate, who had been lucky enough to be ill when the ship sailed, rented a tug and investigated the sighting. He reported finding only a dark iceberg covered with seagulls.

No bodies ever washed ashore and other than the small pieces of wreckage, including spars, the *Chicora* was never found. The ship's dog was reported wandering along the beach near St. Joseph a few days later. The ship's crew, however, was not so fortunate. The *Chicora*, with bodies entombed, likely lies at the bottom of Lake Michigan between Saugatuck and St. Joseph.

The survivors were left to contemplate the ironies: The *Chicora* had been tied up for winter when called into service. The Captain pressed his son to replace the second mate who was too ill to make the trip. And, the saddest irony of all, the message telling the *Chicora* to stay put until after the storm, arrived minutes too late to save her and her crew.

Nixon Waterman wrote "Song and Sigh" commemorating the sinking of the *Chicora*. It was turned into a ballad popular in the lower lakes region of Michigan.

> *"Here's a sigh for the Chicora, for the broken, sad Chicora;*
> *Here's a tear for those who followed her beneath the tossing wave.*
> *Oh, the mystery of the morrow! From its shadows let us borrow*
> *A star of hope to shine above the gloom of every grave.*
>
> (Public Domain)

<<>>

The **Rockaway**. The 106-foot-long lumber schooner *Rockaway* was lost in a storm off South Haven on November 19, 1891, while sailing from Ludington to Benton Harbor. Built in 1866, the *Rockaway* was a scow, a vessel designed with a broad flat bottom for stability. Respected as a workhorse, she spent her time carrying wood products, coal, salt, produce, grain, and packaged goods between the lakes. In 1880 the *Rockaway* was transferred to Muskegon where she was devoted solely to the Lake Michigan lumber industry. Michigan is notorious for its brutal storms of November, and it was the *Rockaway*'s ill fortune to sail directly into one. The captain, first mate, and crew of four stayed with their damaged vessel until they had no recourse but to abandon ship or go down with her. All six aboard were rescued. The bones of the *Rockaway* rest in 70 feet of water, 2½ miles northwest of South Haven.

The wreck of the *Rockaway* was not discovered for almost a century—and then only by accident—when in 1983 the anchor of two fishermen became entangled in an underwater obstruction. To their surprise, the obstacle was the *Rockaway*. The wreck was reported to the Michigan Maritime Museum and became an archaeological site. The wreck is broken into three major pieces on a level plane in approximately 65 feet of water. The ship is now a popular dive site.

<<>>

282

The **Verano**. In the summer of 1995, two shipwreck hunters dove into the chilly waters of Lake Michigan off South Haven in their ongoing seven-year search for the elusive remains of the *Chicora* (See Ghost Stories.) What the divers found was not the *Chicora*, but the remains of the long-forgotten luxury yacht *Verano*. The find brings a past era alive again. Wealthy Chicagoans had money to spend, and a fancy yacht put only a small dent in their huge savings accounts. In exchange, the expenditure bestowed a lavish means of pleasure as they traveled uplake and downlake surrounded by opulence. The yacht changed ownership several times in her 21-year life.

On August 28, 1946, the good times crashed to an end for the *Verano*. Three months earlier Maynard Dowell had become the yacht's final owner. The yacht was in serious need of repair, and Dowell was having her moved to Holland for overhaul in anticipation of a trip down the Mississippi River into the Gulf of Mexico. Three men were aboard for the trip to Holland, two engineers and a cook. None of the three was well-trained to handle the ship, and none knew the peculiarities of the *Verano*.

The yacht never arrived in Holland, and her disappearance was fraught with mystery and speculation. The lake was calm. A large insurance policy had been taken out on the ship. The Coast Guard arrived before the *Verano* disappeared beneath the water.

No one was found aboard. The lifeboat was missing.

A few days later the overturned lifeboat was found upside down with the oars locked in the stowed position. It wasn't long before the bodies of the three men who had been aboard washed ashore. One victim had his life jacket on backward.

Investigations, then and subsequently, have speculated the reasons the *Verano* sank. Foul play was never established, and one potential cause for the tragedy suggested the *Verano* was not seaworthy. She had been known to leak and list in the past. Another factor that could have doomed the craft was her inexperienced crew. The *Verano*'s broken remains—two large engines and a dashboard with the keys still in the ignition—now lie off South Haven in about 55 feet of water.

<<>>

Flight 2501. Fifty-five passengers bound for Milwaukee and Seattle boarded a Northwest Airlines flight on June 23, 1950. They settled into seats unaware that this would be the day that they died.

Captain Robert Lind and two other crew members aboard the DC-4 had everything under control. Travelers had nothing more to worry about than whether they could nod off during the red-eye flight. Over Lake Michigan, in an area often referred to as the Great Lakes Triangle (Manitowoc, Wisconsin, and Ludington and Benton Harbor Michigan are the three triangle vertices), Lind experienced severe turbulence. (See Lake Michigan Triangle under Shipwrecks/Ludington.) He was instructed to drop to 3,500 feet to avoid an eastbound flight which was likewise contending with violent wind gusts.

Lind radioed that he would reach Milwaukee by 11:37 p.m. That was the last transmission from flight 2501. The plane vanished.

More than 71 years later, the whereabouts of the aircraft and the circumstances of the crash remain a mystery. Searchers found an oil slick, a fuel tank, seat cushions, luggage, and an airline logbook floating in the lake several miles from shore near South Haven.

The U.S. Coast Guard Cutter *Mackinaw* assisted in the search. Captain Carl G. Bowman, skipper of the *Mackinaw,* told the United Press at Detroit by radiotelephone that his men found small body parts including hands and ears. At the time, the crash was the worst aviation tragedy in American history.

Northwest Flight 2501. Courtesy of Wikipedia.

• THE FAMOUS OR INFAMOUS WITH TIES TO SOUTH HAVEN

Liberty Hyde Bailey was born in 1858 in a simple frame house in South Haven. Bailey was a world-famous botanist and horticulturist who attended Michigan State Agricultural College (now Michigan State University) and developed a curriculum that is still used for horticultural training. His home in South Haven is a museum. (See listing under Museums.)

<<>>

Pamela Lynn Fanning Carter was born in South Haven on August 20, 1949. Carter was the first Black woman elected a state's attorney general. She served as Indiana Attorney General from 1993 to 1997.

<<>>

David Lawrence Gumpert was born on May 5, 1958, in South Haven. He became a major league baseball pitcher for the Chicago Cubs, Detroit Tigers, and Kansas City Royals. He was Rookie of the Year for the Tigers in 1983.

<<>>

Becky Johnston, an American screenwriter, was born and attended public schools in South Haven. Among her screenplays are *Under the Cherry Moon, The Prince of Tides*, and *Seven Years in Tibet*.

<<>>

Drakkar Don Klose was born on March 9, 1988, in South Haven. He is a mixed martial artist. He had a standout wrestling career at South Haven High School where he won a state championship in 2005.

285

<<>>

Mark Lenard was born Leonard Rosenson. Primarily a TV actor, his most famous role was Sarek, father of Spock, in the science fiction Star Trek franchise. The son of Russian Jewish immigrants, Abraham and Bessie Rosenson, Mark was raised in South Haven where his family owned a tourist resort.

<<>>

Daniel Keith Ludwig, born June 24, 1897, in South Haven was a businessman and billionaire who in 1982 was #1 on the Forbes 400 Richest American's List.

<<>>

James C. McCloughan was born on April 30, 1946, in South Haven. For bravery as a soldier in the Vietnam War, he was approved for the Medal of Honor by President Barack Obama. The medal was presented by President Donald Trump. After his military service, he returned to South Haven and taught high school and coached.

<<>>

Kennedy McIntosh played high school basketball at South Haven High. He played college basketball at Eastern Michigan University. At 6' 7" tall, he was the 15th pick the Chicago Bulls in the 1971 Draft. He played forward.

<<>>

Audrey Niffenegger was born on June 13, 1963, in South Haven. Her debut novel, *The Time Traveler's Wife* was published in 2003. It became a best seller.

<<>>

Arthur D. Walker Jr. was born on November 24, 1933, in South Haven and attended school there. He graduated from South Haven High School and then attended the University of Michigan. He played seven years of professional football in the Canadian Football League (1955-1961).

Kaliesha West was born on February 11, 1988, in South Haven. She became a professional female boxer and the former three-time WBO Female Bantamweight and IFBA Super Bantamweight Boxing World Champion.

<<>>

D'arcy Elizabeth Wretzky-Brown was born May 1, 1968, in South Haven. She was the original bass player of the alternative rock band, the Smashing Pumpkins and is credited on their first six studio albums. She left the band in 1999.

● BOOKS AND MOVIES WITH TIES TO SOUTH HAVEN

Michigan Maritime Museum, ***Maritime South Haven 1900-1950*** (Illustrated). A history of South Haven between 1900 and 1950 when it transformed from a rough commercial port into a beautiful tourist attraction.

<<>>

Bea Kraus, ***A Place to Remember: South Haven—A Success from the Beginning***. History of Southwest Michigan beginning in 1830 (2013). The paperback includes 180 photos and covers the development of the Jewish resort era.

<<>>

James Ollgaard, ***South Haven by the Big Blue Water: Historical Walking Tour***. South Haven is a twenty-first century town that prides itself on its rich heritage, its tree-lined streets, and old architectural treasures. Each building tells a story. This book recounts some of those stories as it creates a historical walking tour.

<<>>

V. O. van Heest, co-founder of Michigan Shipwreck Research Associates based out of Holland, Michigan, authored ***Fatal Crossing*** (2013). She recounts what is known of the crash of Northwest Airlines Flight 2501.

(See Shipwrecks and a Plane Crash in this section.) Author and explorer Clive Cussler of the National Underwater Marine Agency teamed up with van Heest, and they embarked on a quest to solve the mystery of the plane's disappearance. They reviewed evidence, carried out further research, and talked to relatives of the victims. What they discovered led them in an unexpected direction. They never found the lost plane, but unearthed a few surprises in the archives. Van Heest creates a heart-rending account of the victims' last few hours.

• Ghost Stories

Ghost of Al Capone's Mistress. At night, if you walk through Hawks Head Cemetery in South Haven, you may see the ghost of Al Capone's mistress, Flora. She is said to be buried there, but little more is known. Researching Flora is not easy. Capone had more mistresses than can reasonably be counted, and many of them are unknown to history. Capone spent his recreational time along Lake Michigan's coast, so the tale of a mistress buried at Hawks Head is easy to believe. Chimes are said to herald her appearance. A dim red light has been spotted near the middle of the cemetery. Beyond that is anyone's guess. Maybe Capone had her killed because she was unfaithful. That also seems to be a recurring theme among his lovers. It would also explain why she might be unhappy with the way she died. Hard to imagine Capone would do it the quick and easy way.

<<>>

The South Haven Keeper's Ghost. As she entered the ramshackle old house, Dr. Susan Scully[6] was greeted by a chilly draft and chillier foreboding that she was not alone. The floorboards creaked under her light step. Torn curtains covered streaked windows. A stream of sunshine

---

[6] Names have been fictionalized since they differed in various accounts. Details differ depending upon who is telling the story.

peeked through the shreds and illuminated dust mites in the stagnant air.

A university scholar and doctoral student, Scully researched old lighthouses. She had received a key to let herself in and permission to study documents kept in the South Haven, Michigan, keeper's house. The dwelling perches on a bluff overlooking a 35-foot red lighthouse situated in Lake Michigan.

Dr. Scully did a quick inventory of the structure. It appeared maintenance had been an afterthought. Armed with notebook and pen, she tightened her sweater about her and dove into her work. She pulled out old ledgers, diaries, journals, letters, and other documents.

Susan read for hours. Night closed in. She had committed mountains of information to memory and had filled one binder with notes from the piles of papers spread out before her on the table. She laid her head down for a moment, intending to rest her burning eyes before putting the materials away. She planned to leave and return another day. She hadn't considered that she might doze off, but fatigue overcame her.

Susan awoke to moans and crying. Remnants of my dreams, she thought. The keeper's dwelling was dark except for a small sliver of moonlight that fell across her research and convinced her she was awake. She fumbled for the chain on the desk lamp. She pulled it, but no light rewarded her effort. Her fingers explored the table for the telephone she had seen earlier. Lifting the receiver, she heard no dial tone. She rose to feel her way out of the building. The shadowy interior of the keeper's house raised goosebumps on the flesh of her forearms. Before she took her first step toward the door, a gut-wrenching scream pierced the silence.

Susan responded with her own shriek, so powerful that it left her breathless. When she managed to take air into her lungs, she shouted, "Who is there?"

A second wail shook the walls before it was joined by a chorus of garbled words from men, women, and children. Susan made out: "Help," "Take my child," "Please, Captain, save my baby," and "Goodbye, my love." The rest was unintelligible.

Dr. Scully tried to run, but fear paralyzed her legs. The voices continued, stronger and stronger, pleading to be saved. A gush of air slammed her. The room grew colder, but Susan began to sweat. Her gooseflesh turned to an icy mist on her skin. A bearded figure wearing a Civil War uniform and holding a cane in one hand floated close and landed inches from her trembling body. Existing in a different dimension, it seemed unaware of her presence. The apparition's left leg was amputated at the knee. A wooden peg replaced the missing limb. It tap, tap, tapped against the floor, moving the wraith closer to the groaning crowd.

Around the Captain, lurched misshapen, grossly deformed, corpse-like figures. Some wore hooded black cloaks. Crashing waves and splintering wood muffled their cries. Bodies floated and clung to pieces of debris. Susan tried to convince herself this wasn't real. It was useless. She saw a sinking ship with a gaping hole in its port side. She watched as the peg-legged skipper stepped into a small boat and rowed toward the terrified crowd hanging from the deck of a great steamer.

The hooded creatures lowered the coverings from their heads revealing leathery skin drawn tight over skulls with gaping holes where eyes had once been. Lips contorted into deathly grins.

The crowd pitched toward the wooden-legged man in the boat. "Captain, how could you leave us to die?" The macabre assembly chanted its indictment.

"I did not leave you. I did what I could." The Captain slumped for a moment before continuing toward the steamer. "There were too many. Stop torturing me. Be off with you. Can't you be grateful for those I saved?" The Captain's voice cracked. He begged his tormenters for mercy. He thrust his cane about to protect himself from the groping hands that reached out when he was within touching distance. As he struck them, creatures fell to the floor of the ship.

As the image of the scene came closer, Scully recognized the captain from a picture she had seen earlier that day. It was Lars Johansson, a former keeper who had saved many shipwreck victims during his tenure at the lighthouse. An equal or maybe greater number, he watched die as he damned his inability to prevent their drowning.

Dr. Susan Scully wondered if she was seeing hell. The Captain's eyes hooked on hers, and he appeared to have shifted dimensions. He turned from the crowd, swung his cane in Susan's direction, and limped closer. "I suppose ye, too, hold me accountable?" he asked.

"No, no. I'm not part of this. You are a dream." She struggled to return from the horror, but her efforts proved futile against the advancing captain. With a vicious strike of his cane, he slashed through her shoulder, and the wooden weapon came out the other side. She felt nothing. Susan realized his world couldn't entwine with hers. That knowledge gave her strength. She picked up her notebooks and edged toward the door. The specter followed, cursing and lunging. When she closed the door behind her, he stayed inside the house. She hoped she had all the information she needed because she knew she'd never return to this place possessed by unearthly creatures.

The rest of the story: With ghost stories, the facts often float around in the netherworld and are shaped as much by innuendo, speculation, and good storytelling as they are by truth. In this strange and haunting tale, none of the names applied to the captain in any of the accounts could be verified. None was listed as a lighthouse keeper in South Haven. However, a few astonishing coincidences can be confirmed: The lighthouse keeper with the longest tenure in South Haven was Captain James Donahue who tended the lighthouse for thirty-five years. Before he became a keeper, Donahue had enlisted in the 8th Michigan Infantry and fought in the Civil War from 1861-1864. He lost a leg in the Battle of the Wilderness. His 1874 appointment as lighthouse keeper at South Haven was compensation for his loss.

South Haven Lighthouse on a stormy day.
Photo Courtesy of Gary Martin, www.coastalbeacons.com.

While lighthouse keeper, Donahue was elected village president. During his service at the lighthouse, several ships went down in Lake Michigan near South Haven. He retired in 1910 after saving at least seventeen lives. Hailed as a hero, newspaper accounts claim he often jumped into icy water to save struggling victims, and he earned a silver medal in recognition of his courageous acts. His death in November 1917 may not have freed Donahue from the keeper's dwelling. His body is buried at Lakeview Cemetery in South Haven, but there is a mystique that suggests lighthouse keepers' spirits are tugged to remain at their post. Today, the Michigan Maritime Museum uses the old South Haven keeper's house as an archive and research facility. Many who have researched in the museum report sounds of footsteps when no one is present, self-opening doors, and other sounds for which there is no explanation.

27. BENTON HARBOR

Benton Harbor had a 2020 population of 9,742. Often called the twin to its resort and tourist-oriented sister, St. Joseph, Benton Harbor has strong ties to agriculture and industry.

Originally named Brunson Harbor, Benton Harbor was founded in 1860 by Sterne Brunson, Henry Morton, and Charles Hull. The men had to dig a canal to the harbor to develop the site on the banks of the St. Joseph River and make it livable and productive.

The home of the Henry Morton family is a registered Michigan Historic Site and the oldest home in the city. It provided shelter to four generations of this early founding family.

Benton Harbor was marshy swampland bordering the Paw Paw River, when in 1863 the three founders platted the village. The city was later renamed Benton Harbor in recognition of Thomas Hart Benton, a Missouri senator who is credited with supporting Michigan's 1835 bid to become a state.

Many famous people were born in Benton Harbor including two actor/comedians, Arte Johnson and Sinbad; three professional basketball players, Anthony Miller, Quacy Barnes-Timmons, and Robert Whaley; a jazz pianist, Gene Harris (in whose honor there is a festival each summer); a rhythm and blues singer, Jerome Woods; and professional wrestler, Bobo Brazil. (See The Famous or Infamous with Ties to Benton Harbor for more information.)

Benton Harbor was home to the City of David, the third oldest religious community in the United States. The City of David had a famous baseball team that is part of Benton Harbor's historic roots.

• MUSEUMS

The Morton House Museum, 501 Territorial Road, is said to be "The Home of Benton Harbor History." Housed in the oldest building in Benton Harbor, it provides exhibits that tell the story of the city from its beginning through today. Morton House was built in 1849, by pioneer Eleazar Morton and his son, Henry. Henry's son, J. Stanley Morton helped the area's steamboat industry prosper. The Mortons were large landowners and held many public offices in Benton Harbor.

Stanley deeded the house to the Federation of Women's Clubs which, in addition to using it as a clubhouse, started the museum in the early 1960s. The Morton House Museum board now operates the museum. The Morton House is a registered Michigan Historic Site.

<<>>

Van Buren County Historical and Heritage Museum, 58471 Red Arrow Highway, a 20-minute drive from Benton Harbor to Hartford. The museum is located in the historic 1884 Van Buren County Poorhouse and contains three floors of historical memorabilia, a log cabin, blacksmith works, and a gift shop. Seasonal.

<<>>

Water Street Glassworks and Dorris Akers Gallery, 140 Water Street, located in the historic Hinkley Building. Talented artists create fire arts including blown glass, fused glass, stained glass, enamel, and lampwork jewelry that they sell in their gallery. This is a teaching/working gallery. Small and interesting stop.

● BEACHES, PARKS, AND TRAILS

Jean Klock Park, Klock Road exit off M-63. Amenities: Lake Michigan beach, paved parking, boardwalk, volleyball courts, pavilion, shelter with picnic tables, concession area, playground, bathhouse, and observation tower.

<<>>

Rocky Gap County Park, 1100 Rocky Gap Road, overlooking Lake Michigan from a bluff in Benton Township. The Park has 1,100 feet of Lake Michigan frontage and a swimming beach. Panoramic views and perfect sunsets await you at this small, quiet park along the shoreline. Amenities include an observation deck, picnic tables, vault toilets, and a parking lot.

<<>>

Sarett Nature Center and Brown Sanctuary, 2300 Nature Center Road. The sanctuary is a 300-acre wildlife preserve located on the floodplain of the Paw Paw River. It includes ponds, marshes, and swamp forests in a large wetland area. It is home to interesting wildlife, including the great horned owl. The Brown Sanctuary is located about a mile downstream from the Nature Center's headquarters and is the place for birdwatchers. The rare black tern and the American bittern have nested here. In addition, you will spot ducks, geese, rails, coots, gallinules, and green back herons. Trails are open every day dawn to dusk. Building hours are limited.

● OTHER STOPS TO CONSIDER

Lake Michigan Shore Wine Trail. Locals claim "it's a shore thing" you'll find great wine and great times along the trail. More than a dozen area wineries open their doors to tasting. Wineries dot the coast from Holland to the Indiana border. (For additional information see listing under Other Stops to Consider in Holland.)

<<>>

The Mendel Center at Lake Michigan College, 2755 East Napier Avenue. A welcoming venue with fine acoustics, and comfortable seating. Parking is easy and close, and the lineup is worth checking out.

<<>>

Benton Harbor provides other attractions including golfing, miniature golf, brewery visits, cruises, tours, and U-pick farms

● SHIPWRECKS

The **Havana**, a 135-foot two-masted schooner, was lost on October 3, 1887. She carried bulk cargoes during her career. The *Havana's* first scrape with trouble was near Port Huron in Michigan's Thumb. She was salvaged and repaired and put back into service. She was less fortunate on her next brush with disaster. On October 3, 1887, the *Havana* was bound for St. Joseph with a load of iron ore. Captain John Curran encountered rough waters and was unable to safely steer the *Havana* into the St. Joseph Harbor. The hold took on water, and the captain unsuccessfully signaled a tug. The *Havana* foundered. Three of the crew—Captain Curran, the ship's cook, and another seaman—drowned after they scrambled onto the rigging and clung to the mainmast. It fell dumping them into the water. The tug *Hanna Sullivan* rescued the other four crewmen.

Today, the *Havana* lies in approximately 52 feet of water eight miles north of Benton Harbor about one mile from shore. She has broken apart leaving the hull, keelson, centerboard, and more for divers to investigate.

• The Famous or Infamous with Ties to Benton Harbor

Muhammad Ali. He claimed he was the greatest and the world came to believe him. Muhammad Ali was born Cassius Marcellus Clay Jr. in Louisville, Kentucky, on January 17, 1942. After he retired from the ring, he rested his weary and pummeled bones on a farm in Berrien Springs, a small community about eight miles from Lake Michigan. Ali had owned the place for 27 years. He liked it because there was no traffic and few people. Rumors long persisted that Al Capone owned Ali's farm in the 1920s and buried some of his ill-gotten gains on the property. Ali's cornerman, Drew Brown, hoping to find treasure, searched Ali's homestead, but came up empty-handed. If the farmhouse was owned by Al Capone, someone else held the title for him. A records search shows no Capone in the chain of title. It is speculated that the wife of one of Capone's bodyguards held the farm in her name. (See Al Capone under Sawyer in this guide.)

There is no adequate way to summarize in a paragraph or two the life of this three-time, world-heavyweight, boxing champion of the world. He was a braggart although most of his claims bore at least a resemblance to the truth. He was charming, witty, and wrote outrageous poems that garnered him attention in the press and brought a sense of liveliness to the sport.

By age 18, young Clay won Olympic gold and developed an acute social consciousness. His first wife quoted him as saying,

"I was young, Black Cassius Marcellus Clay who had won a gold medal for his country. I went to downtown Louisville to a five and dime store that had a soda fountain. I sat down at the counter to order a burger and soda pop. The waitress looked at me. 'Sorry, we don't serve coloreds,' she said. I was furious. I went all the way to Italy to represent my country, won a gold medal, and now I come back to America and can't even get served at a five and dime store."

The story ends with Cassius Clay, who had been sleeping with the medal and proudly wearing it everywhere, throwing the meaningless gold trinket off a bridge. Ali, himself, does not confirm the bridge part of the story; he simply recalls losing the medal. Either way, his political conscience was stirred by a waitress at a coffee counter in Louisville.

He converted to Islam and was given the name Muhammad Ali by Muslim patriarch Elijah Muhammad. It meant "beloved of Allah." Ali was a conscientious objector to the War in Vietnam. He said he had no reason to kill men he did not even know. For his refusal to serve in the armed forces, he was stripped of his title and boxing license and was not allowed to fight professionally for more than three years. Ali went into exile. He appealed his conviction and remained in the public eye.

His boxing matches are legendary, especially his bouts against Sonny Liston and Joe Frazier. His career resulted in a total of 61 fights, of which he won 56. Of those 56, 37 were knockouts. Movies and books have been written about him. History has painted this incredible athlete with a softer, kinder brush than the newspapers and tabloids of the day.

In Southwest Michigan, he lived a modest life for one who called himself "The King of the World." He had a pool and a pond and a security gate with an intercom. He seemed content to play with his adopted son; perhaps making up for the time he did not spend with his older children. After his retirement, Ali devoted himself to worldwide humanitarianism. He spent winters in Arizona where he died in 2016. He remained a devout Sunni Muslim and lent his name and presence to hunger and poverty relief, supported educational efforts, promoted adoption, and encouraged people to respect and try to better understand one another. Perhaps that is as much his legacy as his boxing.

<<>>

Quacy Barnes-Timmons was born in Benton Harbor on September 26, 1976. She played college basketball at Indiana and professional basketball for the Sacramento Monarchs, Seattle Storm, and Phoenix Mercury of the WNBA. After her playing career, she became Eastern Illinois' women's head basketball coach.

<<>>

William Richard Berry was born on September 14, 1930, in Benton Harbor. He was a jazz musician, best known for playing trumpet with the Duke Ellington Orchestra in the 1960s. His father was a bass player, and the family spent most of their time traveling. As an infant, he slept in his father's bass case under the bandstand.

<<>>

Houston Harris is better remembered by his ring name Bobo Brazil. He was one of the first successful African-American professional wrestlers and credited with breaking down barriers of racial segregation in the sport. He lived in Benton Harbor and played baseball in the Negro Leagues for The House of David before he began wrestling. He was working at a steel mill when he got his chance to try wrestling.

<<>>

Wilson Chandler was born on May 10, 1987, in Benton Harbor. He played professional basketball for the New York Knicks where he was their first-round draft pick in

2007. He also played for the Denver Nuggets before going to the Chinese Basketball League.

<<>>

Gene Harris was born in Benton Harbor. He was known for his soulful, blues-drenched piano style. From the late 1950s through the late 1970s, Harris was part of the jazz trio, The Three Sounds. After a short retirement from touring, he returned to record many albums for Concord Records. An annual festival in Benton Harbor continues to honor Harris and his music.

<<>>

Earnest Lee Hudson was born on December 17, 1945, in Benton Harbor. He has an impressive acting career and appeared in dozens of film and television roles, but is best known as Winston Zeddemore in the *Ghostbusters* film series.

<<>>

Arte Johnson (Arthur Stanton Eric Johnson), the comedian most famous for his characters on *Rowan and Martin's Laugh-In*, was born on January 20, 1929, in Benton Harbor. While working in New York City, he impulsively joined an audition line and, to his surprise, was cast in a revival of *Gentlemen Prefer Blondes*. His two most memorable characters from Laugh-In are the Nazi soldier and Tyrone F. Horneigh.

<<>>

Julie Krone became the first female jockey in the National Thoroughbred Racing Hall of Fame in 2000. She was born in Benton Harbor on July 24, 1963. In 1993 Krone became the only woman to win the Belmont Stakes, a Triple Crown race, after which ESPN gave her an Espy Award as the year's top female athlete.

<<>>

Iris Floyd Kyle was born on August 22, 1974, in Benton Harbor. She is an extremely successful professional female bodybuilder with more than a dozen titles including ten overall Ms. Olympia wins and seven overall Ms. International wins.

<<>>

James Mangrum was born on March 30, 1948, in Benton Harbor. He went by the stage name Jim Dandy and was the lead singer for the American Southern rock band Black Oak Arkansas. He is known for his raspy voice, long hair, and wild, sexually explicit stage antics, sometimes imitating sex with a washboard that accompanied his singing.

<<>>

Anthony "Pig" Miller was born in Benton Harbor on October 22, 1971. The 6'9", 225-pound guard played basketball for Michigan State University. He was selected by the Golden State Warriors in the second round, 12th pick of the National Basketball Association Draft in 1994. He played professional basketball from 1995 to 2005 for the LA Lakers, Atlanta Hawks, Houston Rockets, and Philadelphia 76ers.

<<>>

Charles Willard Moore was born on October 31, 1925, in Benton Harbor. He became an architect, educator, and writer. He won the American Institute of Architects Gold Medal in 1991. He has been called the father of postmodernism.

<<>>

Sinbad was born David Adkins on November 10, 1956, in Benton Harbor, the son of a preacher. Sinbad became a standup comedian and an actor. He played Coach Walter Oakes on *A Different World* and hosted his own show, *The Sinbad Show* in the early 1990s. Sinbad is ranked 78 on Comedy Central's list of the 100 Greatest Standup Comedians of all Time.

<<>>

Ruth Mae McMahon Terry was born in Benton Harbor on October 21, 1920. She was a singer and became a film and television actress from the 1930s to the 1960s.

<<>>

Chester "Chet" Walker played high school basketball for Benton Harbor High. He earned the nickname Chet the Jet for his speed, and he played starting forward on the 1966-67 Philadelphia 76ers team as a teammate of Wilt Chamberlain. Walker was a seven-time all-star. In 2012 he was inducted into the Basketball Hall of Fame.

<<>>

Lyman Munson Ward was a colonel in the Union Army during the Civil War. He was nominated and confirmed for appointment to brevet brigadier general in 1866. On January 19, 1909, he died in Benton Harbor and is buried in the local Crystal Springs Cemetery.

<<>>

Robert Whaley was born on April 16, 1982, in Benton Harbor. He was voted Mr. Basketball of Michigan even though Benton Harbor missed winning the championship the year he received the honor. He was selected by the Utah Jazz as the 51st pick in the 2005 National Basketball Association Draft.

<<>>

Jerome Woods, known as Rome, was born in Benton Harbor on March 5, 1968. His first singing experience was in the church choir. In high school, he joined a rhythm and blues band, Fire & Ice and toured regionally both as a solo artist and with the band. He dropped out of college and moved to California to further his career. RCA heard his demo and signed him. His first album, *Rome*, was released in April 1997, and made it to number 30 earning Rome gold certification. Two years later he released *Thank You* and then *Soul Snatchers*.

Books

Muhammad Ali, **The Greatest, My Own Story,** (Illustrated). In his own words, the heavyweight champion of the world shares the battles he faced in and out of the ring. The memoir is edited by Nobel Prize-winning novelist, Toni Morrison.

<<>>

Alex Kotlowitz, **The Other Side of the River: A Story of Two Towns, a Death, and America's Dilemma**. This novel about a Black teenaged boy murdered and dumped in the river opens ugly wounds and fosters accusations. St. Joseph is a prosperous lakeshore community and ninety-five percent white. Benton Harbor struggles economically and is ninety-two percent Black. The cities of St. Joseph and Benton Harbor, separated by more than the St. Joseph River struggle to solve the mystery and find justice.

<<>>

Elaine Cotsirilos Thomopoulos, **St. Joseph and Benton Harbor** (Images of America). Through more than 200 photographs, this book documents St. Joseph's and Benton Harbor's development from the time when pioneers first struggled to create a community in the wilderness.

Movie

Ali. The 2001 American biographical sports drama focuses on the ten years between 1964 and 1974 in the life of Muhammad Ali. He gains the heavyweight title from Sonny Liston, converts to Islam, becomes an outspoken critic of the U.S. policy in Vietnam, is stripped of his title, returns to fight Joe Frazier in 1971, and regains the title from George Foreman in the Rumble in the Jungle fight of 1974.

28. St. Joseph
Including Berrien Springs

St. Joseph had a 2020 population of 7,511. It has been flatteringly called "The Riviera of the Midwest." Its lakeshore is sprinkled with dune formations. Further inland lush countryside produces some of the nation's finest orchards and vineyards. Southwestern Michigan is the largest non-citrus fruit-growing region in the nation.

In 1679 French Explorer La Salle and 14 fellow adventurers constructed a fort on a bluff overlooking the St. Joseph River. They did not stay long, and the area remained unsettled except for a mission established in about 1700 at the mouth of the river. It was described in Catholic Church records as "The Mission of St. Joseph of Lake Michigan." St. Joseph was the Patron Saint of Canada which, at that time, was called New France. New France sent Jesuit priests to convert Native Americans living in the area.

In 1691 the French built a fort and fur trading post about 21 miles from the current city of St. Joseph. Fort St. Joseph remained an important trading post from 1691 to 1781. Pottawatomie migrated to the area in 1721 and were active in the fur trade.

Four flags flew over Fort St. Joseph before the fortification was vacated. In 1761 the British captured it from the French during the French and Indian Wars. In 1780 Americans raided and temporarily claimed the stronghold. The Spanish captured the fort in 1781 after a group of French and Native Americans asked Spanish Governor Cruzat to authorize an attack on the fort. The Spanish Governor believed gaining possession of the fort would diminish British control in the region so he agreed to support the effort. As a result, the Spanish flag briefly flew over the garrison. However, the British quickly reclaimed and held the fort until the signing of Jay's

Treaty on November 11, 1794, but by then it was no longer a thriving post and trading center. After the British abandoned Fort St. Joseph, it fell into ruin and was overtaken by forest. It is currently an archeological site.

William Burnett was the first European settler in the area. In 1805 William Hull was made governor of the newly formed Territory of Michigan. The largest Native American settlements at that time were in the northeast portion of St. Joseph County and the southeast part of Kalamazoo County.

Legends passed on by Native Americans to the European settlers, and by the settlers to their children, suggest fierce battles took place between various tribes for possession of the land in this area. The fertile soil produced abundant maize, the dense forests provided plentiful game, and the lake was full of fish.

The last battle is believed to have been fought in 1801. The Pottawatomie had lived peacefully for a long time with their neighbors, the Odawa of Kalamazoo Valley. The Shawnee, motivated by their desire to possess the rich wilderness land, allegedly broke the peace. They carried out a sneak attack on the unsuspecting Pottawatomie, defeated them, and attempted to drive them from the area. As the Pottawatomie fled, they carried with them Princess Mishawaka, daughter of the fierce Shawnee leader, Chief Elkhart. The story says the princess found happiness with her scout captor. The Pottawatomie, eager to regain their land, struck an alliance with the Odawa of Kalamazoo County and the Odawa of the Grand River Valley area. The strength of the three tribes drove out the Shawnee, and peace returned.

In the early 1800s, an elderly enterprising Native American chief established a toll station on the old trail near Mottville and charged travelers a fee to pass.

It is believed that European settlers introduced the Native Americans to whiskey, and by 1821, supposedly under its influence, Odawa Chief Topinabee sold most of what is now St. Joseph County to the settlers. The terms of the deal provided the Odawa with annual payments of $5,000 a year for 20 years, $1,500 a year for a blacksmith and a teacher, and $1,000 a year forever.

There was a growth spurt after the Carey Mission Treaty of 1828. The developing crossroads was named Newberryport in honor of a prominent businessman who lived there. The village incorporated in 1834 and was renamed St. Joseph.

The city became the permanent county seat in 1894, about the same time resorters and tourists began discovering St. Joseph. Hotels sprang up to accommodate visitors, and the Silver Beach Amusement Park opened to provide entertainment.

The area's rivers and streams feed the St. Joseph River contributing to its grandeur. Steamers, freighters, and pleasure boats have long found the St. Joseph River an ideal Lake Michigan port.

• MUSEUMS

Box Factory for the Arts, 1101 Broad Street, is set in a historic factory building originally constructed at the turn of the century to manufacture containers for various decorative and specialty purposes. The business continued to perform that function until 1989. The Berrien Artist Guild purchased the Williams Brothers Paper Box Manufacturing building in 1995. The Guild's enthusiastic artists converted the old structure into a multi-use arts facility, called it the Box Factory for the Arts, and deemed it a place where arts are celebrated. Two floors of the 55,000-square foot multi-use art center include artist studios, galleries, a performance stage, classrooms, an art shop, meeting space, and more. Visitors are invited to watch artists create their work.

Browse the studios and shop for one-of-a-kind items for themselves or to give as gifts.

<<>>

Curious Kids Museum, 415 Lake Boulevard, (across from Silver Beach), and Curious Kids Discovery Zone 333 Broad Street. [At the time this guide was being compiled, both Curious Kids Museum and the Curious Kids Discovery Zone were temporarily closed due to COVID-19.[7] The goal of closure was to ensure the safety of the children for whom these venues are a resource. The staff constantly monitors the situation and hopes to open soon. Check social media or the website for updates. The museum staff can't wait to hear giggles again!]

Voted Reader's Choice *Best Museum in Southwest Michigan* and *Best Place to Take Kids*, the two locations are steps from each other. The museum is hands-on and encourages kids to touch, see, hear, smell, and even taste with over 100 exhibits and activities spread over two floors. Children are drawn to the Toddle Farm, Farmers Market, Curious Kids Veterinarian Clinic, GEO Kids, Kids Space, and Face Paint. The second floor encourages creativity through its exhibits which include Emergency Vehicles, Bubbles, Construction Junction, Super Speedway, Physics of Sound, Simple Machines, the *S.S. Cruizer*, What If?, and the Sandbox.

The Curious Kids Discovery Zone is geared for ages 3-12 years old with special exhibits including the Lighthouse Climbing Tower, Lake Michigan Water Table, Water Power Tower, Wave Table, Pin Table, Whisper Dishes, and more.

<<>>

Fort Miami Heritage Center, also known as the Priscilla U. Byrns Heritage Center, 601 Main Street (Corner of Main and Market Streets). This Greek Revival Building, on the site of the historic First Congregational Church,

---

[7] Curious Kids opened in July, 2021, but given the uncertainty of COVID-19 variants, it would be wise to confirm that it remains open before planning your visit.

incorporates architectural elements salvaged from local houses scheduled for demolition. The Center promotes historical preservation, education, and research that relates to Benton Harbor, St. Joseph, and the surrounding region. They strive to help visitors create a personal/emotional connection with the past to see the present and future more clearly. An exhibit hall, research library, and gift shop are on the premises.

<<>>

Gallery on the Alley, 611 Broad Street, is the place to check art and fine crafts from 175 American artists who offer a wide selection of jewelry and other art in mediums from whimsical to fine art. The gallery features junkyard dogs and cats by Yardbird, Story People prints, sculpture, books, clocks of Leonie Lacouette, art glass, Me2U fused glass, and other works from the country's most talented artists, all beautifully displayed in this charming gallery.

<<>>

Krasl Art Center, 707 Lake Boulevard, has brought people and art together for 25 years. Monthly exhibitions, trips, and a gallery shop. In 1962 a handful of local artists explored creative ways to get their art noticed. They held a clothesline art exhibition along Lake Bluff Park. After that exhibit, those artists formed the St. Joseph Art Association, which in 1979 received funding from George and Olga Krasl that allowed them to build the Krasl Art Center. The Center's 17,500 square feet of space has public galleries, art-making studios, a black-and-white wet darkroom, and a permanent collection of 41 sculptures.

<<>>

Twin City Players Theatre, 600 West Glenlord Road. One of the oldest continuous performing theatre groups in Michigan, founded in 1932, TCP has performed for almost 90 years. Community theatre at its best, the performers tackle both comedy and drama and give top-notch entertainment.

● Beaches, Parks, and Trails

Knauf Park and Nature Trail, 3000 Washington Avenue, access off Vineland Road at June Trace, ends at Niles Road. Knauf Park offers a 2.4 mile moderately trafficked out and back trail plus parking, benches, picnic area, information about the trail, and one of the points of access. The trail takes you through a wide range of habitats in a minimal amount of acreage (34 acres). Many plants and creatures find a stream, forest, marsh, or meadow suited to their tastes.

<<>>

Kiwanis Park and the John and Dede Howard Skatepark, Pearl Street near Langley Avenue. Amenities: picnic tables and shelter, playground, basketball and tennis courts, and also home to the John and Dede Howard Skateboard Park, an in-line skating, skateboarding, and BMX biking facility.

<<>>

Lake Bluff Park, 201 Lake Boulevard, runs along downtown St. Joseph. Unparalleled views of Lake Michigan, Silver Beach, and the St. Joseph River. Amenities include a walking trail, picnic tables, benches, and historic monuments.

<<>>

Lion's Park Beach, below the bluff in downtown St. Joseph, south on Lions Park Drive. Amenities: parking and sidewalks, sheltered pavilions, grills, playground, restrooms, and a view of the St. Joseph piers and lighthouse. There is no lifeguard and swimming is discouraged at this beach.

<<>>

Lookout Park, Lakeshore Drive off Hilltop Road, north of Hawthorne Avenue. Amenities include views of Lake

Michigan, picnic facilities, and a viewing deck. This is not a swimming beach, but you will get the closest approach to the bluff. It is a place for picnicking, relaxing, and lake watching.

<<>>

Riverview Park, 2927 Niles Road (south of St. Joseph). A 107-acre park located in a bend of the St. Joseph River. The park has baseball fields, playground equipment, picnic shelters, boat access, and nature trails.

<<>>

Silver Beach County Park, 101 Broad Street, below the bluff in downtown St. Joseph. Silver Beach County Park is located at the mouth of the St. Joseph River and offers a clean, wide beach with 2,450 feet of Lake Michigan frontage. Almost 1,600 feet of the frontage are dedicated to public swimming in the summer. Amenities include men's and women's bathhouses, bike racks, playground, volleyball courts, visitors center, and swimming beach.

<<>>

Tiscornia Park, 80 Ridgeway Street, north of St. Joseph River Channel off Upton and Marina Drives. Amenities include a public beach and access to the North Pier and lighthouse, dunes, a pavilion, fishing, picnic area, restrooms, and a place to fish.

Park in St Joseph. Courtesy of Bob Royce.

St. Joseph/West Basin Marina provides 90 rental slips and ten transient slips. The marina is a publicly accessible waterfront facility that provides space to moor or dock boats and yachts. In addition to docking and storage, the Marina provides services such as fuel and marine supplies, maintenance service and boat repair, and bilge and sewage pumping.

● OTHER STOPS TO CONSIDER

Nye's Apple Barn, 3151 Niles Road, Exit 27 off I-94. Farming since the late 1800s, Nye's has fruits and veggies (apples, peaches, raspberries, strawberries, grapes, sweet cherries, pears, plums, pumpkins, zucchini, cucumbers, tomatoes, peppers, eggplant, gourds, and squash) as well as cider, jams, jellies, honey, salsa, syrup, and take 'n bake pies.

<<>>

Silver Beach Carousel, 333 Broad Street. In an earlier life, Silver Beach was once visited for its amazing amusement park with boardwalk, midway, pavilion, and carousel. The carousel was a prized feature. People came from all over to ride—or just see—the authentic-looking horses, each a work of art. Then the amusement park closed. The people of Southwest Michigan missed their unique carousel and began figuring out ways to purchase it and put it back in the park. It was not meant to be.

Original Silver Beach Carousel. Courtesy of Pixabay Free Images.

The original carousel had already been disassembled and moved to a new home in Washington State. The Carousel Society opted to obtain another carousel, but it had to be special if it were to replace the original. Meticulous research and planning went into the project and today the new carousel brings joy to another generation of admirers. The carousel opened in 2010 and the millionth rider climbed onto her chosen horse in 2017. The steed she chose was decorated in an MSU motif.

<<>>

Whirlpool Compass Fountain and Splash Pad, 333 Broad Street. The fountain is 200 feet in diameter and sprays water 35 feet high. Located next to the carousel at Silver Beach, the jets spray 10,860 gallons of recycled water every 15 minutes. Kids of all ages love this alternative for cooling off on a hot summer day. Best of all, it's free.

<<>>

There are a few dozen shops and galleries to explore downtown. Antiquing, fishing charters, fruit farms, boating, swimming, restaurants, and much more will vie for your attention in St. Joseph.

● LIGHTHOUSES

St. Joseph North Pier Outer Lighthouses and **St. Joseph North Pier Inner Lighthouse**, North Pier Street. The Outer Lighthouse perches on the north breakwater at the mouth of the St. Joseph River. The structure is a round, cast-iron plated 35-foot-tall tower topped by a round watch room and a 10-sided lantern room. Toward the middle of the pier sits the St. Joseph North Pier Inner Light. The two lights are connected by an elevated catwalk that extends from the shore to the outer light.

The original St. Joseph lighthouse was lit in 1832, just months after the first lighthouse on Lake Michigan commenced operation at Chicago. In 1859 a new two-story lighthouse with a frame keeper's dwelling and a square tower rising from one end of its peaked roof took over safeguarding the waters around St. Joseph. This second light was roughly 48 feet tall, but because it sat on a bluff, it gave a focal plane of 101 feet above lake level. In 1864 the color of the light was changed from white to red to distinguish it from other lights along the coast.

The mainland light was discontinued in 1885, and the position of keeper was eliminated until 1889 when the mainland light was reactivated. In 1904 the War Department extended the north pier. Today's range lights on the north pier were constructed in 1907. The steel framing of the front tower tapers slightly from its base to its nine-sided lantern room.

The rear tower is a 24-foot-square steel structure with a pyramidal roof surmounted by an octagonal tower. The pier's original steam whistle was transferred to the lower portion of the new structure. A diaphone fog signal was installed in the rear tower in 1933.

The original 1859 lighthouse was razed to build a parking lot. In May 2008, the St. Joseph Pierhead and Inner Lights were deemed excess by the Coast Guard. They were offered at no cost to eligible entities. After some negotiating about what would be done with them and how they would be preserved, the pier lights went to the City of St. Joseph. The lights needed a great deal of restoration and fundraising began to raise money for the project.

Today, St. Joseph and Grand Haven are the only piers on the Great Lakes that retain their range lights and catwalks. A commemorative stamp with the St. Joseph Pier Lights was issued in 1995.

St. Joseph North Pier Light during a winter storm.
Courtesy of Gary Martin, www.coastalbeacons.com.

In his book *America's Lighthouses: An Illustrated History*, Francis Ross Holland Jr. wrote, "They are called lakes, but from the lighthouse point of view they have virtually all the characteristics of the ocean."

• SHIPWRECKS

The **Desmond**, a wooden-hulled propeller, went down on December 8, 1917. The ship sold sand it extracted from the bottom of Lake Michigan. December is late in the season and the *Desmond* was on her last trip of the year when Captain Emil Thorsen departed St. Joseph in the afternoon headed northwest for Racine with a load of sand. Gale winds blew the *Desmond* off course, hurling

314

her into the path of a nasty squall blowing high waves and subzero temperatures.

Thorsen realized the danger and headed for the safety of the Chicago Harbor. Everyone aboard feared this would be their last trip—not for the year, but of their life. A survivor later said crew members tried to persuade the captain to run the ship on a beach, but he refused. He had been sailing for thirty years and never lost a ship. He declared that if the *Desmond* went down, he would go down with her.

The continued rocking of the waves shifted the cargo of sand causing the *Desmond* to list to starboard. The crew shoveled furiously to get the ship back on an even keel. They were inspired by the lights they saw in the Chicago Harbor. Surely with safety so close, they would be rescued.

At 2:00 a.m. the ship developed a leak in the stern. The engines had to be shut down to operate the steam pumps. The crew continued working all that long terrifying night to keep their ship afloat. At the same time, they frantically tried to get someone's attention to their plight. Water was gaining on them. One of the coal bunkers collapsed, and pieces of coal clogged the pumps and siphons.

The Captain decided his only chance to save his ship was to launch a lifeboat and row for help. He desperately needed a tug to haul them in. As the lifeboat headed away, the *Desmond* tipped on its side, and its stack hit and capsized the lifeboat, throwing its occupants into the water. The eight men still aboard the *Desmond* scrambled up top as their vessel tipped.

The *Desmond* floated that way for several hours, buying them critical time. The men still aboard the ship threw ropes to the five they spotted floundering in the icy water. Captain Thorsen and Frank Kipper managed to grab the ropes and were pulled alongside the ship, but

Thorsen froze to death as he lay there. Kipper survived, along with the eight still on board. They were rescued by the tug, *William A. Field*. The *Desmond* finally sank at 7:00 a.m. Seven men died in the disaster.

● THE FAMOUS OR INFAMOUS WITH TIES TO ST. JOSEPH

Caryl Chessman was born on May 27, 1921, in St. Joseph. He died in the San Quentin gas chamber 38 years later. His given name was Carol, but he later changed the spelling to Caryl. Shortly after his birth, the family moved to California. Caryl suffered from asthma and was a sickly child. He contracted encephalitis which he claimed changed his personality and led to a life of crime. He rebelled against the family's strong Baptist values. He committed minor crimes—stealing food and other necessities to help his parents survive the Great Depression. His father lost several jobs and attempted suicide on at least two occasions. His mother was paralyzed in an auto accident when Caryl was eight.

From petty theft, Caryl graduated to grand theft auto. He was sent to reform school, released, stole another car, joined a gang, and escalated to robberies and shootouts with police. He served time in San Quentin and Folsom and hardened himself to a life of crime that included raping and robbing his way through life.

In 1948 California had a law called the Little Lindbergh Law which made kidnapping a capital offense and defined it as moving a victim and causing bodily harm. In a robbery attempt, Chessman stopped a young couple, and dragged the female victim 22 feet from the car before assaulting her. The circumstances stretched the definition of kidnapping, but Chessman was sentenced to death. The law was repealed by the time the trial began, but the repeal was not applied retroactively.

Chessman spent 12 years on death row. During his incarceration, he wrote four books, *Cell 2455, Death Row*; *Trial by Ordeal*; *The Face of Justice*; and *The Kid Was a Killer*. In addition to seeking public sympathy through his writing, Chessman argued against the death penalty. He gained worldwide support for his antideath-penalty campaign from influential people including Eleanor Roosevelt, Billy Graham, and writers Aldous Huxley and Robert Frost.

After eight stays of execution, Chessman's appeals ended. He was executed on May 2, 1960, a month short of his 39th birthday.

<<>>

Nina Davuluri attended high school in St. Joseph before becoming the 2014 Miss America and then a television reality show host.

<<>>

James Frey, author, was outed on Smoking Gun website for fictionalizing a large part of his memoirs including details about his criminal past. One incident mentioned was a 1986 train-automobile accident in St. Joseph Township.

<<>>

Harry T. Gast Jr. was born on September 19, 1920, in St. Joseph. He served in both houses of the Michigan Legislature where for the last 18 years of his services, he chaired the appropriations committee.

<<>>

Sean Giambrone was born on May 30, 1999, in St. Joseph. He got his first acting stint in a McDonald's commercial when he was nine years old. Later jobs included the role of Adam F. Goldberg in the sitcom, *The Goldbergs* and Ron Stoppable in the Disney Channel version of *Kim Possible*.

<<>>

Larry Darnell Gordon, a criminal handcuffed and in a sheriff deputy's custody, was being escorted from a holding cell into the St. Joseph Courthouse on July 11, 2016. He faced a number of charges that carried possible life sentences. Gordon's handcuffs were locked in front, not with his hands behind his back, and there was no link to a belly chain to limit his movement. He attempted escape, disarmed the deputy, killed two bailiffs, injured the deputy, and attempted to take hostages. Court officers responded by shooting and killing Gordon.

<<>>

Michael Joseph Green was born on October 13, 1917, in St. Joseph. A devout Catholic, he became a bishop of the church and served as an ordained priest for the Diocese of Lansing. He was later named the Titular Bishop of Trisipa and Auxiliary Bishop of Lansing. He attended all four sessions of the Second Vatican Council from 1962 to 1965.

<<>>

Doris Keane, a live-theatre actress was born on December 12, 1881, in St. Joseph. She was educated primarily in Europe.

<<>>

Rachel Renée Russell was one of five siblings born in St. Joseph. She is the author of the best-selling children's book series, *Dork Diaries*.

<<>>

Craig Smith was born on August 11, 1975, in St. Joseph. He started his career as a standup comedian where he developed his voice. He then started doing voices including that of Sonic the Hedgehog from the *Sonic* series.

<<>>

The Uptons of Southwest Michigan. The Uptons were an influential family instrumental in bringing Whirlpool to the Benton Harbor-St. Joseph area. Emory and Louis Cassius Upton helped create the precursor to the modern washing machine. They described their appliance as a labor-saving device designed to make a woman's life easier. The homemaker could relax in a rocker and pull a handle that moved the agitator back and forth. The invention was dismally received.

Louis' father was Cassius Marcellus Upton. He was likely named for the antislavery leader Cassius Marcellus Clay (October 19, 1810-July 22, 1903), who served the abolition movement. Although Clay came from a Southern slave-owner background, he risked his career, wealth, and life for the abolitionist cause. Why Upton was named for an abolitionist leader is unclear.

The better-known Cassius Marcellus Clay is the heavyweight champion who converted to Islam and took the name of Mohammed Ali. Ali also had ties to the St. Joseph-Benton Harbor area of Michigan. (See Mohammed Ali under The Famous or Infamous with Ties to Benton Harbor.)

Frederick Upton, grandnephew of Louis and uncle to supermodel Kate Upton, was a Senior Vice President of Whirlpool Corporation. He was a politician and served in the U.S. House of Representatives.

<<>>

Karen Ziemba, Tony award-winning actress and dancer, was born on November 12, 1957, in St. Joseph.

● BOOK AND MOVIE WITH TIES TO ST. JOSEPH

Kelly Pucci, ***Hidden History of St. Joseph County***, Quirky stories about the forgotten history of St. Joseph County, including fishing for diamonds, saloon bashers, and Lakeside Cemetery which provides the final resting place of more magicians than any other cemetery in the world.

<<>>

Kill Me If You Can, starring Alan Alda, was a 1977 television movie about the life of Caryl Chessman (also called *The Caryl Chessman Story*). (See The Famous or Infamous with Ties to St. Joseph.)

• GHOST STORIES

The Ghost Skater of Hickory Creek. Hickory Creek runs south of St Joseph. Sometimes—especially in days past—there had been enough water in the creek to allow ice skating. There is nothing unusual about someone wanting to skate by moonlight on frozen winter waters. The thought could be quite enchanting, but what a young Harvey Seasongood claims he saw as he stood caught in the barbs of a fence facing the river was anything but delightful.

Seasongood and his buddies had stayed out later than they were supposed to that winter night. The sun had set and darkness crept in to fill the spaces between the ghostly trees. As a phantom skater glided close, the frightened children dispersed up the ravine. Seasongood's jacket snagged on the barbs of a fence, and he was caught, facing the oncoming figure. Fortunately, the skater didn't seem to notice the young boy, or if he did, must have been uninterested.

Seasongood swears he saw the skater and describes the figure floating by as an enormous specter clad in black tights and wearing a skull cap. The creature had cloven hooves, and if that wasn't quite enough to terrify the youngster, the skate blades flashed green sparks and blue flames. The phantom leaped over a bridge while shrieking macabre laughter. More ominous was what Harvey noticed that sent a second wave of shivers up his spine; the skater cast no shadow under the bright moonlight.

The tale has since been repeated around campfires and by parents trying to mold their children's behavior by fear. "Be home before dark or the skater of Hickory Creek may get you." A local newspaper breathed life into the tale when on January 30, 1863, columnist William Ast made it a front-page story told to him by Seasongood.

<<>>

The Mansion Grille Ghost. The now-closed Mansion Grill began its life as home to the Smith family from Chicago. The house was built in 1892 as their summer home, and from what we know, it was a place of joy and renewal for them until 1929. That gloomy year the stock market crashed, and Mr. Smith, dejected and inconsolable, jumped from a building to his death. The widow Smith sold the property to Otis Colby in the early 1930s. The Colby family operated a used car lot to the north of the house. The Colbys also operated a produce stand across the street on the lakeside for many years. The house became known as the Colby Mansion. The family remained in the house for sixty years, celebrating many happy occasions, including their 50th wedding anniversary, within its walls.

In 1990 the home was purchased as the site for an upscale restaurant. The new owners spent nearly three years renovating and preparing the mansion for its new incarnation. The goal was to restore the magnificent old home to its original splendor.

Apparently, the resident ghost, likely that of Mr. Smith, appreciated the renovations which made him feel at home. He continues to inhabit the basement. He is a shy and considerate ghost and the current owners only became aware of his presence through a book about ghosts in the Midwest.

29. STEVENSVILLE

Stevensville had a 2020 population of 1,141. The town was named for Thomas Stevens who purchased 160 acres of land there in 1869. Mr. Stevens struck a deal with the Chicago and West Michigan Lake Shore Railroad

Company to have a railroad depot built on a portion of his property. The contract required the depot to be named after Stevens, and per the terms, he was to be paid $1 for the land. By having a depot located at this spot, Mr. Stevens assured himself transportation to get his fruit crops to market.

Stevens had the land platted in 1870, but the plat was not recorded until 1872, and an additional decade passed before the Michigan Senate formally acknowledged the Village of Stevensville as a chartered village in 1893.

Another early Stevensville pioneer was John Beers who came to the area from New Jersey in the same year as Stevens. After a failed peach crop, Beers entered Medical School at Northwestern University and later returned to Stevensville to set up practice. In addition to farming and practicing medicine, Beers was an active politician, serving as a state senator and in many lesser positions.

• BEACHES, PARKS, AND TRAILS

Glenlord Beach, 3000 West Glenlord Road, Exit 23 off I-94, north on Red Arrow Highway and west on Glenlord Road. Overlooking Lake Michigan from an observation deck on a high bluff, you can enjoy the most spectacular views in all of Southwest Michigan. Picnic tables and restrooms available. Swimming is not allowed at this site because of beach erosion.

<<>>

Grand Mere State Park and Nature Area, 7337 Thornton Drive, Exit 22 off I-94. The 1,000-acre park has a nature center that covers slightly over a third of that acreage. The nature area is a favorite place for birdwatchers. At the entrance, there is parking, and the beach is about ten minutes down the self-guided path. You will need a permit that can be obtained at Warren

Dunes State Park. Amenities include shelters, pit toilet restrooms, and paved trails. The path winds along the dunes (sand and tall grasses) to the lake. Grand Mere is not far from Warren Dunes, but the feeling of the two parks is entirely different. If you are seeking a social beach experience, Warren Dunes is more appropriate. For the nature lover who enjoys the rustic, Grand Mere might make you happier.

<<>>

Lincoln Township Park and Nature Center, 5575 South Roosevelt Road, Red Arrow Highway and Notre Dame Road just south of Stevensville. Amenities: boardwalk, access to the beach, picnic area, and restrooms.

Stevensville: Early Days.
Courtesy of the Village of Stevensville.

30. BRIDGMAN

Bridgman enjoyed a 2020 population of 2,213. In the late 1600s, the French became the earliest European explorers to the area. They found dunes, marshes, and forests awaiting them on the shores of Lake Michigan. It took another century and a half before the first settler, John Harner, arrived in 1834. Known then as Laketon, the small village grew around the sawmill.

The village was renamed Charlotteville to honor the wife of a prominent citizen, Charles Howe. However, in 1870 George Bridgman plotted an area about a half mile east of Charlotteville and named it after himself. Bridgman had the good fortune or good sense to plot his land directly in the path of the Chicago and West Michigan Railroad, a situation that gave rise to growth in Bridgman and the decline of Charlotteville, the latter eventually disappearing altogether.

At the end of the nineteenth century, Russian and German immigrants began populating the area and working on fruit farms and in other industries. In 1949 Bridgman became a city, and today it covers three square miles. The lake attracts tourists by the hundreds in the hot summer months. Permanent residents are drawn to upscale living in beautiful homes built on the dunes. A sidewalk connects the community with Weko Beach making the walk to the beach an easy one.

● MUSEUM

Historic Courthouse Square, 313 North Cass Street, in nearby Berrien Springs. An 1839 log house, courthouse, sheriff's office, jail plaza, and the Herb and Heritage Garden. Also a museum shop. Open seasonally.

● BEACHES, PARKS, AND TRAILS

Warren Dunes State Park, 12032 Red Arrow Highway, south of Bridgman, Exit 12 off I-94. Warren Dunes is almost 2,000 acres of park with varied terrain. Rugged dunes rise majestically above Lake Michigan. Tower Hill dune soars 240 feet above lake level and is the focal center of the park that beckons more than a million visitors a year. Amenities include picnic tables and shelter, concession store, playground, restrooms, swimming beach, and trails for cross-country skiing and hiking. Sandboarding and hang gliding are favorite activities in the park. Two campgrounds can be reserved: Warren Dunes Modern and Warren Dunes Semi-Modern. Warren Dunes Modern, on the inland side of the dunes, is within walking distance to the beach. It offers 200 campsites. Warren Dunes Semi-Modern is smaller and more rustic. It provides 30 campsites, some with more privacy and others that are fairly close together. There are also three cabins. These campgrounds are packed to capacity in the summer months, so you'll need reservations. Take insect repellant.

<<>>

Weko Beach, 5239 Lake Street, Exit 16 off I-94, then north on Red Arrow Highway, and west on Lake Street. Amenities include 900 feet of Lake Michigan beach, concessions, beach house, changing areas, restrooms, boat launch, volleyball, boardwalk, and two magnificent dunes. There are 70 campsites with electricity, 48 that have water, 25 rustic sites, and four camping cabins available. *Taps* is played each night at dusk on summer evenings.

<<>>

Lake Michigan Shore Wine Trail. The Lake Michigan Shoreline is dotted with wineries. (For information see listing under Other Stops to Consider under Holland.)

<<>>

Bridgman has charters, farm-fresh produce markets, U-pick orchards, breweries, wineries, and a host of water activities.

31. SAWYER

Sawyer is a census-designated place that had a 2020 population of 1,344. In the mid-1800s, Silas Sawyer, an Ohio judge, decided it was time to leave the bench and experience a more tranquil lifestyle. He purchased 100 acres on which he intended to create an orchard. Before he planted fruit trees, he cut the original timber and hauled it to the nearby pier for shipment to Chicago.

Sawyer has remained an agricultural center, and lovely vineyards grace its rolling fields. Today Sawyer is known for its proximity to the Warren Dunes. (See Parks, under Bridgman.) A few antique shops provide the traveler with a diversion from the lake, dunes, and beach, although none can compete with the area's natural beauty as a tourist draw.

It is the northernmost village in the group of eight collectively known as Harbor Country.

● BEACHES, PARKS, AND TRAILS

Covert Park Beach and Campground, 80559 32nd Street, next to Warren Dunes between Sawyer and Bridgman. (See Parks, Beaches, and Trails under Bridgman.) This township park offers ¼ mile of private sandy beach. It is both a day-use and camping park. Day use provides picnic tables, grills, and restroom facilities. The entrance to the campground is down a lovely, short drive along a tree-canopied road. Amenities: water and electricity, bathhouse, store, picnic tables, playgrounds, dump station, ice, firewood, and new camping cabins.

● ANOTHER STOP TO CONSIDER

Local Harvest, formerly Joe Jackson's Michigan Fruit Stand, 12120 Red Arrow Highway. Although the market has changed ownership, it has been a farm produce market for as long as many people can remember. It first opened in the 1950s and was taken over by Joe Jackson in the late 1980s. Joe ran the popular fruit stand for 30 years and made it famous in the area. After Joe's passing, the market closed for a few years. In 2010 Local Harvest reopened the market and is working hard to restore it to its prior popularity. They partner with local farmers to provide the freshest selection of fruits and vegetables, local honey, and a wide variety of other products including baked breads, jams, jellies, salsa and flowers.

Fruit and Vegetable Stand.
Courtesy of Bob Royce.

• THE FAMOUS OR INFAMOUS WITH TIES TO SAWYER

Al Capone has numerous connections to southwestern Michigan. Historians don't dispute that. However, since gangsters don't leave a clear trail or make their movements easy to trace, pinpointing where he skulked the shores and sands is open to speculation, some fact, some legend, and maybe even some creative fiction. Capone is alleged to have owned a home on Flynn Road in Sawyer, and the area around Sawyer is rife with tales of the notorious gangster, so this is an appropriate place to provide a few stories about the best known of all bootleggers and his links to Lake Michigan.

Chicagoans, including Capone, merely had to step out their back door to find themselves in the middle of Michigan's lakeshore playground. They left behind the seediness, pressures, crowded conditions, crime—all that went into creating the angst of the big city—and relaxed on pristine beaches as beautiful as those found

327

anywhere in the world. Capone's life is written in ink on the pages of Chicago history; it is written much less indelibly in the sands of Lake Michigan's Gold Coast where he came to play, unwind, and sometimes hide.

It is irrefutable that Capone was a murderer, racketeer, drug dealer, pimp, brothel owner, bootlegger, political boss, gambler, and perhaps the most successful gang leader in history. And yet, we are captivated by this cocky killer. To a select few, he was a modern-day Robin Hood. Unlike Robin Hood, though, he generally took from everyone and left a trail of murder and mayhem in his path.

In 1917 at the age of eighteen, Al Capone earned the nickname he would carry throughout his life. He was waiting tables at the Harvard Inn in Brooklyn and was enthralled by a beautiful Italian girl sitting in his section. Al was not sure if it was her body or her face that tantalized him most; his eyes were riveted on her. With the brash ignorance that accompanied his youth, he approached the table, leaned toward the stunning woman, and blurted in a voice loud enough for her brother, sitting next to her to hear, "Honey, you have a nice ass, and I mean that as a compliment." By today's standards that is not the raunchiest thing one can imagine, and as Al suggested, some women might have been flattered.

But Frank Gallucio, the outraged brother, leaped to his feet. Frank was drunk and much smaller than Al. But he had the courage of liquor on his side. He also had a four-inch knife which he immediately brandished at Al. Gallucio aimed the knife directly at Al's neck and made his first stab. Al was hardly fazed by the cut and moved closer to Gallucio, who got in two more slashes along Al's cheek. Then with uncommon good sense Frank grabbed his sister by the hand and made a hasty exit before Al, who was trying to stanch the flow of blood, could come after him. As the scars healed, they left white, jagged ridges along Al's left cheek, and the gangster remained sensitive to his disfigured face. He turned his head when cameras focused on him so they captured his right, non-scarred side.

Gallucio, fearing for his life, went to Lucky Luciano who mediated the beef between the two hoodlums. The justice meted out by Luciano required Capone to apologize to Gallucio, adding insult to the very real injuries that would brand him Scarface forever. It was a learning experience for the young Capone—there were times when he needed to shut his mouth and control his temper.

By 1920 Chicago was the second-largest city in the United States with a population of 2,701,705. That same year, on January 16, the 18th Amendment, known as the National Prohibition Act, made it illegal to manufacture, sell, or transport intoxicating liquor. Rowdy, rapidly growing, Chicago was ready for Al Capone. He arrived one year later in 1921. He was not the only bootlegger in Chicago, but he dominated the business. There was Capone, and then there was everybody else. Capone did not like everybody else.

Every gangster needs a safe house, and Capone is alleged to have had one in Southwestern Michigan. He crossed the border from Illinois, drove north to a house plunked down in the middle of nowhere, and was ready to hole up and keep a low profile. Some accounts suggested the location of this hiding place was on Purgatory Road. Maybe that's a little too poetic. It is more likely it was near Constantine at the intersection of Preston Road and Harvey Street. The house is gone, but a small bunker in the side of the hill is said to remain.

The most famous home Capone reportedly owned in Michigan is the farmhouse later purchased by Muhammad Ali. Title to this 88-acre farm on Kephart

Lane in Berrien Springs is believed to have been held in the name of Charlotte Campagna, the wife of one of Capone's bodyguards. Whether it was truly Capone's home is open to speculation, but the stories are persistent, and Muhammad Ali never denied them. Instead, Ali added a few of his own details.

The Twin Gables Hotel & Restaurant (currently the Hotel Saugatuck, a Michigan Historical Landmark) operated in Saugatuck during the 1920s and was a regular stop for Capone and his gang. It presented them with a win-win situation: sell bootleg liquor to the owner and enjoy a bit of carousing. A bullet hole in the bar's wall is reputed to have been made by one of Capone's thugs defending the honor of the thug's woman from another customer's advances.

Frankfort has its own Capone story. Joe Winkler ran bootleg liquor for Capone in the area, and rumor says a tunnel connected his home to the Hotel Frankfort where his boss stayed when in town. Capone also had reported connections to the House of Ludington Hotel in Escanaba and a home in the Leland area.

In Lakeside, just five miles from Sawyer, Capone played an occasional game of poker with his buddies at the Lakeside Inn. (See Ghost of the Lakeside Inn under Lakeside.) The inn may have been one of the gangster's favorite drinking and gambling spots during prohibition. The inn provided sleeping quarters and entertainment to movie stars and Chicago politicians. Capone loved glitz and considered himself part of the big-city, flashy in-crowd. The Lakeside Inn was his kind of place.

Capone's murders, bootlegging, prostitution, and other crimes went unpunished. It is commonly accepted that from his home in Miami after he moved south, he orchestrated the St. Valentine's Day Massacre. On February 14, 1929, the bloodbath sent seven mobsters of the Bugsy Moran gang to their death. After that,

Capone became known as Public Enemy No. 1. To accomplish the hit, he enlisted the services of Machine Gun McGurn who was more than happy to do a favor for Capone. McGurn studied the movements of Bugsy's gang. He called on Capone's occasional golfing partner, Killer Burke, from St. Louis to lead the group. Although Burke spent much time in Chicago and Benton Harbor, few associated him with Capone. Burke agreed to a fee of $5,000 for carrying out the job. He hired a gunman named James Ray. The slaughter took place in a parking garage at 2122 North Clark Street in Chicago. The assassins dressed as cops, and the Moran gang, obviously believing the charade, lined up against a wall as ordered. It was a brutal machine-gun execution, but the intended target, Moran, was not present.

In December 1929, Burke sideswiped a car on Main Street in St. Joseph, Michigan, and during an ensuing altercation, he fired four shots at a young police officer, Charles Skelley, who was attempting to arrest him. Skelley died in the hospital, and police launched a manhunt for his killer. At that point, Burke vanished for over a year. During his absence, Major Calvin Goddard was carefully examining the bullet patterns from the St. Valentine's Day massacre. He also studied the bullets and shells recovered in the Skelley shooting and matched their markings to the bullets retrieved from the bodies of the massacre victims. When Burke was found, hiding out at his father-in-law's farm in Milan, Missouri, he was happy it was the police and not other mobsters "taking him for a ride." He was extradited to Michigan, where he stood trial and was sentenced to life in prison for killing Officer Charles Skelley. The long arm of the law couldn't touch Capone in that killing.

The income tax evasion trial that finally resulted in Capone's imprisonment was presided over by Judge James Herbert Wilkerson who was intent on bringing the notorious gangster to justice. Capone's men had bribed the entire jury pool. Capone's confident smirk vanished when Judge Wilkerson entered the courtroom and announced, "Judge Edwards also has a trial commencing today. Go to his courtroom and bring me his entire panel of jurors. Take my entire panel to Judge Edwards." With that, the men who were supposed to sit in judgment of Capone left the courtroom, where they were replaced by a new set of prospective jurors whose names had not appeared on any list, and who had not been approached with bribes or threats from the Capone organization. During the trial, Judge Wilkerson hid his young son in Southwest Michigan to protect him from the Capone gang's retaliation. Capone was convicted of federal tax evasion and served seven years in prison.

Al Capone died of syphilis-related complications on January 25, 1947. He was forty-eight and a free man at the time. However, his mind was bedeviled by then, and he was never more than a shadow of his former ruthless self.

<<>>

Carl Sandburg was the People's Poet. Many of his contemporaries found their voices and sought inspiration through association with other writers and poets in London and Paris. Sandburg found his genius near his beloved Lake Michigan and her dunes. He will always be associated with Chicago, but much of his writing took place in his Sawyer and Harbert homes.

Part of Sandburg's legacy was making Chicago real to the rest of the world through his finely chiseled poetic descriptions. The city was alternately the Hog Butcher of the World and the Freight Handler of the Nation. She was a City with Broad Shoulders, a City of Cunning, and at times a Laughing City. He loved her when the fog came in from the harbor on little cat feet. His was an exciting Chicago; a Chicago full of mobsters and bootleg liquor; a city that seduced with opportunities of overnight wealth and shunned with oppressive poverty. Carl Sandburg attempted to capture it all.

Early literary success from *Chicago Poems* and his *Rootabaga Stories*, a book of fanciful children's tales, convinced Sandburg's publisher, Alfred Harcourt, to encourage Carl to write a juvenile biography of Abraham Lincoln. For most of his life, Sandburg had been fascinated by Lincoln and collected information about the Great Emancipator. He had a complete, complex filing system of materials and a ten-volume set of Civil War photographs plus several biographies to start his research. After three years of intense work, the intended juvenile biography ended up a two-volume biography for the adult market.

Sandburg maintained a frantic schedule writing and lecturing, and as a result, his health suffered. He was in his mid-forties and a respected author. He had not taken a vacation since completing the Lincoln biography. He was working on the *Songbag* manuscript and on the road lecturing much of the time.

His wife Lilian, known by her middle name Paula to her husband and friends, looked for a new home where her husband could take life easy and regain his strength. She wanted a place with tranquility and solitude—a place where Carl could restore his soul. She found that place— a summer cottage on Lake Michigan at Tower Hill near Sawyer. She called it Wren Cottage. While Carl was in New York for a month on business related to *Songbag*, she moved the family to their new lakefront property. Regarding the move, Carl told a friend, "I nearly went bankrupt in health" referencing his work on the Lincoln biography. Wren Cottage was his safe haven; the place he rested and recuperated.

Sandburg and his family, which included three daughters he affectionately called his "Homeyglomeys," all loved their Lake Michigan bungalow, but Carl complained about the way, "invaders from Lakeside" transgressed his privacy. Still, by 1927 the Sandburgs decided to live on the Lake Michigan shore year-round. His lecture schedule kept him away from Wren Cottage much of the time, and every spare moment was dedicated to his writing.

Concluding that their current home was too small and the area too heavily populated with summer visitors, they bought a large lot in nearby Harbert in Chickaming Township.

Paula designed their dream home which was to have a special place where Carl could work uninterrupted by the stresses of daily life. There would be his workroom, a bedroom, and a deck where he could write outside when the weather permitted. His suite would be on the third level of the white clapboard home—away from the mundane bustle of an active family. Paula's plans included a fifteen-by-thirty-foot steel and concrete, shelf-lined vault in the basement. Carl's research files, manuscripts, and books could be safely stored in a fireproof and dehumidified mini-fortress.

Sandburg turned fifty on January 6, 1928. He took long walks on the dunes he had grown to love. He described his work to a friend, "I've been laying off and protecting myself from the disease called civilization—amid the sand hills of Michigan." He had reached a point in his life where financial security was no longer a concern. He had earned $7,000 in lecture fees the previous year, the equivalent of what today would be an annual salary of approximately $140,000.

Carl maintained a rather schizophrenic relationship with the lakeshore. He admired its beauty and felt content, but then his compulsive nature would take over, and he'd give in to one or another of his many obligations and leave.

Sandburg was again in robust health and began working feverishly in the family's new home on the secluded Lake Michigan shore. He turned his attention back to one of his favorite and recurring subjects, Abraham Lincoln. This time it was the war years. By 1929 he was so engrossed in his Lincoln project that he rarely left home, even to lecture. He still wrote a column for the *Chicago Daily News*. This was the most prolific and productive period in Sandburg's life. He played guitar and sang. And, of course, he wrote.

Paula, acknowledging although not resenting, the time Carl spent on *The War Years*, raised a goat herd on the extra lot she had purchased next to their home. Carl called it Paula's summer of the "three Gs": garden, geese, and goats. Paula's herd provided the milk that allowed her to make all the family's cheese and butter. The garden contributed string beans, spinach, corn, cantaloupe, squash, pumpkin, and broccoli.

It was a peaceful time for the Sandburgs. Paula's farm ran smoothly, and Carl wrote feverishly. He continued working on *Lincoln: The War Years*, but also began devoting time to an epic 112-page poem, *The People, Yes*.

Occasionally Carl took short breaks and visited with neighbors. Sometimes notables like Frank Lloyd Wright dropped in on the Sandburgs. But in the late 1930s, Carl again returned his undivided attention to *Lincoln: The War Years*. Carl loved working in his dune paradise. Of Lake Michigan, he said, "The Lake performs. The lake runs a gamut of all moods." Sometimes he went into his Crow's nest to watch a sudden, angry storm overtake his lake.

For days at a time, Sandburg lost himself in Lincoln's world. He perched on a sturdy wooden fruit crate and bent over his reconditioned Remington typewriter and pecked away. When the weather was warm, he moved the crates to the third-floor sundeck where he enjoyed the sunshine on his skin as he lost himself in reflection. As a break, he indulged himself in long walks on the beach. He often swam at noon. He drank coffee and smoked a cigar.

By 1938 Sandburg had incorporated every last note and shred of information into a document that was more than a million words long. He was ready to begin editing. His goal was to have the book ready for print in September 1939. Upon publication, Harcourt had to rush a second printing to meet the Christmas demand. Sandburg was awarded his first Pulitzer Prize in 1940 for *Lincoln: The War Years*. With its completion, he admitted, "I'm slowing down. There's a weariness in the bones . . . the heave and the haul, the slime and the scum of a long voyage, is still on me." He was by that time nearly sixty-two years old.

In 1943 Carl turned sixty-five. He was the celebrated author of poetry, biography, children's stories, a folk music anthology, and a news commentary. The house on Birchwood Beach in Harbert seemed strangely quiet with all three of his daughters grown and gone. It was time for Carl to take on another challenge. He had not yet written a novel, and that became his next project. It was tentatively titled *American Cavalcade*.

In 1945 Carl began the novel and decided to move from his beloved home on the Lake Michigan shore. He enjoyed the beauty of each new season, but the severe winters were brutal as they blew down with a fierceness that he no longer wanted to brave. The bleak gray and cold which endured from the fall color change through spring every year made the Sandburgs yearn for a warmer, more accommodating climate.

Paula began searching for a new place to call home. It had to have space for her prize-winning goat herd. There had to be plenty of flowers. She wanted fruit trees. And there had to be privacy and solitude for her husband. She found the perfect place in North Carolina. The beautiful mountains to the north of what would be their new home were a bonus. By January 1946, the Sandburgs left the Lake Michigan shore forever. It had been their home for nearly twenty years. Their family had grown up there. Carl had earned his Pulitzer there. He was sixty-eight. For the man who left school after the eighth grade to help support his family, it was time to move on. The West Michigan shore lost its most illustrious citizen.

Courtesy of Joe Jurkiewicz.

• GHOST STORY

The Ghost of the Timeless Treasures Antique Store. The proprietor of Timeless Treasures was surprised a few years ago when a group of high schoolers stopped by and asked about the ghost that lived in the building. The owner was unable to provide them with much information, and the details were sketchy. The ghost's name was Joe, and what follows is the bare bones of his story.

Joe owned Blackstone Grocery which many years ago occupied the building that later housed Timeless

Treasures. Joe and his wife had a tempestuous relationship.

After one particularly unpleasant disagreement, the distressed wife escaped to Grand Rapids to visit their son. When Joe realized she had truly abandoned him, his emotions kicked into overdrive. He was angry, hurt, provoked, and indignant. More than anything, he wanted revenge. He was driven to confound his wife as much as her leaving had confounded him. Acting on his first hunch, he called one of his wife's friends. He was assured his wife was not there. He did not believe the friend. The thought that his wife played games with him only further infuriated Joe, and he became more agitated. He went into the back room and retrieved his gun. It is unclear whether it was a handgun or a shotgun, but either would have sufficed for what he contemplated.

He sat for a while and reflected on his situation. Joe decided not to just kill himself; he needed to make his errant wife suffer. Joe called their son to see if the son knew his mother's whereabouts. Joe was surprised when his son said, "She's here." Joe asked to speak to her. As she listened, Joe said, "Look, what you have made me do." And with that, he blew off his head. This suicide was believed to have occurred in the 1940s, and Joe's ghost has found no peace since. Maybe it serves him right.

32. HARBERT

Harbert had a 2020 population of 2,830. The tiny community was founded in the 1850s by John Glavin, a local farmer, who was riding a train between Chicago and Detroit and noted the flat, barren land in the area. He thought it would be a good place to locate a train depot. Unfortunately for Glavin, it was a wealthy industrialist from Chicago who had the money to carry out the dream. Along with the village's gratitude, the industrialist was afforded the honor of naming the small town which became Harbert and not Glavin.

Orchards and vineyards were the economic mainstay of the region, and the trains transported the fresh fruits to the final market in Chicago.

Carl Sandburg wrote much of his Pulitzer Prize-winning *Lincoln: The War Years* while living at his Harbert home. (See *Famous or Infamous with Ties to* Sawyer.)

• MUSEUM AND GALLERY

Fort St. Joseph Museum, 508 East Main Street (behind City Hall), Niles. This museum may be worth the time to travel inland a few miles. Its exhibits include pictographs drawn by Sitting Bull, the famous Sioux chief, history of the fur trade, Fort St. Joseph excavation artifacts, ice age fossils, history of prehistoric people living in the area, Victorian decorative arts, Underground Railroad connections, Civil War memorabilia, and artifacts and history of railroads, business, and industry. The museum attempts to tell the complete story of early Niles and its contributions to Michigan and the world. The museum is housed in the Chapin Mansion.

<<>>

Jill Underhill Gallery, 13462 Red Arrow Highway. Outdoor sculptures, oil paintings, fine arts and crafts by many nationally recognized artists. A destination for contemporary sculpture, fine art, and fine crafts. The gallery features metal sculptures of Underhill's husband, John Searles. The gallery is located one-half mile from the beach and two miles from I-94.

<<>>

Judith Racht Gallery, 13707 Prairie Road (near Red Arrow Highway). Each summer month brings a new exhibit of contemporary art. Judith opened her gallery with the intention of creating a high-caliber and diverse art gallery featuring both emerging and established artists from the area. The artwork covered a variety of mediums and was ever-changing. The little shop across the street is part of the gallery and displays primarily textiles, rugs, and quilts.

• BEACHES, PARKS, AND TRAILS

Cherry Beach was deeded to Chikaming Township by the Warren family in 1922. The park offers approximately 253 feet of shoreline, picnic facilities, and a street-level observation deck which is wheelchair accessible. Attendant on duty, and passes are available for parking.

<<>>

The Harbert Road Preserve is located on Harbert Road east of the I-94 overpass between Three Oaks Road and Flynn Road. This 90-acre preserve's amenities include two ponds, wetlands, wooded and open land trails, a shelter, prairie grass fields, wildflowers, and nesting fields for pheasants.

<<>>

Chikaming Township Park and Preserve is located on Warren Woods Road between I-94 and Lakewood Estates. The 263-acre natural area offers trails for hiking, mountain biking, and cross-country skiing. It also provides viewing platforms, fishing pier, picnic area, restrooms, and a community garden. The topography includes uplands, wooded floodplains, 2,800-feet of frontage on the Galien River, and a 5.3-acre lake.

• OTHER STOPS TO CONSIDER

Southwest Michigan offers a winery tour or you can pick and choose the wineries you'd like to visit. (For mor information, see listing under Other Stops to Consider in Holland.)

Antique stores, galleries, fine dining restaurants, and other attractions worth investigating dot the shoreline.

● The Famous or Infamous with Ties to Harbert

Al Capone and Carl Sandburg are included under the Sawyer listing in this guide. However, their lives flowed over into other Southwest Michigan beach towns, including Harbert (Sandburg) and Lakeside (Capone).

The Sandburgs moved from their tiny cottage in Sawyer to their house on Birchwood Drive in Harbert. They called their new home Chikaming Farm. It is perhaps in this home that Carl Sandburg achieved his best writing.

33. Lakeside

Lakeside had a 2020 population of 250. It is believed the early Native Americans named the area north of New Buffalo, Chikaming. In the Algonquin language, the words *Chigike-Chiamiu* translate to *by the side of the great expanse* or more loosely to *on the shore of the sea.* Translations may not be exact, but in this case, on the shore of the sea seems appropriate.

John Wesley Wilkinson arrived at Chikaming in the 1850s and established Wilkinson's Trading Post and Boarding House, both of which were lucrative local businesses for many years. The small community was named Lakeside in 1874.

The economic history of the village was similar to that of so many others along the Michigan coast. Forests drew the attention of lumber barons seeking to make a fortune, and some realized their dream and grew rich. When timber was depleted farming took over. The sandy, somewhat acidic soil, was perfect for growing fruit.

Eventually, however, most coastal towns realized their fortunes lay in the establishment of resorts where the wealthy built second homes. Tourists, who flocked to the beautiful beaches to wade in the water, play in the sand, and watch the sun set majestically in the west, brought a much-needed infusion of money to the area. There are antique stores, galleries, and other specialty stores that will gladly help you part with some of your cash.

• MUSEUM AND GALLERY

Wilkinson Heritage Museum at Wilkinson Village, 15300 Red Arrow Highway (located in the former trading post built by city founding father John Wilkinson). This little museum houses artifacts from the Wilkinson family and a history of the Lakeside area. Period dolls, furniture, clothing, and jewelry are on display, and visitors can view early photos of the area.

<<>>

Abigail Heche, 14866 Red Arrow Highway. Abigail Heche is highly talented, like her big sister, actress Anne Heche, but Abigail is gifted with a different set of artistic abilities. For 20 years, Abigail has created beautiful, high-end jewelry for stars and common folks alike. She uses quality gemstones and other materials to fashion subtle but exquisite pieces that are inspired by love, the countryside, travel, and the simple life. Her pieces range from uncomplicated sterling silver shapes borrowed from nature to unique one-of-a-kind creations studded with diamonds. Abigail spends summers at her home and gallery in Lakeside and has expanded the shop to include a clothing line and quilts made in collaboration with her mom.

Ghost of the Lakeside Inn. Arthur Aylesworth and his brother first visited the Lakeside Inn Resort on a family camping trip when they were boys. In 1901 they persuaded their parents to buy the inn and the thirty acres of land surrounding it. The total cost of the purchase was $4,500. In 1917 Arthur's father died, and two years later his mother deeded the property to him.

The hotel/inn is located on a dune and stands three stories high with an English basement[8] at the rear. There are half a dozen ground-floor entrances around the perimeter. As far as is known, no architect was involved in the inn's design. It has two large, stone fireplaces, back-to-back, one in the lobby and the other in the ballroom.

Arthur Aylesworth operated the hotel and owned significant other property in the Lakeside area. He was always buying, mortgaging, and selling land. The inn had beautiful gardens and a mini-zoo in the back with a pet bear, raccoon, deer, goats, and peacocks. During its heyday there was gambling just off the lobby, and boatloads of alcohol were consumed inside its walls during Prohibition. Supposedly, bootleggers' vessels from Canada beached in front of the hotel, and guests waded into the lake to help unload the cases of whiskey. It is alleged that Al Capone visited the place to relax. (See the Famous or Infamous with Ties to Sawyer.)

Arthur was a world adventurer who traveled extensively in South America and Alaska. He produced films about his game hunting expeditions. He also toured with Buffalo Bill's Wild West Show, operated a gambling hall and bar in Las Vegas, and married and divorced

---

[8] An English basement is an apartment on the lowest floor of a building, often a townhouse or brownstone. It is usually partially below and partially above ground level and is often call a garden apartment. It has a separate entrance from the rest of the building.

Florence Young, the sister of movie star, Clare Kimball Young.

During the 1930s, Aylesworth went bankrupt more than once but somehow managed to maintain ownership of the inn until the 1950s. After divorcing his first wife, he married an actress named Virginia Harned. Mrs. Harned-Aylesworth toured the country in the play, "The Woman He Married," produced by her husband. Years before her death, she was shot and wounded by Arthur who insisted it was an accident. Sentiment in the local community ran contrary. No charges were filed and both Mrs. Aylesworth and the marriage survived. During a massive rehabilitation of the inn in 1995, a bloodstained towel with Aylesworth's initials was found hidden in a wall.

During the later years of his life, Aylesworth, whose second wife had predeceased him, still lived in the inn. He became a lonely figure watching a tiny television set in the lobby until sleep finally numbed his mind. At about 10:00 p.m. each evening, the handyman who lived in an outbuilding behind the inn was awakened by the ghost of Virginia Harned-Aylesworth. She urged the handyman to go inside and awaken Mr. Aylesworth and tell him it was time to undress and go to bed. Through subsequent decades, many visitors have detected the presence of the ghost of Mrs. Aylesworth—especially in or near Room 30.

There is less agreement over whether there is also a male ghost on the premises, presumably Mr. Aylesworth. A guest at a wedding in the ballroom swears she observed Mr. Aylesworth's silhouette with a pet raccoon on his shoulder. All indications suggest these are harmless ghosts, pleased to continue residing in their inn. It seems that even bankruptcy, death, and familial squabbles—if shooting a spouse can be called a squabble—cannot keep them away.

In an interesting aside to the ghost story, Aylesworth eventually lost the inn to foreclosure by the Niles Bank. He died in the University Hospital at Ann Arbor, where no one knew his illustrious background. His cadaver was almost used for experimentation by medical students. A doctor from the hospital mentioned, during a phone conversation with the township lawyer of Lakeside, that one of their citizens had died at the hospital. When people from Lakeside realized what had happened, several men went to Ann Arbor to claim the body which was then buried in a plot Ayesworth had purchased at the Lakeside Cemetery.

The Lakeside Inn. Courtesy of Samuel Darrigrand.

34. Union Pier

Union Pier had a 2020 population of 628. In 1861 John Gowdy moved from his home in New York to the site that would become Union Pier. He was immediately struck by the lush natural beauty of the forests surrounding him. Spectacular trees measuring up to five feet in diameter and sometimes 60 feet to the lowest branches represented a source of cheap lumber; Gowdy saw a fortune waiting to be harvested.

Capitalizing on the potential fortune required finding a way to cut the mighty giants and then transport them to market. Gowdy and his partners resolved the first problem with no more than strong backs and a few simple tools.

Getting the felled trees to Chicago, their logical destination, presented a thornier dilemma. The savvy businessmen recognized the need for a ship to haul the cargo and a pier for docking. They set about constructing a 130-ton schooner on the beach and then built Union Pier at the foot of Berrien Street to provide their ship with docking facilities. The pier ultimately gave its name to the area.

Success seemed a foregone conclusion, and the area prospered. With growth came a larger sawmill and a new industry, a brick factory.

The horrific Chicago fire of 1871 increased the demand for cordwood, timber, and bricks. Union Pier was financially secure until the depletion of the forest coupled with the washing away of the pier forced the village to look for a new economic foundation. The fertile soil left in the wake of forest removal was perfect for fruit farms and agriculture.

The 1900s brought an even more lucrative business— one shared by all sister beach cities on Michigan's West Coast—exclusive resorts and tourism. Chicagoans needed to get away more than they had needed bricks and lumber.

Today, time is clarified by Southwest Michiganders as Michigan time to distinguish the more relaxed pace enjoyed by resorters and tourists from the more frazzled pace felt in the Windy City. Of course, there is a literal difference because of the time difference between

Michigan (Eastern Time Zone) and Illinois (Central Time Zone).

• GALLERY

Local Color Gallery, 16187 Red Arrow Highway. This bright and colorful gallery displays the work of over 90 artists, many of them local. The art includes paintings, fine crafts, jewelry, furniture, pottery, photography, sculpture, glass art, and more. Styles range from contemporary to delightfully whimsical. Prices range from very affordable to an investment in art.

• OTHER STOPS TO CONSIDER

Tiny Union Pier is close to many activities in Southwest Michigan, including the wine trail tour (For additional information see listing under Other Stops to Consider in Holland), breweries, museums, galleries, shopping, cruises, parks, beaches, camping and more. Look under the listings for nearby towns and cities to find more than enough to fill a busy vacation schedule.

• SOMEONE FAMOUS WITH A TIE TO UNION PIER

Jesse Owens once owned a home in Union Pier and spent many summers there. His parents named him James Cleveland Owens. He was the seventh of eleven children of sharecropper, Henry Owens, and his wife Emma. Jesse was the grandson of a slave. He was first called Jesse by a teacher who did not understand when he said his name was J.C.

Owens' junior high track coach, Charles Riley, found young Jesse on a playground and put him on a track team. Riley became Owens' inspiration and mentor. Owens practiced before school because he had a job in a shoe repair shop after. He attended Ohio State University and got his first taste of fame at a Big Ten Track Meet in

Ann Arbor on May 25, 1935, when he tied the record for the 100-yard dash and set world records in the long jump, 220-yard dash, and the 220-low hurdles. His performance, rendered in less than an hour, is still considered one of the most amazing athletic achievements of all time. At Ohio State, he was a member of Alpha Phi Alpha, the first Greek fraternity established for African-Americans.

In the 1936 Olympics, Owens represented the United States. Adolf Hitler saw the games as a way to showcase

Jesse Owens at 1936 Olympics. Public Domain.

Nazi Germany to the rest of the world. He did not intend them to promote the triumphs of African-Americans whom he considered inferior. He called the dark-skinned children of German women, Rhineland Bastards, and their mothers he labeled whores and prostitutes. In *Mein Kampf,* he denigrated these children as a black disgrace. Hitler was dismayed and shocked when Owens won four gold medals: the 100-meter dash, long jump, 200-meter dash (he beat Matthew Robinson, Jackie's brother), and the 4x100 meter relay. Jesse's records stood until the 1984 Summer Olympics when Carl Lewis won medals in the same events.

A story in the papers at the time of his victory noted that Hitler shook hands only with the German athletes who won medals and left early to avoid shaking hands with Cornelius Johnson, another African-American. In spite of Hitler's politics, the crowds in Berlin applauded Owens enthusiastically. Owens came back to the United States and had to ride a freight elevator to a reception in his honor at the Waldorf Astoria. Of the slight by the

German Chancellor, Owens commented, "I wasn't invited to the White House to shake hands with the president either."

After his incredible athletic victories, Owens had difficulty earning a living. He was a sports promoter, forced to rely on theatrics to keep his job. He challenged and defeated a racehorse, later explaining that there was a trick to beating a racehorse; he had to find a high-strung horse that would be startled by the pistol, giving Owens a good start.

By the 1920s, Union Pier had developed into a tourist resort. Its proximity to Chicago, where Owens was engaged in public relations, allowed him to enjoy his home and still be close to his job. Owens was Union Pier's most famous resident—the one who used to run like the wind on its beaches. Posthumously, he received honors that had eluded him in life: The Presidential Medal of Freedom in 1976 by Gerald Ford and the Congressional Gold Medal in 1990 by George H. W. Bush. A 1999 Irish postage stamp bore his image, and a street in Berlin was renamed for him. Owens, a heavy cigarette smoker, died of lung cancer at age 66.

<<>>

John Dillinger once said, "I guess my only bad habit is robbing banks. I smoke very little and don't drink much." When the heat—both kinds—was too great, Dillinger used to flee Chicago and escape to the cooler beachfront areas of southwestern Michigan. He was a guest at the Prusa Resort, and the local gas station frequently serviced his car. Dillinger was dead before his thirty-second birthday.

35. NEW BUFFALO

The 2020 population of New Buffalo was 1,088. Today, New Buffalo serves as the cornerstone to Lake Michigan's

Beach communities. It is a harbor town bustling with the activity of its public beach, lake and riverside parks, boat launch, and marinas. Condos and yachts predominate the landscape.

In earlier years, Native Americans prized the land and water around New Buffalo for its bountiful fishing and hunting. The lake and rivers provided a water highway for canoes. The Miami, Iroquois, and Pottawatomie fought for control of this area with the Pottawatomie victorious. The riches of the land tempted French fur traders, who were later followed by missionaries intent upon converting the Native Americans.

In 1834 Captain Wissell Whittaker, bound for Chicago, tangled with one of Michigan's notorious Storms of November, and the gale afforded no mercy. The waves hurled the schooner, the *Post Boy*, ashore near current-day Grand Beach. The ship was a total loss, but captain and crew miraculously made it to safety and struck camp before starting for St. Joseph to report the wreck of their ship.

On his way, the captain was awed by the beauty of the New Buffalo Harbor. Besides finding it physically stunning, he considered its utilitarian potential as a port so great that he argued it could rival Chicago.

In 1835 Whittaker returned with friends and family and began buying land and laying out plans for a city. He gained partners in his endeavor, and the land quickly rose in value. The project proceeded according to Whittaker's dream until the severe 1841 winter brought an end to his speculative land development. After that, New Buffalo, which Whittaker had named for his prior home of Buffalo, New York, struggled for many years.

The Michigan Central Railroad was completed in 1849 and helped the economy rebound slightly. However, it was not until the turn of the century that the area gained recognition for its resort potential and began catering to tourists and summer residents.

Michigan recognized New Buffalo as the "Gateway" to the state and in 1934 built a tourist information center there. (See the next listing in this guide). Its current location on I-94 remains the busiest tourist center in Michigan.

In the 1960s, harbor dredging began and by 1975, New Buffalo's safe harbor was ready to offer sanctuary to boats seeking refuge from storms. The harbor never became serious competition to Chicago as Whittaker had dreamed, but the prime travel destination is busy with marine activity.

Specialty stores and unique eateries line the streets. The lakefront park is a charming place to watch the sailboats or a sunset, or perhaps feed the wild gulls, geese, and ducks that flock there to take advantage of tourists' generosity.

• GALLERIES

Courtyard Gallery, 813 East Buffalo Street. Original upper end, high-quality fine art, including paintings, bronze, blown glass, photography, and more.

<<>>

Wow Art Gallery, 529 East Buffalo Street. Primarily contemporary art, the gallery is operated by Rick Ott and Angela Reichert. Ott displays acrylic abstracts and Reichert creates mixed media collages. The gallery also exhibits the glass, ceramic, sculpture, and jewelry pieces of about 30 other artists. The business does not post hours so you have to check to see if they are open on any given day, although Rick says they are open most of the time.

Theatre

New Buffalo Performing Arts Center, at the high school, 1112 East Clay Street. A 450-seat capacity venue for summer theatre and concerts. Call for further information.

● BEACHES, PARKS, AND TRAILS

Backroads Bikeway, country roads for the cycling enthusiast. Most routes are mapped from nearby Three Oaks, but several run through New Buffalo and Lakeside, and you can pick them up or join there as you travel the coast. Twelve different trails range from 5 to 60 miles, offering fun for the beginner and experienced rider as they cycle through picturesque hills, alongside streams, farms, and meadows.

<<>>

City Beach, 100 Marquette Drive. Sandy beach. Parking fills up early. Otherwise, a great spot to put your beach chair, watch the water activity, and get a view of the Chicago skyline.

<<>>

Galien River County Park, 17424 Red Arrow Highway, offers a boardwalk along the river. Great place to explore the marsh area and surround yourself with nature.

<<>>

New Buffalo Lakefront Park and Beach, at the end of Whittaker Street across the bridge. Designated swimming areas along the 800 feet of Lake Michigan shore, picnic tables, grills, playgrounds, an 18-acre natural area, snack facilities, restrooms, and a pavilion.

<<>>

New Buffalo Municipal Marina, 100 West Water Street, located in the harbor at the end of Whittaker Street. Offers transient docking; no reservations, first come, first served. Has a boat maximum length of 55 feet. Amenities: showers, water and electric hookup, and pump-outs.

<<>>

New Buffalo Public Boat Launch, 200 Marquette. Offers 24-hour a day access to Lake Michigan from its eight ramps.

<<>>

New Buffalo Township Memorial Park, 17425 Red Arrow Highway. Amenities include playground, splash pad, hiking trail, picnic facilities, and restrooms.

● The Famous or Infamous With Ties to New Buffalo

Roger Brown was an artist and painter often associated with the Chicago Imagist groups. He had a distinctive style of painting, but he was equally known for his social commentaries directed at religion and politics as well as art. In adult life, Brown had a home and studio in New Buffalo. He drew inspiration from his Michigan dune property and commissioned his partner, architect George Veronda, to design his residence and the studio on that land. Studio and dwelling were completed in 1970 and both donated to the School of the Art Institute in Chicago in 1995. In 2004 Brown was inducted into the Chicago Gay and Lesbian Hall of Fame. The Roger Brown Study Collection and Art AIDS America Chicago, a landmark exhibition, explored how the AIDS crisis impacted art and culture. He died in 1997.

<<>>

Laurent Novikoff was born in Russia in 1888 and graduated from Moscow's Bolshoi Ballet School in 1906. He danced alternatively between the Diaghilev (1909 and 1919-1921) and Pavlova's company (1911-1914 and 1921-1928). He emigrated to the United States and became a citizen. He was ballet master at the Chicago Opera from 1919-1933, and at the Metropolitan Opera in New York from 1941-1945. He opened a ballet school in

New Buffalo and died there in 1956. He is buried in Pine Grove Cemetery in New Buffalo.

• GHOST STORIES

The Ghost of the Taylor Heath Salon. It is after the sun goes down and everyone has left for the day that the ghost or ghosts of the Taylor Heath Salon are most at unrest. Whether it is the darkness, the moon's rays streaming through the upstairs windows, or just being left alone, the disembodied souls, who struggle to escape this earth, wander about the salon trying to find their way. The staff and clients report numerous encounters with the spirits that haunt the salon. No one knows what causes the agitation of their resident ghosts, only that they make themselves known in disconcerting ways.

One evening, stylist Jennifer Kasper (all names changed throughout this story) remained late to finish up Margie Howard's shampoo and cut. They were the only two living souls remaining in the salon that night. Jen guided her client to the shampoo bowl and began lathering Margie's hair. Kasper heard the unmistakable jangling of keys and the rattle of the door up front. She had locked that door, so she tried to ignore the suspicious sounds until Margie, who heard the ruckus over the whoosh of running water, insisted, "There's someone up there." Reluctantly, Jen went to investigate, but there was no one else in the building. The front door was locked, just as she expected it would be.

Another evening, as darkness crept in, Karen Phillips remained in the building finishing paperwork long after her co-workers had left. She turned off the music that provided a pleasant backdrop to the day's busy activities. Quiet enveloped her, and she was heavy in concentration when the sounds of footsteps and gnarled mumbling filtered down from the first room at the top of the stairs. Initially, Karen wondered if someone had accidentally been locked in that tiny room. But she knew that was not possible. She continued working, dismissing the noise as the result of an overactive imagination. Then she heard an unmistakable cough. Karen was neither fainthearted nor easily rattled, but she grabbed her purse and vamoosed.

The ghost sometimes says "Hi," to employees who look up to find no one there. These occurrences are so frequent that clients hearing unexplained noises remark, "Oh, the ghost is here."

When a former owner of the building stopped by, the staff questioned him about the odd occurrences. He shared peculiar experiences from the time he lived in the building. He heard noises like children crying upstairs. Doors opened. He checked and found no one there. Unfortunately, he could not explain who the ghosts were, or why they continued to rustle about the haunted building.

<<>>

Hannah's Restaurant. This popular restaurant serves food that brings 'em in by the busload, but behind its cheery façade lurk the ghosts of two former residents who lived there when Hannah's was a magnificent and expansive home in this lovely harbor town.

James Janata brought his Czechoslovakian bride to her dazzling new domicile shortly after they were married. Mrs. Janata proved a handful. A former beauty queen, whose stunning looks captivated and enthralled her bedeviled husband, she felt a sense of entitlement. Her inexhaustible expectations left the beleaguered James weary and frustrated by his inability to satisfy her whims. Her demands were so relentless that the sweet-natured James, worn-down and heartsick, swore he would return in the afterlife to haunt her. It is suspected that he carried out his threat and that until the day she died, James capitalized on every opportunity to make his widow as miserable as she had made him during his life.

If Mr. Janata's ghost spends time in his former residence, it may be that he has enjoyed the warm, friendly feelings that have settled there since Mrs. Janata's death.

After the Janatas lived there, Hannah's became home to a rugged sea captain who sailed from the port at New Buffalo. While at sea, the captain lived a stark life barren of any luxury. He can hardly be blamed, then, if he wanted a grand and opulent home to make up for the deprivations endured while sailing. He heard of a newfangled, ostentatious luxury item known as a bathtub. The captain took a trip to Chicago to purchase this extravagance, and once installed it became the object of his great admiration. So much so, that even in the afterlife the captain came back to gaze upon its beauty. He appeared in the bathroom, occasionally wearing his skipper's uniform, and fondly, but vacantly, staring at his tub. He is a bit melancholy and causes no harm, although he may have shocked and dismayed ladies bathing as he looked on.

36. NEW BUFFALO WELCOME CENTER
Located at 11630 Wilson Road, New Buffalo.

The first book of this three-part series of Traveler's Companions, *Exploring Michigan's Sunrise Coasts,* provided information about the Welcome Center in the southeast corner of Michigan. Since Michigan's Welcome Centers are amazing, it is appropriate to end this third book with the Welcome Center that should be your first stop if you travel the state in reverse order, the New Buffalo Welcome Center in the southwest corner of the state. Located just across the border from Illinois on 1-94 west, this is the state's busiest welcome center. It provides plenty of parking and a grassy area—for you, your children, and even Fido if your dog is lucky enough to be accompanying you—to stretch, run, or walk. There is a playground and clean restrooms.

You are greeted by knowledgeable staff with an abundance of brochures, maps, and up-to-the-minute information at their fingertips. They can warn you of current construction work, road closures, and weather blips. They will also assist you with hotel or campground reservations.

There is a shop inside for souvenirs and snacks. The center earns its name as a *welcome* center—everyone employed goes out of his or her way to give you a hearty Michigan' welcome and offer assistance. If you have a travel question or problem, they do their best to answer or resolve it.

APPENDIX ONE: FIVE FABULOUS RECIPES FROM THE SUNSET COAST

Since restaurants are not listed in this guide, it seemed only fair to offer you a taste of West Michigan's Sunset Coast, and a way to do that was through recipes.

Baked Brie with Dried Michigan Cherries or Michigan Caramel Apples

<u>Ingredients</u>

    1 round (8 ounces) Brie cheese, cut in half diagonally
        sliced French bread baguette or crackers

<u>Cherry</u>

    ½ cup dried Michigan cherries
    ½ cup chopped walnuts
    ¼ cup packed brown sugar
    ¼ cup brandy or unsweetened apple juice

<u>Caramel Apple</u>

    1 Tbsp butter
    ½ cup chopped, peeled firm Michigan apple (Braeburn, Gala, or Granny Smith)
    ¼ cup sweetened dried Traverse City cherries
    ¼ cup packed brown sugar
    2 Tbsp chopped shelled pistachios or pecans
    2 Tbsp brandy or apple juice

<u>Directions</u>

1. Preheat oven to 350°. Put one half of Brie into 9" pie pan.

2. For Cherry Brie: Combine cherries, walnuts, brown sugar, and brandy; spoon half over cheese. Add second round of cheese and add remaining fruit mixture.

3. For Caramel Apple Brie: Melt butter, add apples and other ingredients and cook in microwave 3 to 4 minutes. Spoon half of fruit over brie, add second round of brie and remaining fruit.

4. Bake 15-20 minutes or until cheese is softened. Serve warm with baguette or crackers. Baguette slices can be toasted if you prefer.

Michigan Senate Bean Soup

In addition to the Michigan navy beans, this recipe calls for many veggies produced in Michigan. The vegetables don't have to come from Michigan, but if you live in the state, chances are they are locally grown.

<u>Ingredients</u>
1 pound dry Michigan navy beans
1 meaty ham bone or 1½ pounds ham hocks
1 cup chopped Michigan onion
1 cup chopped Michigan celery
1 cup thinly sliced Michigan carrots
2 cloves garlic, minced
¼ cup chopped parsley
1½ cups Michigan potatoes, peeled, and cut into small chunks
1½ tsp salt
1 tsp pepper
1 tsp each nutmeg, basil, oregano
1 bay leaf

<u>Directions</u>
1. Cover beans with 6 to 8 cups water. Boil 2 minutes. Remove from heat; cover, let stand 1 hour. Add 2 quarts of water and ham bone. Simmer 1½ hours.
2. Stir in remaining ingredients. Simmer 20 to 30 minutes until beans are tender. Remove bay leaf. Remove ham bone, trim meat from bone, and add to soup. Serve hot. Leftovers freeze well.

Notes:
You can bring the beans to a boil per step 1 and let soak overnight to make sure they don't end up hard. You can add a cup of mashed potatoes to thicken the soup.
Yield: 3 quarts.

Blueberry Walnut Salad
with Raspberry Vinaigrette

<u>Ingredients</u>
1 (10 ounce) package of mixed salad greens
1 pint fresh blueberries
¼ cup walnuts
½ cup raspberry vinaigrette salad dressing (Recipe below)
¼ cup crumbled feta cheese

<u>Directions</u>
In a large bowl, toss the salad greens with the blueberries, walnuts, and raspberry vinaigrette. Top with feta cheese to serve.

Raspberry Vinaigrette
<u>Ingredients</u>
1 cup fresh raspberries
1 Tbsp white sugar
⅔ cup balsamic vinegar
¼ cup olive oil
1 Tbsp honey
½ tsp salt

<u>Directions</u>
1. Mix raspberries and sugar in a bowl; set aside until mixture is juicy, about 10 minutes. Mash berries with fork until liquefied. Pour berry mixture into a jar with a lid; add balsamic vinegar, olive oil, honey, and salt. Cover jar with lid and shake until dressing is mixed well. Store in refrigerator.

<u>Notes</u>
You can substitute goat or bleu cheese to change the flavor. You can toast the walnuts before adding to the salad to bring out the nutty flavor. You can make with spinach instead of mixed lettuce. This is a versatile salad that uses two delicious Michigan products: blueberries and raspberries.

Gingered Carrot & Kale Ribbons

<u>Ingredients</u>

8 large carrots (about 2 pounds), peeled

¼ cup vegetable oil

3 slender leeks (white parts only) thinly sliced, washed, and dried

1/3 cup golden raisins, coarsely chopped

2 cloves garlic, finely chopped

2 Tbsp finely grated fresh ginger

1 Tbsp finely grated lemon zest

1 Tbsp lemon juice

salt and pepper

4 large kale leaves, tough stems removed and leaves thinly sliced

<u>Directions</u>

1. Using a vegetable peeler, slice the carrots into long, thin ribbons.

2. Warm oil in a large skillet over medium heat. Add the leeks and cook, stirring frequently, until softened, about five minutes. Add the raisins, garlic, ginger, lemon zest, and ½ tsp salt. Cook, stirring, for one minute.

3. Add the carrots, kale, and ½ cup water and cook, stirring or turning with tongs, until softened, about ten minutes. Add the lemon juice and season with salt and pepper.

Pearl's Chocolate Pecan Pie

Recipe Courtesy of Chef J.W. Pascoe
Pearl's New Orleans Restaurant in Elk Rapids

<u>Ingredients</u>

4 eggs
¾ cup sugar
1 cup dark corn syrup
½ teas salt
1 Tbsp vanilla
1¼ cups pecans
¼ cup melted butter
2½ Tbsp cocoa powder

2 single pie crusts

<u>Directions</u>

1. Line two pie pans with crusts and prebake pie shells for ten minutes before filling.
2. In a mixing bowl combine eggs and sugar. Add corn syrup, salt, vanilla, and pecans.
3. In a separate bowl, stir together melted butter and cocoa powder. Mix to dissolve, add to pecan mixture. Blend well and pour into the two prebaked pie shells.
4. Bake pies at 325 degrees for 45-60 minutes. Let cool before serving. Top with whipped cream or ice cream.

APPENDIX TWO: THREE INLAND TRIPS WORTH A TOURIST'S TIME

This guide focuses on Lake Michigan—its shore towns and places to visit along the Sunset Coast. If you are a tourist new to Michigan or a Michigan resident who simply hasn't visited your home state treasures, there are many inland spots you should put on your bucket list.

Hartwick Pines State Park, located near Grayling in the center of the state. This public recreation area covers 9,673 acres of old-growth forest of red and white pine. There is a museum, visitor center, exhibit hall, and camping.

<<>>

Fredrik Meijer Gardens and Sculpture Park, 1000 East Beltline Ave NE, Grand Rapids. Modern sculptures in a stunning botanical garden.

<<>>

Michigan State Capitol, 100 Capitol Avenue, Lansing. One of the first state capitols to be topped by a dome, the State Capitol Complex is visitor worthym and tours can be arranged.

Michigan State Capitol. Courtesy of Pixabay Free Images.

ACKNOWLEDGEMENTS

Exploring Michigan's Sunset Coasts is my way of thanking Michigan for a safe, nurturing, and memorable childhood.

What started as a single guide with an expected three hundred pages ended up more than 900 pages spread over three books. So much appreciation for my home state.

My husband, without whose help I never would have finished this project, is even happier than I am to see this undertaking completed. Now maybe I'll start doing my share of the housework.

I thank Jennifer Granholm, Jessie Voigts, Paula Chinick, Julaina Kleist-Corwin, and Kathi Hyatt for their kind words.

Working on these travel books gave me a special appreciation for the generosity of strangers. Along the way, some of those strangers became friends. Gary Martin permitted me to use his incomparable photos. The cover of book one features the Edwin H. Gott crossing under the Mackinac Bridge. Known primarily for his lighthouse photographs, Gary's image of Big Red enhances the front cover of book three. Visit www.coastalbeacons.com to see more examples of his amazing work. Tim Trombley gave me permission to use his gorgeous photograph of Spray Falls on the front cover of book two. To see more of Tim's photography, go to www.greatlakesphotography.net.

To the business owners, museum staff, chambers of commerce, historical societies (including the Omena Historical Society for the photo of Ms. Sweet Tart), librarians, and residents along the Michigan coasts who shared their time and stories, I say thanks.

In no particular order, I am indebted to Margie Lampel, Susan and Joe Jurkiewicz, Kanda McKee, Vee Byrum, Neva Hodges, Lani Longshore, Gretchen Goehmann, Jordan Bernal, Diane Herron, Maureen Scully, Julie Rosas, George Cramer, Nina Rosas, and especially Violet Moore who is the CMOS expert extraordinaire. She is also a walking encyclopedia of useful information for any writing endeavor.

ABOUT THE AUTHOR

Julie Albrecht Royce was born in Lexington and raised in the small town of Sandusky in Michigan's Thumb. After retiring as a Michigan First Assistant Attorney General, she turned to her love of writing and authored two travel books: *Traveling Michigan's Thumb* and *Traveling Michigan's Sunset Coast*, both were published by Thunder Bay Press.

She has written two novels, *PILZ* a crime thriller, and *Ardent Spirit*, the fictionalized biography of Magdelaine La Framboise, an Odawa-French fur trader born in 1780.

Ms. Royce has written magazine articles, has been included in several anthologies, and has had stories published in the *California Writers Club Literary Review*. In her three-book travel series: *Exploring Michigan's Sunrise Coasts*, *Exploring Michigan's Upper Peninsula Coasts*, and *Exploring Michigan's Sunset Coasts*, she comes full circle back to her love of Michigan and the Great Lakes.

www.ingramcontent.com/pod-product-compliance
Lightning Source LLC
Chambersburg PA
CBHW071446140726
47997CB00005B/1607